T0365156

BEVERLEY ANN FARMER

Perhaps

BALBOA.
PRESS

A DIVISION OF HAY HOUSE

Balboa Press books may be ordered through booksellers or by contacting:

Balboa Press
A Division of Hay House
1663 Liberty Drive
Bloomington, IN 47403
www.balboapress.com.au
1 (877) 407-4847

Because of the dynamic nature of the Internet, any web addresses or
links contained in this book may have changed since publication and
may no longer be valid. The views expressed in this work are solely those
of the author and do not necessarily reflect the views of the publisher,
and the publisher hereby disclaims any responsibility for them.

The author of this book does not dispense medical advice or prescribe the use
of any technique as a form of treatment for physical, emotional, or medical
problems without the advice of a physician, either directly or indirectly. The
intent of the author is only to offer information of a general nature to help
you in your quest for emotional and spiritual well-being. In the event you use
any of the information in this book for yourself, which is your constitutional
right, the author and the publisher assume no responsibility for your actions.

Any people depicted in stock imagery provided by Thinkstock are models,
and such images are being used for illustrative purposes only.
Certain stock imagery © Thinkstock.

Print information available on the last page.

ISBN: 978-1-4525-2748-2 (sc)
ISBN: 978-1-4525-2749-9 (e)

Balboa Press rev. date: 06/11/2015

PERHAPS, PERHAPS, PERHAPS.

The pallor of the winter season so often seemed to envelop these hills that surrounded us.

In contrast, in the long, lazy summer months, there was the exquisite blue created by the vapor exuded from surrounding gums.

Together, both would form part of the canvas for the picture of my early life.

Here, in this tiny valley, my childhood memories would be created and multiplied.

How fortunate I was to be born in these beautiful Blue Mountains, to this family, at this point in history.

The Blue Mountains Three Sisters- Shirley, Fay and Beverley?

It was here also that my parents had first come together --within a short distance of what was to become their final resting place.

PERHAPS I should commit my recollections of my childhood to paper.

PERHAPS you, one of my children, or my children's children, and my children's, children's children, may like to share my memories.
I know I would like to share those recollections with you.

PERHAPS you will come to know me a little better as I introduce you to some of your ancestors and try to acquaint you with the lifestyle I enjoyed as a young person.

May I take your hand?

Let us begin.

Allow me to start with some family history from the time of the arrival of your ancestors to Australian shores.

I will commence with <u>WILLIAM O'NEILL </u>(Neil) alias Keating.
(It should be noted that the different spelling of surnames was very common in relation to early records as many scribes were unable to spell correctly due to a general lack of education. I have not been able to verify the addition of the alias or when or where it originated).

Henceforth I will refer to our man as <u>WILLIAM O'NEILL.</u>

<u>WILLIAM O'NEILL </u>was a convict.
He had been born c1782 four miles west of a town called Glenealy (Gleann Fhaidhle) in the county of Wicklow, Ireland.

This way to Wicklow

Country House in Wicklow Area   *Glenealy Cemetery*

At the end of the 1790's <u>WILLIAM</u> married <u>SARAH MORNING</u> (BORN 1773), the daughter of <u>GARRET MORNING</u> and <u>MARY OWENS</u> from Ahoule, who themselves had been married in Wicklow parish on January 18th, 1772.

Although some registers of births, deaths and marriages exist from 1747 they are frequently gapped due to the reluctance of Catholics to publicly announce their affiliation with the then outlawed religion.
It was also common practice for the invading English to raze the Catholic Churches to the ground, thus destroying the church records within.
The churches were not always rebuilt as was the case in nearby Ashby where the stones from the destroyed church were re-built as a grotto.

Ashby Grotto

As so much of the local activity, and culture, revolved around the local church in those times the desecration also served to destroy cohesion within the community.

The invaders encouraged spying on neighbors and the division of families and as a result preservation of local history and customs were fractured.

Many locals, dying from starvation, became 'turncoats' and supported the invaders in return for sustenance.

WILLIAM and SARAH had six children, all of whom were born in Wicklow, Ireland.

Jane c1804
CATHERINE c1806
John c1807 (Died 1807)
William c1810
Michael
Anne c1817

CATHERINE was baptized May 26th, 1806.
Her godparents were John Cullin and Mary Hicks (I obtained this information from Wicklow Family History Centre).

NSW Immigration records of 1854 show that CATHERINE was born at Ballykillavine, County Wicklow, situated east of Glenealy.

On the 10th August, 1835 in Wicklow, Ireland,
CATHERINE married JOHN DOWDELL.

Witnesses were Catherine McGrath and William Neil.

4

The children of this union were:-
Maurice 1835 John 1837
WILLIAM 1839 (Baptized 12-12-1839)
Rose 1842 (Baptized 6-7-1842)
Sarah 1844 (Baptized 10-3-1844)
Michael 1846 (Baptized 20-6-1846)

JOHN senior died in Ireland.
Daughter Rose was kidnapped and disappeared in the forest in 1852 as a young girl.
No trace of her was ever found (family history and ship's records).

During a trip to Ireland in 2008 I visited Wicklow and verified that WILLIAM had been baptized in the St Patrick's Church which is perched high on Kilmantin Hill close to the jail where WILLIAM was held prior to being sentenced at Naas, to transportation.

Said jail building is now a museum and as I wandered from cell to cell, wondering how WILLIAM had felt at the prospect of being banished to an unknown land at the time of his sentence, I experienced a range of emotions.

Wicklow Gaol.

An appointment with a resident genealogist furnished me with some information, not least of which was the 'good fortune' of WILLIAM.
I had always felt him unlucky until the genealogist explained that WILLIAM'S crime (stealing of a mule) carried a much lesser punishment than if he had stolen a horse, as the punishment for that crime was the penalty of instant hanging!

There were obviously extenuating circumstances and in this case it was because WILLIAM had his farm confiscated by the English and he was given a very brief time to vacate the small holding

With a wife and children he loaded his few meagre possessions onto the livestock and set out for the home of his father-in-law, Garret Morning.

He was followed, arrested and charged with stealing the mule which was now considered the property of the English occupying forces who were acting on behalf of the English Crown.

He was jailed in Wicklow before being sent to nearby Naas.

In March, 1821 at Naas, County Kildare, WILLIAM received a sentence of seven years transportation to NSW having been found guilty as charged.

He boarded the convict ship "Isabella 2" that sailed from Cork on November 4th, 1821 arriving in Sydney on March 9th, 1822.

The ship carried two hundred convicts.

The warrants of the Lord Lieutenant of Ireland for the ship Isabella' described WILLIAM as 'a stout person, laborer, aged forty five."(He was forty that year.) Convict indents describe him as a "forty year old ploughman, 5'5 inches tall, hazel eyes, dark hair and sallow complexion."

WILLIAM was sent to Parramatta upon arrival before being assigned as servant to John Blaxland at "Newington" east of Parramatta.

Gregory, the brother of John, was one of the first men to cross the Blue Mountains with Lawson and Wentworth in 1813.

In 1823, WILLIAM applied through petition to Governor Brisbane for permission for his wife and family to be brought from Ireland at the Government's expense.

He stated his family was in the care of his father-in-law, Garret Morning, in the Parish of Dundrum, County Wicklow, Ireland.

Wicklow Docks 18ᵗʰ century.

Wicklow's St Patrick's Catholic Church perched on Kilmanton Hill.

The recommendation was furnished by a pioneer Catholic Priest, J.J. Therry.
The request was refused due to a lack of support material, namely a 'good conduct' certificate.

A second application was forwarded to Governor Brisbane suitably supported by Reverend Michael Maguire, RC Pastor of Wicklow Abbey, A.C. Coates, JP. and Alex Carroll, JP., both of Wicklow.

WILLIAM described his behavior since arriving in the colony thus "Since been assigned servant to William Blaxland I have conducted myself with strict propriety."

In June 1827 WILLIAM again forwarded a petition to the new Governor Darling.
He stated since being in the employ of John Blaxland he had "always manifested good, uniform and industrious conduct."

John Blaxland supported his claim and testified "William Neal has lived with me and is capable of maintaining his wife and children."

On June 27th, 1827 "WILLIAM NEAL, alias Keating" of 'Isabella' was granted a ticket of leave provided he remain in the Parramatta district.

He was now able to buy land, employ himself and enjoy some measure of freedom.

Four months later WILLIAM gained employment with Doctor Ross of Windsor and he applied for and was granted a change in his address to that region.

The Colonial Secretary granted permission for him to reside in the Windsor District on October 16th 1827.

In the 'Sydney Gazette' May, 1828 a report of a theft from one WILLIAM NEALE of South Creek, Windsor was featured.

Three escaped members of a chain gang had escaped and they not only stole from WILLIAM but threatened to kill him.

WILLIAM, with the help of others, pursued the escapees and overtook them. They were subsequently charged and sentenced to transportation for a further seven years.
I have endeavoured to find a true record of this incident without success.

On June 27th, 1828, WILLIAM NEAL, alias Keating, formerly of ship 'Isabella2' received a Certificate of Freedom.

The NSW Census of 1828 listed WILLIAM NEALE as being free of servitude, employed by James Rodgers at "Ludenham" farm (owned by John Blaxland), Bringilly district, near Mulgoa, NSW.

In 1830 WILLIAM'S wife, SARAH, and their two daughters, arrived in Sydney as free passengers on the convict ship "Forth 11" on October 12 of that year.

Jane was then twenty-six and Anne, thirteen.
They had travelled with seven other convict's wives and nineteen children, together with one hundred female convicts.
They had embarked from Cork on June 3rd, 1830.

A daughter, Catherine, had remained in Ireland as did WILLIAM 11 and Michael, all of whom would migrate at a later time.

It is interesting to note that Sarah and her daughters carried 'seven petticoats, four shifts, four pairs of stockings, seven handkerchiefs, ten caps and four aprons' in their luggage and these items were augmented by Government supplies of 'three pairs of shoes, three bonnets, two gowns, two petticoats, four shifts, four pairs of stockings and three handkerchiefs.'

Jane would marry John Green on April 30th 1831 in the Parish of Narellan, NSW the ceremony having been performed by the Rev. Thomas Hassall.
(John was a convict who had been transported to Australia on the ship "Mellish" in 1829.
He was granted a Ticket of Leave on May 1st 1838 and a Conditional Pardon on April, 1844).

They would have eleven children all of whom were born at Mulgoa, NSW.

The children were:-
    James 1832
    William 1834
    Michael 1835
    Catherine 1836
    Sarah 1838
    John 1839
    Mary Anne 1841-1841
    Mary Anne 11 1842
    Jane 1842
    Thomas 1845
    Francis 1847

As shown in the Penrith Catholic Church register <u>WILLIAM</u> and <u>SARAH</u> were sponsors for the baptism of their granddaughter, Jane Green, on the 5th of December 1842.
{Jane would die following an accidental fall from a dray on Christmas Eve, 1869](aged sixty-seven) at Tumut NSW, where she was buried].

It is known that <u>WILLIAM O'NEILL</u> had been granted the lease on a large pastoral run "Gunningbar" in the Wellington district of NSW near the Bogan River in 1848.
This run was of 16,000 acres or 24 square miles.

In the lists of licensed occupants of 'wastelands' of the Crown in Wellington district it was shown that <u>WILLIAM O'NEILL</u> paid ten pounds for the years ended 30th June 1848 to 1853.

His stock list in 1851 included 830 sheep, 20 horses, 510 cattle.

At this time <u>WILLIAM O'NEILL</u>, residing at Jerry's Meadow near Lowther, NSW, bought 200 acres at Antonio Creek near Lowther Creek, Hartley district, NSW in 1852.
The sales were held at Hartley and records show he paid 200 pounds. When he selected the 200 acre valley the surveyor described it as "red black soil and excellent pasture."

<u>WILLIAM</u> had hoped to establish a stud farm for breeding horses.
This undertaking was not a great success and general farming was undertaken.

WILLIAM'S son, WILLIAM 11 purchased 50 acres adjoining his father's farm on June 16th, 1852 for the sum of ninety-seven pounds.
In 1852 WILLIAM'S stock-lists included 4,782 sheep, 550 cattle and 21 horses.

Lists from 1853 include 4 horses, 640 cattle and 1, ooo, sheep and an addendum "now of John A Gardiner."

WILLIAM'S son, WILLIAM 11, (who had arrived in NSW in 1842) had joined his father as shown in the documents recording his marriage.

In September 1853 the run "Gunningbar" was transferred from WILLIAM O'NEILL to John Gardiner whose father was the first settler at Antonio Creek, Hartley.

The story has been handed down through the family that WILLIAM, when living in the Wellington property had, during a drunken episode, signed over his holdings and stock to Gardiner following a bet during an all-night card game.

Despite attempts to rescind the transfer the law at that time afforded no protection and, in consequence, WILLIAM lamented losing everything he had worked so hard for and family history suggests he broke his heart.

WILLIAM was in receipt of a letter informing him of the arrival of his daughter, Catherine Dowdell with her three sons Maurice, William and John. The letter' dated the 16 instant, demanded further payment for the upkeep of the family who were housed at the Parramatta Depot.

After a lapse of 33years Catherine had missed being re-acquainted with her Father by days.

He had died just five days previously at his residence in Hampton.

[handwritten letter]

WILLIAM, was aged seventy-three.

He was buried at the Hartley Cemetery near the fence on the Great Western Highway.

The details on his headstone are incorrect as they state he died March 24, 1853 whereas Probate documents state he died 24th March, 1854.

Grave

William O'Neill's headstone at Hartley cemetery. Difference in year of death date shown on probate records and headstone of William O'Neill. Hartley church records did not record his death

WILLIAM'S wife, SARAH, was known to be alive in 1842 but no details of her death are available at this time.

WILLIAM'S will dated 14th March, 1853, left 'a freehold farm of 200 acres, premises, team of bullocks and dray, a horse cart and horses in number about 40' to be shared between his two sons WILLIAM, and Michael.

BRIDGET MADDERN, a free settler from Ireland, had joined her convict brother, Peter, who resided in the Lowther district of NSW.

It was there she met English convict HENRY ENGLAND, who at seventeen years of age had been transported from England to Australia for stealing.

After a brief courtship, and in keeping with the law for ex-convicts, the couple sought permission to marry as documented below.

Details of the couple include name, age, name of transportation ship, sentence, date of bans, name of Clergy as follows. (right hand page fourth from the top).

Henry England 27 Porcher life

Bridget Maddern......26 Agnes Free

(This document was obtained from the Archive Authority of New South Wales)

My Great, great Grandfather CONVICT Henry England,
who married Bridget Maddern, the parents of Annie.

John England brother of Annie

As stated, <u>ANNIE</u> was the daughter of <u>BRIDGET MADDERN</u> and <u>HENRY ENGLAND</u>, an ex-convict of Miles Flats near Lowther, NSW.

<u>Annie England, had been born at 'Lowther Park' where her parents were employed on the 3rd of December, 1849.</u>

<u>On the 28th of February, 1867 Annie married William Dowdell who had been born in Glenealy,County Wicklow, Ireland, in 1839.</u>

The wedding took place at St Bernard's Catholic Church, Hartley.
<u>ANNIE</u> was eighteen years old (B 3-12- 1849) and <u>WILLIAM</u> was ten years her senior (B. 1839).

Copy of Marriage Certificate of William and Annie Dowdell 1867-

A copy of the marriage certificate of Annie and William.

Annie at the door of the old Wattle and Daub Dowdell House

innie Dowdell at back of old Off Flats house

WILLIAM and ANNIE had ten children. They were:-
SARAH JANE-1868
William-1869
John-1871
Henry-1893
Maurice-1875
Michael-1878
Joseph-1880
Thomas-1883
James 1885
Mary Catherine

THE NEW DOWDELL HOUSE. Joe Mrs Forsyth Tom Will Jnr Annie

<u>*MRS. ANNIE DOWDELL*</u>
Born at "Lowther Park", Lowther near Hartley, N.S.W on 3.12.1849
Married William Dowdell at St Bernard's Church, Hartley on 28.2.1867

<u>*WILLIAM DOWDELL*</u>
Born at Gleanealy, Co.Wicklow, Ireland in 1839.

Following her eighteenth birthday, in 1887, <u>SARAH JANE</u> was permitted to cut her hair for the very first time.

Her birthday gift from her family was a silver, horseshoe shaped locket.

A thin plait was made from the hair and it remains in that locket which was entrusted to my Dad when Granny, (Sarah) died in 1955 and given to me when he died.

The Dowdell Family at Annie's funeral in 1930

William and Annie Dowdell's 10 children:

Sarah Ryan, William, John, Henry Dowdell (standing), Maurice, Michael, Joseph, Thomas, James Dowdell and Mary Kirwan - at their mother's funeral in 1930.

Sarah Ryan, William, John, Henry, Maurice, Michael, Joseph, Thomas, James and Mary Kirwin.

Sarah

*Joe and Maggie &
Gwen & Ray*

Mary Catherine

SARAH JANE, the eldest, would marry GEORGE BERNARD RYAN (Junior), known as 'Barney', who had been born on May, 2nd 1865 at The Meadows, Hazelgrove.
The wedding was conducted at Bathurst in 1892.

SARAH and 'BARNEY' did not enjoy a happy union and the spacing of two years between the children will attest to the family history that Barney would leave after a big disagreement and would not appear for 'a year or so'.

Then he would return and SARAH would become pregnant with the next child.

BARNEY stayed until the baby arrived, and the next big argument took place, and he'd be off again.

They didn't live together after Aunty Doll (Ann Elizabeth) was born and nor did they divorce because both were very strict Catholics and divorce was considered such a mortal sin in the eyes of the church that it warranted ex-communication.

So, for forty odd years (with emphasis on the odd) they were man and wife in name only. (Barney did however have a female friend in Lithgow who bore him a son years later!)

Sarah and Mary   *Sarah Jane and Jim's dog Spot*

PERHAPS, one day, I should look for a compassionate religion less dominated by stupid man- made rules.

*'Barney' Ryan with his horseteam Main Street,
Lithgow. 1910 with plant from Hoskin's.*
*'Barney' was contracted to move Hoskin's Iron and
Steel Works to Port Kembla, NSW.*

Grandfather had felled and transported the timber for the original Jenolan Caves House from Kanimbla Valley and was later to win the big contract to transport the original Hoskin's Iron and Steel works from Lithgow to Port Kembla.

It was during one of his trips down the valley that he came in contact with a huge splinter which was deeply embedded in his arm.

By the time he drove the horse team many miles through the virgin bush to seek medical help, the arm had become gangrenous and necessitated amputation.

Despite this obvious handicap his reputation as a horseman did not diminish.

Dad, <u>JAMES FRANCIS RYAN</u>, had been born on July 23ʳᵈ, 1902 at Off Flats, Via Hampton, NSW.
He was the fifth surviving child of Sarah Jane Dowdell and Bernard George RYAN.

As stated, his siblings were Henry, Julia Agnes, Arthur, Winifred Ellen and Ann Elizabeth.

When Dad was introduced to his new younger sister (aged two) he refused to call her Ann and kept calling her 'Dolly'.

When other family members called her Ann, or 'the baby', Dad would scold them by shaking his head and in a loud voice tell them in no uncertain manner that 'it' was a doll.

Consequently the name 'stuck' and she would be known as 'Dolly' all of her life.

Hampton School 1914
Dick Rushworth, Harry Ryan, Tom Griffiths, Ham Boyd, Mick O'Neill, Jim Rushworth, Tom Dowdell, Ted Marshall, Everett Hughes, Perc Wilson, Fred Rushworth, Norman Kelly, Ernie Rushworth, Alf Hughes, Hubie Hughes, Jimmy Ryan, Sep Boyd, (past and present students of Hampton school)

Dad attended a bush school at Hampton and was a very bright student.
He described to me the joys learning from his old teacher who came to school on a horse that he tethered near the door of the old schoolhouse.
The horse would punctuate the lessons with frequent snorts and farts that 'smelled like new mown hay' and much whinnying as it swished its tail to keep the flies at bay.
The horse shared the abundance of flies that tethered horses seemed to attract, with the small band of students.
Each morning began with a nature lesson and the kids were sent to 'scramble' outside for something interesting, be it a plant, insect or rock.
The teacher would form his lessons around the treasures.

He told me of the earthern floor that frequently sported puddles of rainwater and the ill fitting window that allowed wind and water to enter the building.

Dad was really well versed in a variety of subjects including French and Latin, history, astronomy and all aspects of the English language, and was very articulate and well-read for a man who had had such limited opportunities. He was also the best writer I had seen and I aspired to write like him.
Dad won a scholarship to secondary college but couldn't take it due to lack of money.
He didn't even have a pair of shoes of his own to wear to the interview.

Dad told me how he loved having birthdays and his very special birthday treat. He was allowed an extra slice of bread on which he dribbled hot, black tea then sprinkled sugar on the birthday specialty.

Dad and friends.

Dad and friends.   *Sarah Paddy Doll Frank Cullen Reg Laurie Hubert Ken*

Art Trix Sarah   *Uncle Burwood and Dad*   *Aunty Doll & Reg*   *Dad's cousins Vera & Molly Kirwin*

Dad would occasionally treat himself to this 'dish' even when it wasn't his natal day.

Each time he did so I would feel overwhelmed remembering the small fatherless boy whose birthday was celebrated with such simple fare.

I promised myself that in the event of my having children they would always have at least a birthday meal to show how special they were.

PERHAPS Dad will share the anniversary of his 90th birthday with a special great-grandson, Joel Antony Farmer, whose name will be entered on the family tree on July 23rd, 1992.

Dad was an appealing little chap who early on demonstrated a way with horses.

He sometimes accompanied Granny Ryan to Wilson's Half Way House in Hampton when she delivered the laundry.

Here Granny would also buy staples like flour and sugar from the adjoining produce store.

She would ask for credit until the end of the month when she was paid for the laundering she had done.

One particular day as Dad tended the horses that were being changed over to take the travelling coach to the Caves, he was approached by a beautiful lady dressed in red.

The 'red lady' struck up a conversation and wanted to know all about the young boy.

Dad told her his life story with unabashed honesty.

The lady became overwhelmed.

She took out her purse and gave Dad the princely amount of two pounds!

(To give you some idea of the value of the gift a good pair of expensive shoes could be purchased for less than one quarter of that amount, ie five shillings).

Dad went to the store owner to pay Granny's account with the windfall only to be informed that the 'lady in red' had already settled the account.

After leaving school, Dad followed his father's occupation of operating his own horse team.

In his late teens he won the contract to extend the railway line in Sydney's west to Fairfield and employed his eldest brother, Harry, to work for him. Like his father before him, he always had a natural fondness for horses and even the horses employed in the mines (the pit ponies) he later encountered in his working life were special friends who were seasonally treated to the tiny coddlin -moth infested apples that grew in our yard.

Dad and his horse team extending the rail-line to Fairfield NSW.
Uncle Harry is standing on the left.

Lithgow Waratah Football Club-(Dad Front, second from left) 1922

Dad's eldest brother, Henry (Harry) had married Carrie Dawson.
The children of this union were Shirley (known as Hampton Shirley) and Jim.
Sister, Julia Agnes (Cis) married Frank Cullen.
They had five sons, Reg, Laurie, Hubert, Ken and Douglas.
Arthur married Bridget (Trix) and four children are registered in this family.
They are William (who was adopted by Art,) Elizabeth, Bernard and Faye (known as Blackheath Faye).
Winnifred Ellen married Burwood Rolfe and they had two children, Ray and Gwen.

The youngest, Dolly, (Ann Elizabeth) married local grazier, Patrick James Curran.

Sarah ? Paddy Doll ? Burwood Tom Curran Cis,Old Tom Curran, Frank Mary

Art Paddy Doll Bridesamaid
Gwen Rolfe Marguerette Evans

Aunt and Uncle (Aunty Doll
loved this photo of her dress!)

Lowther Church Mission Currans & Sarah Jane & Mary(Far right)
(Aunty Doll and Uncle Paddy were on their honeymoon.)

My parents, James and Vera, had met at a dance at Corney's Hall in Lidsdale,
NSW when Mum was sixteen and Dad, twenty-two.
After two years they became engaged.
They could not marry until my Dad had finished paying for a house in
Blackheath that he, and his brother Arthur, were buying for their mother,
Sarah Jane Ryan, so, for four long years their courtship endured.

I once ask Mum why she was attracted to Dad and she admitted begrudgingly
'Because he was so 'dashedly' handsome'.

He must have been something special as I had never before heard such a
description and I haven't heard it since!

The completion of the railway to One Tree Hill in 1868 (Later named Mt
Victoria) led to the opening up of the Western district.
In 1869 the line to Lithgow, via the Darling Causeway, Bell and the remarkable
engineering feat of the Zig Zag railway, saw great advancement.

This rail link allowed exploration of coal deposits of Lithgow and Wallerawang
and beyond to the Western Plains where the pastoral industry would be
established.

Dad began working in the coalmines around Lidsdale just before he met Mum.

He would mine for black coal.

Dad at work down the mine!

He was to study at the Lithgow Technical College at night and gain his Deputy Certificate and for a time managed the mine where he worked. (Brown's Mine)

He periodically upgraded his First-aid qualifications and remained as officer for many years.

He was to be associated with the industry well into his sixties, frequently being summoned back after his retirement to relieve a staff member who went on holidays or who had become ill.

When Dad was employed in underground mining he wore a miner's lamp on his hard hat.

The miner's lamp smelled strongly of cordite.

Dad wore the hat with the lamp ablaze as he peddled off to the 'pit' at some unearthly hours in the morning to turn on the pumps.
The pumps had to be engaged to clear out the water before the miners were lowered to dig the coal with picks and shovels.

Dad also lowered the pit canaries in a small cage attached to a rope to check the air for gases.
If the birds died while down the shaft then it was unsafe for the men to work.

Later Dad would work in an Open Cut Mine called Newcom. (David would join him and serve his Fitting and Turning Apprenticeship there).

As kids we were amazed at the size of the equipment that was brought up to our little village to operate the massive mining exploration when Newcom first began.
(Standing next to a giant Euclid tyre when you are small is a Lilliputian moment).

In Birmingham England in March, 1829 JOHN WHITE was born.
He would marry ELIZABETH JACKSON (Born Derbyshire, June 1832) in 1850.

In 1853 with their new daughter, Harriet, they set sail as assisted migrants aboard the 'William Fortune' for Australia.
William, a carpenter and wheelright, found work with Cobb and Co Coaches in Campelltown, NSW.
For the next two years they lived in that district before moving west to Emu Plains where they lived for the next twelve years.

Five further children were added to the family during this time including SARAH (1855), George (1857), Emily (1860), Mary (1865) and Amy (1866).

The parents decided to again move west with the newly extended railway network and travelled in the first train to convey passengers to Mt Victoria.
They continued business at Hartley with Cobb and Co for a further two years deciding to move west again.
Reaching "Delectable" Lidsdale, however with its "enchanting surrounds and rose tinted prospects for the future" they decided to remain.

These comments were quoted by family members in family documents. With mail coaches, teamsters and drovers passing through, Lidsdale was a flourishing little centre.

JOHN and ELIZABETH added Joseph (1868), Maria (1871) and John Jnr (1873) to their family.

The White Family Members

Amy (Born 1866) and family Lidsdale c1904

John died in May, 1889. Elizabeth died June, 1922 aged ninety.
Both are buried at Piper's Flat cemetery, Wallerawang.

In 1876 at Hartley, NSW, <u>SARAH WHITE</u> married <u>JAMES NOLAN</u>.

Two sons were born of this union.

They were William Henry (1876) and <u>GEORGE ARTHUR</u> (1878).
Both boys were born at Hartley.
An illegitimate daughter, Maud, had been born to Sarah in 1873.

St Johns Wallerawang

GEORGE ARTHUR NOLAN married ROSE GRACE
TOMLINSON at St Johns Church, Wallerawang, in 1904

My Mum, Vera Nolan, was born at Lidsdale, NSW on November 14th, 1908. She was the second surviving child of Rose Grace (nee Tomlinson) and George Arthur (Toby) Nolan.

Her siblings were Ernest, Peter, Lily, Violet and Douglas.

Mum as a baby

Mum attended Wallerawang Public School.

Her life had not been easy as Grandfather Nolan was not very fond of working at a steady job, though he did spasmodically work in the mines and was later to experience the effects of a lung disorder contracted by miners.

He was generally regarded as a grumpy old man and was inclined to 'throw around his weight' to both Granny and his children.

On one such occasion when Granny was the object of his wrath fourteen year old Uncle Ernie picked him up and carried him outside and threatened him with some of his own medicine.

Grandfather never raised his hand again until he was diagnosed with Dementia and he began to be physical with Granny.

Dad intervened and had Toby committed to an institution for the remainder of his life.

The family was very poor and, as the eldest girl, Mum had to look after her younger siblings and do more than her share of chores.

Peter Vera Ernie and Lily c1917

As soon as she was able she left school to become a 'domestic' at an inn that served Cobb and Co coaches en route from Lithgow to Mudgee.

She worked alongside her best friend, Ilma Joyce Hill and fifty years later they were still laughing about the antics they got up to.

At fifteen Mum interfered in a domestic argument when her boss struck his wife.
Mum threatened the boss with the broom and he chased her.
Mum insisted the wife should retaliate. "The mongrel has to sleep sometimes" she insisted.
The boss never hit his wife in front of Mum ever again.

Mum's wage was given to Granny to help the family and the small allowance she was given was saved to buy bits and pieces for her "Glory Box".
(A 'Glory Box" was a trunk or drawer or cupboard where the girls stored linen, crockery and small household goods that would be used in home-making when a girl married.)

Ilma and Mum in their fashionable swimsuits Hill's house. 1924

Mum's Dance Fan

Mum was a little 'tacker' when the family had a visit from Uncle Bill Nolan.

A conversation took place about the amount of gold remaining in the Cox's river.
Grandfather boasted that he had found several small nuggets and gold dust that he had stored in a small bottle.

He went to get the bottle to prove his claim and returned to display the bottle that was completely empty.
He was indeed upset that those contents had disappeared.

He consulted Granny who denied any knowledge and he then called the kids.

Mum was looking very guilty and Grandfather took her aside to question her further. Mum started to cry before she answered his direct question, "Did you take it Vera?"
She shook her head before blurting out "I just wanted to have a gold lining so I swallowed it all."

When she was barely a teenager Mum had a crush on a young man named Jim Murphy who was a boarder at Granny's.
He hailed from New Zealand.
He had a sister at home whose name was Nellie and Mum began corresponding very occasionally.
This friendship would endure throughout their lives.
On Mum's bucket list was the desire to travel to New Zealand to meet Nellie 'someday'.

Nellie Murphy and husband, Ern

Perhaps in the future Mum will share her birthday with someone of significance- like a boy named Charles who was born to be King.

When my parents married on December 21st, 1928 they were attended by their best friends, said Ilma and Jim White, (Mum's cousin) for whom they had been best man and bridesmaid the previous week.

The foursome then all travelled to Sydney to share their honeymoon!

Mum wore a cream crepe-de-chine dress in a straight "flapper" style with cap-sleeve, hemline just below the knee and adorned with a lowered, gathered hip line with an 'apron' of the same material that featured a 'V' shaped trim of wide coffee lace.
A large brimmed hat and matching shoes completed the outfit.

As best man Dad had worn a pale suit but for his wedding day he was decked out in a dark dinner suit and bow tie and in his buttonhole he had a sprig of orange blossom made of wax.
Mum would keep this little memento of that day until her demise.

Vera and Jim 1928

Mum once told me she had a perfect figure for her day-------flat like an ironing board!

Sixty years after Mum and Dad's wedding day Great-granddaughter Caide Louise, in my presence, chose 21ˢᵗ December 1988 for her arrival at Donnybrook, WA.

Dad in his wedding finery

Ilma and Jim & Ernie
and Hazel & Wilson Lad   *Ernie and Hazel*

Back home in Lidsdale my parents set up house in the front rooms of 'Braeside' next-door to Mum's old home.

This large rambling home was then owned by the Nottle family but had previously been the home of Mum's grandmother, <u>SAR AH</u> <u>NOL AN.</u>

They had a bedroom, entrance/dining room, small, cosy lounge- room, tiny kitchen and use of the shared bathroom.

Duncan Street in 1929

They lived there, until their Californian bungalow was completed around the corner in Duncan Street in time for my eldest sister, Shirley Joyce, to be born there on December 30th, 1929.

Shirley was a popular name of that period and Joyce was to honour Mum's pal, Ilma Joyce Hill.

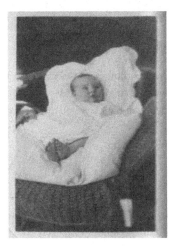 

Shirley Joyce 1929   *Mum & Shirl*

On February 14th (St Valentine's Day) 1931, Fay Elaine was welcomed at the same venue.
Granny Nolan often said the girls were like 'chalk and cheese' as Fay was skinny and blonde and Shirl was plump and very dark.

Shirl was attractive and Fay plain.
Shirl was outgoing and Fay shy.

Fay and Shirley 1931

Shirl and Fay   *Shirley Joyce*

Years later when I questioned Granny why she thought this was so she told me she thought the stork might have gone to the wrong house.
I scoffed at the suggestion as I knew darned well babies weren't delivered by storks.
Everyone knew they were found in cabbage patches.

Silly Granny.

Despite the horrific deprivations caused by the Great Depression my parents managed to eke out an existence for their family though they were to reveal at the celebration for their 50th Wedding Anniversary that they nearly lost their house at that time.

I was aware growing up of the high regard Dad had for Mr Nuebeck who was a local mine owner.
What I didn't know was that he had financed our home during that difficult time.

Dad took any work he could get and food rations were augmented by chickens and eggs, home grown veggies and fruit, jams and preserves, milk, cream and butter from the cows.

My Grandfather Nolan would catch eels from the river down our street and many rabbits were also on the menu.

Dad loved fishing and the local streams bore more than the playful platypus.

Occasional visits from Aunty Doll and Uncle Paddy were welcomed as they supplied extra fruit, veggies, meat, eggs, spare coupons and gifts of clothing for the girls.

Much worse off was our Uncle Ernie and his wife Aunty Hazel, and baby daughter, Vonnie, who lived in Portland.

With no work they were in the daily dole queue to get a handout of soup from a charity organization and like many others they were reduced to eating a strange variety of foodstuffs not normally contained in the diet.

(One favourite at the time was to make soup from some types of grass, and cook nettles for a vegetable).

Portland Nolan's special weekly treat was a small piece of meat delivered by the butcher and paid for by my Mum and Dad.

Ilma Hill's sister, Ivy, was to be married and she invited Shirl to be flowergirl.

Shirl at our front gate in Duncan Street

41

The gold painted flower basket that Shirl carried lived on top of the wardrobe in the back room for as long as I can remember.

We were lucky to get fresh milk from Granny.
We kids would take the big Billy-can up in the morning and collect it in the afternoon every day as we grew older.
It was the common practice to swing the can around in an arc above your head without spilling a drop.
After tea Mum would place the milk in enamel dishes on the cooling fuel stove.

The following morning she would remove the pans from the now cold stove and we would use the the egg slide to heap the thick scalded cream onto our cooked porridge.

PERHAPS I will have a cholesterol problem when I grow up!!!

Granny Nolan & Jim Bourke   *Lily and Ron*

George Albert

Doug & Roy Corney

Peter   *Violet and Raymond*

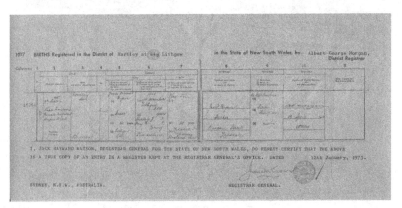

My Birth Certificate written in Dad's hand

I was born on March 16th, 1937, at Sister Thompson's Private Hospital, Cupro Street, Lithgow, third daughter of the Ryan's.

"Look at me. I can now sit up by myself"
Beverley four and a half months 1937

(Later, we would be joined by our brother, David James (8- 1- 1943).
Both David and I were born in a hospital while our sisters were born at home.

As the third child, and after two daughters, my parents had 'ordered' a boy who was to be called Patrick James --because I was due on St Patrick's Day, March 17th and because Uncle Paddy had driven all the way from Lowther to take Mum for her Doctor's visits in Lithgow and my eventual arrival.
The James was to honor Dad.

The best laid plans............!

Mum had not enjoyed a very comfortable pregnancy having 'hurt' her back when she was five months gestation with me.
I believe she slipped a disc in her back as she could still accurately describe the pain many years later.

To help her with the two little girls Mum had some years before employed a local lass named Jean Edwards.
When her pregnancy with me was confirmed, she contacted the now married Jean about coming to work for her again.
A letter arrived from Jean to say she herself was having a child.

45

When Jean had previously been employed by Mum she had met a young man named Fred Taylor from Lithgow when he delivered a load of coal to our house from Dad's mine.

A friendship commenced, became a courtship and they had ultimately married.

They would become significant people in my life.

My name, Beverley, was a uni-sex name (meaning 'beaver meadow') my Mother had noticed in a publication.

The month prior to my birth a plane crash on the border of Queensland was the big news.

A relative, Bernard O'Rielly, had witnessed the passage of the plane from his property in Lamington National Park, south west of Beaudesert in Queensland.

He was sure the search party had headed in the wrong direction when they set out.

Bernard was a wonderful bushman and after the news came through that the search party had not been successful he took one of his horses and some supplies and headed for the area he figured the plane would be.

As chronicled in the book and movie 'Green Mountain', Bernard found the plane wreckage, male victims and two survivors, one of whom bore the name of Beverley.

Reading the newspaper that had so engaged Dad's interest, Mum saw the name and decided on the remote chance she would have a daughter that she would consider the name.

When I was born my parents were so disappointed they didn't name me for four days.

Much later I nursed with the sister who cared for me in those days, Sister Ethel Writer, who imparted this information.

'Ann' was after my Aunty Doll and my great- grandmother, Annie Dowdell.

I always felt I would have liked to have been named Annie Elizabeth like Aunty Doll.

PERHAPS, in years to come, I may live on Beaudesert Road in Queensland

We were all breast fed.

It was Mum's belief that fat babies were bonny babies, but I was never fat. PERHAPS when I am much older????

Mum insisted that each of her babies have their own new cane pram and layette.

Bev and Marie Bourke

My pram, with me in it, was taken to tennis meetings, picnics, dances, the local township and family gatherings.

One favoured picnic spot was Kerosene Vale that held great fascinations for picnickers who loved to closely examine the fantastic collection of Aboriginal Art that was referred to locally as 'Blackfella's Hands'.

We were so ignorant of the ancient history before us we did nothing to preserve the wonders and over a period of time they were chipped from their ancient home and destroyed.

Gone forever were the numerous sized hands, colored in a variety of ochres, together with the many representations of trees, plants and a variety of reptiles and animals.

The detailed fish, kangaroos and snakes were drawn as though the artist had looked at them during an xray.

Later Philistines took to painting their hands with modern paint and plastering the area with their own prints.

Such inexplicable ignorance-and a fair reflection of what little significance our Aboriginal history was given for far too long.

In later years I marvelled at the exquisite remains of my baby layette that were kept in tissue paper in Mum's wardrobe.
The fragile white cotton and lace that I wore for my christening (given to me by my godmother Great Aunty Mary Catherine, the only sister of Granny Ryan) a quilted cot eiderdown in rose pink satin (a thank-you gift from Uncle Ernie and Aunty Hazel for all the gifts of meat), a pink silk crocheted jacket, bonnet and bootees made by Mrs Bell in Lithgow (Mrs Bell later had twins, Graham and Beverley Ann named after me), a pink crepe de chine frock given to me by Aunty Doll and Uncle Paddy, numerous tiny pillow slips lovingly fancy-worked in pastel cottons and even some pink trimmed bibs and a silk and wool shawl.
(My first jewellery was also kept in a safe place and was never worn after infancy.
The tiny gold chain bracelet has a small heart locket that bears many indentations created by small teeth.
My gold baby brooch was oval in shape with my birthstone, an aquamarine, mounted in the 'corner').
As the first grandchild Regina inherited the fragile treasures which proved to be a disaster when Fay, with no appreciation of their uniqueness, failed to show any special care and as a result they were all ruined by her throwing them in the washing machine!

Mum was very, very disappointed and I recall feeling cheated and sad when she shared the news.
She shook her head and said "I looked after those things for all of these years and you bloody kids come along and destroy them".

I was quick to reply that we weren't all the same.

Me in pink 1938

At the time of my birth an historical event of unprecedented proportions was being enacted in England.

The previous December the King, GeorgeV, had died and his eldest son, David, the Duke of Wales, had been named King in accordance with tradition. David had not behaved in a manner reflecting his position and had moved in a 'fast' crowd and had enjoyed the favor of several society matrons.

He then met a previously divorced American woman during a skiing trip with his current mistress and he fell madly in love with her.

Her name was Wallis Simpson.

As the new head of the Church of England Church David was expected to exemplify Church rules which included non- acceptance of divorce and thus he was refused permission of the Parliament to consider marriage to Mrs. Wallis Simpson who was still married to her second American husband anyway.

He was issued with three alternatives, one of which was the remote possibility that he should abdicate as King.

Much to everyone's shock and horror David announced he could not accept the onerous task of being the King without Mrs Simpson by his side.

In consequence of these tumultuous events that had never before taken place in history the second eldest brother in the Royal family, the shy and stuttering Albert, became the reluctant King George the VI.

Days following Mrs Simpson's divorce she and David married in exile with not one member of the Royal family in attendance.

In May 1937 Albert became King George VI. (The name taken was in honour of his father, George V.)
His once very close brother was refused an invitation and it was later revealed that the two had differences about money when David had falsified details of his personal wealth and extracted an ongoing generous allowance from the Royal coffers which George felt he did not warrant.

David would return to visit his Mother but the new Duchess was not welcome in England until her husband died and, in accordance with his wishes, his remains were brought back to England for burial.

She would be interred alongside her husband some twenty years later.

On one of the rare occasions we were allowed in the front room we were visited by Granny's sister, Aunty Marion.
Aunty Marion arrived from Sydney in an impressive auto mobile driven by a uniformed driver.
She was quite old and was beautifully dressed.

We were on our very best behavior and were fascinated that this was our Granny's sister though we had met another sister, Edith, whose son, John Lloyd, was a teacher.

After she left there was considerable discussion between Mum and Granny about the sadness in Aunty Marion's life.

Mum lamented the fact that they had not shared an encounter she had with Aunty Marion's former fiancé.

It appears that as a young woman Aunty Marion was betrothed to a local man from Wallerawang.

Her trunks containing her trousseau and belongings were brought up by horse and wagon from Wolgan Valley to Granny's house.

The wedding finery was prepared and donned by the prospective bride on the appointed day.

A horse and sulky, driven by Grandfather Nolan, then took the bride to St John's Church in Wallerawang.

All was in readiness when the minister announced that the bridegroom had changed his mind and the wedding would not take place.

Aunty Marion was devastated and in her mortification she resolved to go as far away as she possibly could.

She caught the only train that day that left from 'Wang and it happened to be going to Sydney.

She had never been there before and knew no one.

Upon arrival at a Sydney suburb, which she mistook as Sydney itself, she spoke to the Stationmaster telling him of her situation and on his advice she went to the nearest church and begged the Minister for help.

He directed her to a local Doctor's residence where the man's wife had taken ill and he was in need of help in the house.

Marion nursed the wife with compassion and care, and then stayed on long after the wife died as a professional housekeeper until the elderly Doctor himself deteriorated in health.

Marion nursed him until his very last day.

As she prepared to move out to a new post she was shocked to learn that the Doctor had left all of his worldly goods to her, including several Sydney houses!

She never had to work again.

(At thirty seven Marian married Mathew Drummond.
She was believed to have adopted a son in later life about whom I know nothing.)

Whilst out walking with me in my new pram, in the nearby township of Wallerawang, Mum encountered a gentleman named Mr Henning.

He stopped and offered his congratulations on my arrival and then kindly acknowledged my sisters, bidding them 'good afternoon'.
Shirl responded appropriately with the good manners expected of her.
Fay flatly refused.
Mum admonished her and demanded she display good manners saying "You know very well who Mr Henning is."
"Yes" piped up Fay. "He's the mongrel who jilted Aunty Marion."

Mum was deeply embarrassed and Fay was dutifully dealt with.
Mum called in at Granny's on her way home to share her mortification and Granny suggested Fay remain with her for a while until Mum cooled down.

After Mum had gone Granny gave Fay three pence and a big hug!

Mum, Dad and Aunty Lily Bourke

One month after I was born Mum's sister, Aunty Lil gave birth to a daughter, Marie Enid.
Marie was a sister for Jim and Ron.

Cousins Marie, Ron and Jim Bourke 1937

One of my earliest memories is being toted on the shoulders of my father, Jim Ryan, as we walked down 'the lane' after an annual Christmas tea at Granny Nolan's.

As the festivities wound down we would climb up onto Granny's bed until the adults decided to leave.

Dad would then hoist me to his shoulders with instructions to put my head down so we could fit through Granny's little doorways.

I would circle his head with my arms and rest my head on his.

Years later I described this memory to Mum and she dismissed me by saying I was too young when this took place and I couldn't possibly remember.

But I DO.

I also recall being on Dad's back as a jockey while he, on all fours, played the horse who 'galloped' up and down the front hallway.

The floorboards of the hallway had been stained and polished until finances allowed the purchase of a hall carpet runner.

The carpet improved the temperature of the area and lessened the sound of walking.

Athough the runner covered the floor from door to door it left an eight inch gap on either side.

Mum was opposed to the 'rough-housing' but her fears of an injury to our person or her precious ornaments up on the shelf were never realized.

There was much squealing, noise and laughter during these playtimes.

The front door sported lovely stained glass to match the front windows in Mum and Dad's bedroom and the lounge room.
Deep red roses and green leaves formed the pattern and on bright sunny days the colors were reflected down the hallway that led to the dining room.
Above the dining room door to the hallway was wooden fretwork that resembled lemons on a stick!
(The same woodwork was repeated on the tall occasional table in the corner of the dining room opposite the wireless).
The walls of the hall were wood paneled four fifths of the way up then plastered the remainder of the way.
The narrow shelf that delineated the change of materials held many little treasures of china vases etc.
The plaster ceilings resembled tiny shells.
In the dining room the wood paneling stopped at waist height.

In the dining room several 'push open' French windows featured bottom panels of coloured glass, so popular in Californian Bungalows.

11 Duncan Street, Lidsdale

One memorable day Mum took delivery of a special dinner set for which she had for years saved coupons.

It was an Orchid Pattern set manufactured by Royal Doulton in England.
It was packed in straw within a large packing case and had been sent from Sydney by train.
Our neighbor, Mr Hughes, collected the box from the station and delivered it to the front room at our house.
Mum placed a sheet on the floor to collect the straw and began to unpack each cherished piece.
I watched until I became thoroughly bored-- there were endless pieces, and I went outside to play with my dolls and the cane chairs on the back cement verandah---with the tiny coffee cups newly unpacked!

After all, the size of the cups was perfect for tiny hands.
Mum came out to check on my whereabouts and couldn't believe what she saw.

Playing 'cups of tea' with her dolls was three-year-old Beverley Ann, displaying consummate good taste in fine china.

Controlling her natural urge to dive on the valued pieces, Vera calmly suggested I might like to play with her and share a cuppa.
I readily agreed and she was able to fake the procedure and collect the cups to 'do' the washing up.

That dinner set was only used on two occasions.
Once was for my wedding breakfast and the other for my Dad's wake.

It was shared by Shirl, Fay and I at Mum's request but the infamous coffee set was left to me intact.
Now I can play with it whenever I wish.

PERHAPS when I grow up I will drink only from fine china.

Vera's Orchid Pattern Dinner Set

Beverley Ann in her new apron(.Nearly three).

Dad had his bike to get to work or visit the local township.
Being wartime there were very few cars, no rubber for tyres and no available petrol.

The cost of buying a car was absolutely prohibitive for the working class though we did have an old 'T' Model Ford truck in the shed that actually belonged to the Wallerawang Golf Club.

(No car industry had been introduced into Australia, so any vehicles here had been imported from overseas.
The ships that would have transported them were now employed in 'war matters' being converted to 'war ships').

I remember the numerous rides on Dad's bike as we travelled to Wallerawang. I was perched on a green cushion that was tied to the cross bar, riding side-saddle.

I loved being encircled by Dad's arms as I held the upturned handle- bars.
A small, spare miner's lamp with that distinctive carbide smell, was mounted on the front of the bike to light the way when it was dark.
If it was extra cold, and it often was, Dad would cover my small hands with his.
The cold air would make my tiny nose tingle and sometimes I would have to raise a hand to rub the tiny, freckled mound.
Dad would encourage with conversation like "Hang on Bill. We won't be long."

Sometimes he whistled or hummed as we moved along.

Now here I must make a confession.
As we rode along and I rested my head against his chest, I would hear Dad's heart beating and the faster we went the quicker his heart would respond.
Naturally I assumed the legs operated the heart and only people who rode bikes had one!
With such comprehension of how the human body work there is no doubt I should share this knowledge.

PERHAPS I should be a nurse when I grow up or even find a job teaching anatomy and physiology!!!!!

How Dad's Heart Worked

Fay's eighth Birthday Fay, Uncle Doug and Bev

We rode up to the corner and onto the cement road which had been constructed by unemployed men during the depression in the early thirties.

Around the bend to the right where Mudgee Road forked, over the rattily old bridge that spanned Cox's River, past the beautiful sandstone St John's Church and Wallerawang Public School.

On the other side of the road was an old church converted now to a residence (where lived a boy named Laurie Oakes who would grow up to be the most powerful political journalist of his day), and, further on, the racecourse, then the golf links, before a big hill to Wallerawang township.

A railway station, War Memorial, two hotels and two shops, a few old houses and the Co-op constituted this bustling metropolis' shopping area.

The population lived beyond the main street but it was to one of the old houses near the hotels that we headed.

The owner was Mrs Frances.

Mary Francis was a business woman and she paid Dad to do her books for her illegal bookmaking interests.

Her house was full of treasures including dolls and vases and pretty dishes and the little candlesticks.

I loved the tassels on the velvet tablecloth and the bobbled edging on the swathe above the mantelpiece whose colors changed when caught in the reflection of the flickering firelight.

There were huge padded chairs with plump, gay cushions.

And a jar of lollies. There were always lollies.

I was tucked up in a blanket on a chaise lounge until it was time to go home.

I often wonder if I was taken as a bit of protection for Dad's reputation as Mum wasn't one to fraternize with the likes of Mary because SP bookying was a criminal offence in those days.

However she, Mum, would be waiting for us to arrive home and if it was later than expected Dad would receive a scolding for keeping me out so late. After a warm cup of milk cocoa I would be wrapped in a blanket warmed by the open fire and tucked up in bed on the sofa in the dining room.

I was soon fast asleep.

Shirl Bev Barry & Dorothy Nolan

Mum insisted we kept very regular hours and she saw to it that we were 'nice and early' to bed every night-though it wasn't always easy for me with my bed being part of the living room furniture.

The compensation was the warmth from the open fire that would be 'banked up' with pieces of coal before the adults went to bed and again when Dad got ready for work in the mornings.

I could doze off watching the myriad of colors the burning coal emitted and the numerous shapes thus formed.

Exceptions to early nights were when there was a dance at the local hall.

We would be wrapped up in a blanket and placed on one of the rows of seats pushed against the wall after the adults had indulged us by dancing with us. That was where we learned to dance. (I'm not that sure they were very successful with me).

Dad had taught me the basics while instructing me as he twirled me up and down the small hallway between our kitchen and dining room.

"One, two, three. One two, three" he would repeat as he waltzed me round.

Of course we wouldn't settle to sleep until after the home-made supper of sandwiches, cream filled sponges and lamingtons etc., washed down with a cup of tea made by boiling the giant kettles on the open fires in the supper room.

On other occasions we would be taken to Granny's to sleep where we could listen to the muffled sounds of the dance band that usually featured piano, violin, drums, and a trumpet.

The versatility of the group was always a source of wonder to me.

They could play any tune.

PERHAPS I will be lucky enough to marry a man who loves to dance with me............then PERHAPS I wont.

My first teacher was Miss Nellie Mugeridge and I was definitely her pet. (Ironically Miss Mugeridge couldn't stand Fay and they would be nasty to each other well into old age).

As I could already read and write when I commenced school I was sent to the other teachers with notes from Nellie while the other students applied themselves diligently.

I still have the certificate I was awarded for the third place in class and a book for the writing prize for that year even though I obviously did less writing than all of the other students!

We learned so many lessons with the aid of our sand tray.

A sheet of iron measuring a yard square had the sides turned up three inches and welded into place.

Bags of sand from the banks of the local Cox's River were collected and taken to the classroom where they were emptied into the trays.

If the lesson was on Geography we made rivers from blue paper, hills from mounds of sand, bridges from balsa wood, trees from cardboard and cotton wool, houses from bark, ponds from mirrors etc.

I could not believe that we were instructed to make a city that was built in the sea.

That sounded unlikely to me as all of the people would surely drown when it rained.

The name of that city was Venice.

I would have to check this out with Dad as I couldn't believe that a city could withstand the test of time over hundreds of years with the tides coming and going without sinking.

We were told the people travelled around in special boats in the streets that were all called canals.

Even the boats were called by another name.

This all sounded too far fetched for my liking.

Dad verified all that we had been told.

He said I may be lucky enough to meet someone who had been there during my lifetime.

PERHAPS I will.

We would create little villages, zoos with tiny metal or wooden animals, jungles like the ones seen in books, cities with sky scrapers constructed from empty match boxes which were also used to make furniture for the doll's house.

I really liked the dressing tables made from gluing three matchboxes together twice, gluing a seventh box in the center to hold them together, cutting a piece of cardboard to fit the top and cutting another piece which was covered with the silver paper from a penny chocolate to make the mirror.

A paper clip made the handles for the drawers.

They were great, strong storage for tiny treasures.

If I had finished my lessons Miss Mugeridge allowed me to sharpen the pencils by turning the handle of a box- like device built for the purpose.

I called it the' whirring' machine.

Just after I commenced school at Wallerawang Public School (aged four) the School held a Fete to raise money for books and there were lots of games of Chocolate Wheels, Lucky dips and Hooplas to name a few.

One of the big 6th class boys, John Farrimond, won a pale green bangle on the hoopla and he gave it to me because I was the littlest child in the school and I wouldn't be able to reach the table to have a go myself!

I kept that bangle until it broke when I was in my teens.

When I was awarded the third place certificate in mid-year and first in the end of year exams that year the presentation was made by our Headmaster, D.D. Metcalf, whose son, Dr Donald, would become world famous for his research work at Melbourne's Walter and Eliza Institute on the investigation of blood cells.

Dr Don was a classmate of Shirl's.

Despite the privations of war-time like rationing of petrol, my relatives once managed to scrounge sufficient petrol to take a rare family holiday together.

The three Nolan' girls' and their families organized a fishing trip.

The mode of travel was one of Lane's buses and the destination was Burrumjuck Dam south of Canberra.

This was indeed a trek of immense proportions in those days.

The body of the bus was cleared of several seats and only enough left for the seated passengers.

Uncle Kevin drove the bus and Aunty Vi sat next to him on the 'dickey seat'.

The tents, a small boat, tins of fuel, numerous fishing rods and any large items were packed up on the roof in a huge luggage rack.

It was summer time and the conditions were ideal for fishing, swimming, lazing, eating, chasing, hiding, boating and generally having a good time.

Marie Bourke and I shared the back seat of the bus as our bed and we would have to wriggle down towards the middle so we could reach each other's toes for 'tickle' games.

There were outdoor fires where everyone sat at night and not a small number of ales were consumed by the group--much to Vera's total disgust.

We roasted potatoes and burnt our noses eating them from their sticks.

We made damper that we smothered with butter and golden syrup.

We ate a variety of fish the men called by names we had never heard.

A small wallaby was transformed into a delicious stew.

There were delectable eels cleaned and cut into lengths about four inches long before being dipped in flour and fried in butter until golden brown.

And the toast!

Thick, golden, slightly smoked and dripping with lashings of butter kept cool in tins suspended on ropes in the dam.

A wonderful time was had by all and many memories stored for a lifetime.

Sadly the photographs of that wonderful holiday are no longer available to me.

PERHAPS those memories will be so vivid they will be recalled in seventy years hence.

Being able to read really well my sisters would demonstrate my skills to visiting older friends.

On one occasion Bonnie and Wilma Murphy called at our house and the girls called me in to read for the assembled group.

The story featured a girl named Penelope and in my lack of experience and knowledge I pronounced the name as Penny-lope.

Each time I said the name the girls held their sides as they laughed long and loud.

I had no idea why they laughed so much at my perfect reading and yet I knew I was being made fun of so I later asked Miss Mugeridge who had me read the story to her.

She hugged me and explained my mistake.

Despite attempts to bribe me to read on other occasions I never let my mean sisters make fun of me again.

Rationing was in place during and after the war.

That meant that each citizen was only allowed to buy a limited amount of clothing, butter, sugar, meat, tobacco, shoes, linen etc.

Each citizen was issued with a coupon book that comprised twelve pages, one for each month of the year.

Each page was divided into small squares on which was printed butter, sugar, tobacco etc.

You could only use your month's allowance of coupons and thus the amount of food you bought was 'rationed' to ensure equity of goods distributed.

It was impossible to purchase these goods without the required number of coupons.

The term 'black-marketeering' was coined to describe any exploiting of the rules and any offence of selling or buying goods at an inflated price without coupons was a chargeable offence.

That didn't mean that blackmarketeering didn't take place.
Essential service people (miners and servicemen) were given free cigarettes and our Dad would save his ration and sell them illegally

Prices would actually be marked as '2/6 (twenty five cents) and two coupons' for example.

It cost fewer coupons to buy material than a 'made' garment so most Mum's sewed their kids gear and l family members had very few clothes.

Mum had one good frock that was changed immediately upon her return home.
She would lightly sponge the underarms of the dress after removing the folded linen hankerchiefs that had been held in place there with tiny gold safety pins, then hang it 'to air' before hanging in the wardrobe.

Each family member was permitted to use one butter coupon per month so it was very common to use dripping, left over from roasting, for the making of cakes, pastries and even for toast, in lieu of butter.
The same limitations applied to sugar, (one half pound per adult per month) so honey was used as a replacement.

Living in the country certainly had advantages as we grew our own veggies, caught our fresh fish, ran our own chickens and had fresh milk, cream, butter and fresh fruit.

During the war it was not uncommon to dig an air-raid shelter in the back yard.

Ours was very 'swish' and well made with timber uprights to prevent the roof from collapse.
Dad, having worked in underground mines, was well informed in the methods employed in construction.
The entrance was gained through an angled door found at the bottom of the three descending steps.
The shelter had benches around the walls that could double as beds if need be, and alcovesin the walls for food.

Metal (used in the war effort) was scarce but my parents had managed to put some tinned food aside in case of a bombing raid and I remember the tins of condensed milk, huge cans of asparagus, melon and lemon and plum jam.
The shelter was situated near the double tank-stand just beyond the back verandah, and occasionally we would descend the steps and play in the dark, dank space.

I can still recall the extreme cold and rich, earthy smell.

It was big enough to house some of our neighbors in Duncan Street and I often pondered which of the neighbors would be invited to join us and who would be excluded.

It was also gazetted that householders have 'blackout' material on their windows so no lights were visible to the enemy at night and our neighbors readily complied.
Ours were made of black material curtains inside the normal ones.
We were so scared if we ever heard an aeroplane coming as we were convinced the enemy had found us.

Mum and her childhood friend, Ilma, had a disagreement and chose not to speak.

Mine was a carefree and secure, but lonely childhood and the only thing missing was a playmate of my own age.
Still I occupied myself talking to the chooks, chasing the cows and Peter, the old horse, making daisy chains, playing make-believe houses with my tea sets and little pans (and a few improvisations like the top of the Primus stove), reading, drawing, designing houses and jewellery, playing shops with the miniature samples of sauces and baked beans and jams found in the Show bags, collecting and blowing birds eggs, playing schools with my dolls, running, skipping and playing hopscotch, singing on the front verandah, dancing, 'driving' the old T Model Ford truck housed in our shed which took me to fascinating lands like China, England where the King lived and that strange wet place called Venice, playing tennis at the courts situated one hundred yards up the lane, running or making frequent visits to special neighbours, dancing in front of the back bedroom wardrobe mirror as I stood in the small hallway where Dad taught us to dance and getting up to mostly harmless mischief.

My Mixmaster!

I loved to identify the numerous local birds by their look and calls.

Magpie, Kookaburra, Ground Lark, Robin Red Breast, Blue Wren, Willy Wag Tail, Rosellas, Sulphur Crested Cocky, Plovers, Sparrows and Honey Eaters were all welcome visitors to the large Pussy Willow that lived outside our kitchen door.

I also had a collection of kites.

Two fine twigs were cut from the pussy willow tree then trimmed to the correct size. Each end was slotted for a short distance before forming a cross shape and binding the sticks with cotton to form a cross.

Strong cotton or fishing line was threaded around the shape and tied firmly. The shape was placed on a sheet of brown paper and the outline cut leaving an extra inch around the edge.

A glue was applied to the excess and the paper folded over the fishing line.

While the glue dried a tail was made from twisting oblong paper pieces to form a bow and these were attached to an extra yard of line before being tied to the base of the now recognizable kite.

A fishing line or ball of fine string was tied to the centre of the structure and carried to the top of the hill for a try out.

The glue used at home was made from mixing flour and water together.

At Aunty Doll's the glue was made from boiling a fresh rabbit's skin for many hours.

It was a most effective adhesive.

Most families owned B B guns and any bird who invaded the fruit trees after having been warned was dealt with.
Even Vera had a B B gun of her own.

The Kookaburras made their home across the lane in a dead gumtree and it was a common sight to see them with a snake in their giant beaks.
On afternoons of inclement weather I was occasionally permitted to turn on the radio to listen to the Argonauts club and listen to the stories of Jason and the Golden Fleece.

The doorknobs of the doors in our house were shoulder height and were made of brass.
Vera kept them shining bright.
They were also useful in removing teeth.
When the infant teeth became so loose they would become a hazard and my parents were concerned I would swallow them while eating they would tie a length of crochet cotton around the offending tooth and attach the other end to the hallway doorknob.
With me a couple of feet away from the knob the door was slammed and the tooth was extracted.

Bev with her favourite dolls especially Nellie the Nurse.
Age 4

I visited neighbors named Nottle's occasionally, then more frequently when I started school and I had a permanent job of taking all the kettles outside to the water tank and filling them.

I was known to get very wet by turning on the side tap too fast at Nottle's on more than one occasion and Aunty Glad would have to go through the 'duster bag' to find replacement clothes until mine dried each time.
Digger took a photo of me dressed in such apparel and gave Mum a copy.
She was horrified to see me dressed in 'rags' and put it in the fireplace ready to burn the next time the fire was lit.
I took it and hid it in a giant cane laundry basket that lived in the backyard laundry.

The basket was so big it was four feet high and as round as a bike wheel and, despite being the palatial home of numerous spiders, it was an ideal hiding place if you didn't want to be found.

Digger's Photo.

The lost photo -Bev

The kettles at Nottles would be placed on the hearth in the old kitchen and lifted up to the stove top as required by a big adult.

The empty ones would be placed on the empty spots on the fender that covered the hearth.

As I grew up a tap was installed in the kitchen-and I became redundant.

Every house had a dresser as no cupboards were built in kitchens at that time. While Granny's was neglected Mum's was kept highly polished. Nottle's was unpainted.

I loved to help scrub that old dresser with Bon Ami powder, turn the wringer on washing days, water the Aspidistras housed in green gallon drums in the middle verandah, choose a book to read from the library and play the lovely old Beale Piano housed in the large front room.

Later there would be exploring the district on bikes, picnics, sport, movies etc.

The wall at the back of our old three roomed school was made from brick and a line representing the height of tennis net was painted across it.
The large yard in front of the wall was evened gravel and was ideal for a practice ground.
Few kids had a tennis racquet in those days.
I was lucky enough to receive a Junior Slazenger Challenge for my graduation from Primary School and I was so proud of that special gift. (WARNING:- Regardless of how old you are do not loan your valued possessions to oldest daughters who may never return them).

Aunty Glad Nottle kept several old racquets at her house and she was always happy for us to borrow them on the understanding that they be returned the same day when we played on the courts at the top of our lane.
The old wooden racquets were always kept in presses that had been made from two wooden squares that were held together with threaded screws that were operated by tightening or releasing the wingnuts.
Some of the racquets were so antiquated they had flattened tops of thick wood and were so heavy we all avoided them if we had a choice.
Our Dad prepared the gravel courts by mixing a combination of lime and water to mark the necessary lines.

He would first roll the surface of the hard court with the heavy roller kept for the purpose.
Many a time we tried to flex our developing muscles by endeavouring to move the huge cylinder of cement with its long iron handle- without success.

At lunch time on some 'tennis days' during the school holidays Mum would bring up trays of freshly made sandwiches and jugs of home- made cordial with cake and cut fruit to follow.
I never had trouble getting a group of kids to join me for a round robin tennis day.

I loved the days when my older boy cousins allowed me to play tennis or footie with them and although they always beat me I gained much strength and knowledge as a result.

The paddock opposite our house had been cleared for use as a football field.

I developed a burning desire to become proficient enough at tennis to beat Shirl even though she played in the local comp and was seven years my senior.
It took me until I was thirteen-but I finally did it.
After that once she went back to beating me as usual.

The one thing I could not do was play inside our house, not even read a book, as Mum did not believe reading to be a valuable past-time.

My Mum was a 'house fanatic' and she would not allow us to help in the house because her standard was so high.
Even if Dad helped us do the dishes while Mum watered the garden she would take all the china from the cupboard and re-wash it.
There was never a wrinkle in the beds and you were not allowed to sit on your bed after it was made or even enter the bedroom without a very good reason.

The front bedroom housed a beautiful 'bedroom suite' in immaculate condition consisting of wardrobe, lowboy, bed and dressing table resplendent with its elaborate mirror.
On the dressing table a full crystal dressing table set lived.
Tray, clock, powder bowls, candle holder and jewel box glistened in the sunlight.

These pieces were placed on one of two duchess sets, one of which was cream with cut worked design edged with gold and brown fancy work and a set in the same colouring stitched on organdie.

On the bed lay a gold, satin bedspread with matching ruched pillows.

These resplendent pieces were carefully removed and folded each evening and carefully draped over a large old cane chair behind the door.

In the winter months their place was taken by a huge felt backed, kangaroo skin quilt.

Numerous skins had been matched and cut into twelve inch squares forming a very attractive, and very heavy, rug.

The rug had been won in a raffle.

In the back bedroom a similar arrangement of furniture was found.

The metal bed was adorned with pretty, porcelain insets that matched the toilet set of jug, dish, soap holder etc that had formerly lived in the old toilet stand.

The dressing table with its oval mirror had large, commodious draws.

The top draw housed a lovely, poker worked Kookaburra box that contained all manner of hair accessories-combs of varying sizes, butterfly clips, hair pins, clips, slides, padding for making hair rolls, brushes, curlers and the like.

There were discarded chocolate boxes for the girl's make-up.

Mum wouldn't hear of their loose face powder spilling anywhere.

The old inlayed wardrobe housed some interesting pieces including two fur pieces, relics of Mum's youth.

One was called a "Fox" fur and was a long, thin piece of fox's skin to which was still adhered the fox's head!

Another was a dainty fur cape made from lappin (rabbit) that today adorns the shelves in my bedroom.

They hung alongside a gaily multi-coloured, striped, blazer that Dad had worn in the 1920's.

There were straw boater hats and old coats that were well out of fashion.

On top of the wardrobe were other relics of days past including that gold cane basket that Shirl had carried at Ivy Hill's wedding.

The special mystery item was a two volumed, leather bound, set of books that were written in a foreign language.

These books were handed down for several generations on Dad's Dowdell side.

I snuck a look occasionally and was indeed impresses with the exquisite, copy-plate handwriting on thick, shiny cream paper throughout the two volumes.

No one could explain the significance of the books- they were just there.

PERHAPS in years to come Dad will be approached by some visitors from Ireland who are conducting a worldwide search for the hand written volumes written by men of the cloth in Ireland centuries ago.

Such men were the only educated people in those times.

Each volume actually contained the history of the county in which the learned gentleman had lived during the English occupation in the eighteenth century. The books were written in Gaelic so the English could not understand them and then entrusted to a highly respected family for safekeeping.

They were considered priceless by the Dublin Museum, hence their worldwide search.

Shirl had a friend in the 1960's who was a Librarian and she mentioned the search to Shirl.

Shirl immediately rang Dad and ask him if he would part with the books in exchange for a considerable sum the Irish were offering for them.

Dad told Mum the story and ask where they were.

He was not happy to learn Mum had burnt both "old musty books that no-one ever looked at" under the copper!

There was always the smell of furniture polish and fresh flowers and home cooking in our house which sounds very inviting, but, there were rooms we were not allowed to enter unless it was a special occasion.

As the house only had two bedrooms the space was limited.

The 'forbidden room' was the lounge room which housed a velvet club lounge suite in autumn colors, a china cabinet in which the Orchid pattern dinner set lived with a selection of Dad's golf trophies including a wooden shield that proudly bore his name as District Champion in Golf, a matching coffee table, large portraits of the family (we referred to it as 'Rogue's Gallery) and, much later, Shirl's piano.

Two paintings of swans also lived there on either side of the ornate little fireplace surrounded with decorated tiles down either side.

Can you believe in a climate like ours that this fireplace was never lit- it would create a mess you must understand!

On the ornate wooden surrounds and mantle piece several little treasures lived.

Two china red-breasted robins gazed down from the higher shelves.

They still bore the price tag of two shillings and sixpence on their base.

A pale blue vase with a black line around its brim (that had been a wedding gift to Mum and Dad) never held flowers in case it would get broken.

We would have been lucky to have entered that room twice a year as Mum believed in 'looking after' special pieces and that meant they were not used.

This was not an idiosyncrasy peculiar to Mum, but a common practice of the day.

Everything in our home was beautifully cared for but rarely enjoyed.

PERHAPS Mum judged her entire worth by her exemplary housekeeping skills.

Her routine never deviated.

Monday was washing day.

She would arise very early in the morning and light the old wood burning copper that had been filled the previous evening with clean water.

Commencing with the white clothes (sheets only came in white) she would boil the articles in the hot soapy water made by shaving the bars of pure soap with a knife over the now bubbling water.

For extra effect, Borax powder would be added

Then, with the aid of an old sawn-off broom handle called a 'copper stick', she would lift the hot, steamy, wet pieces into the adjoining cement wash trough.

Here cold water was used to rinse the suds from the 'stewed' washing.

Being much more modern than many of her peers, Mum had an efficient, hand turning wringer with rubber rollers to remove the excess water from the clothes.

Many of her contemporaries still had a 'mangle' with wooden rollers.

It was considered a treat to be able to turn the handle for this procedure--if we were ever up early enough!

Next the clothes would be plunged into trough number two (by way of the wringer) that contained clean water to which a bluing agent had been added.

Again the wringer was employed and the clothes directed to the large, cane washing basket.

Any soiled clothing was plied heavily with soap and scrubbed against the old scrubbing board found in all laundries of the day.

Some were made entirely of wood and the updated models had insets of toughened glass.

Naturally, ours was in the latter category.

The second load would be sorted and the procedure repeated until the coal dust laden work- clothes were treated.

Finally, the dusters would be washed after lunchtime.

Only the hot, grubby water remained half filling the copper.

This was bucketed out and used to scrub the front and back verandahs and the 'lav' and the dregs left to cool until it could be used to water the plants.

Relying only on the rainwater collected in the tanks, every drop of water was utilized.

Meanwhile the clothes had to be hung out to dry.

The clothes line consisted of a piece of wire stretched between two stout posts that had been sunk into the ground.

As the weight of the wet clothes took their toll the wire line sank down in the middle. This problem was dealt with by 'propping'.

A limb from a gum tree was chosen not only for its length and thickness but for the formation of a natural fork for at the thinner end.

This fork was 'shoveled' to support the wire and was then propped in a small hole scooped from the earth.

If you wanted to remove specific articles from the line you simply lowered the prop to the required height and corresponding hole.

(Granny Nolan's line was located inside her large chook run so it was imperative that the prop not be lowered too far!!)

To avoid the contamination of the larger pieces they were pegged (with giant dolly pegs) nearer the stout uprights and the smalls were designated to the center.

Mum's washing was sparkling white and bright and would have been the perfect sample for a washing-soda adds.

She also used starch liberally and, before the clothes that required stiffening were hung out to dry, she would rinse them in a solution of dissolved starch made by pouring boiling water over the contents of the starch packet and stirring it until it dissolved.
The stiffer the requirement, the more starch added.

If the items were meant to be shiny- like pillow slips or collars, the hot starch mixture was stirred with a wax candle.

Mum had a philosophy that any grime the article encountered would come out in the wash as the starch itself was removed.
I would sometimes eat a piece of starch and the mass would soften in my mouth as it mixed with the saliva and leave a smooth, tasteless, dry, after-taste.
If the starched items dried too soon they were 'dampened down' by being sprinkled with water that was shaken out of a bottle to which a holey top had been attached.
The holes in the top were usually made by punctures from a nail that had been repeatedly hammered through the metal, though it was possible to buy the 'flasher' models of these aids that had a stem covered with thin rubber that enabled any sized bottle to be used for the purpose.
The treated items were then rolled up and wrapped in a towel.
Tablecloths, tea towels, blouses, shirts, pillow slips or pillow shams and the edge of top sheets, pinafores, dresses and aprons all received special attention.

This procedure was imperative for three reasons namely. It lessened the wrinkles, spread the moisture evenly so no dry spots appeared later on the ironed article and ensured the ironing was done the following day before the moulding process took hold!!!

PERHAPS I will derive as much pleasure from starching and ironing when I grow up as Mum did.

At the completion of the washing saga the scrubbing began.
Like everyone else in the country areas no sewerage was available so our lavatory was built down the backyard as far away from the house as possible---for very obvious reasons!

My version of an affluent- I repeat, 'affluent' person, was someone who had a flush toilet.
Even though I wasn't tall enough to reach the toilet chains in vogue in sewered toilets at the time, I want you to know I set my sights high!
I was determined to one day own a modern toilet.

PERHAPS someone will invent a cistern that will be lower down so small fry can reach easily.

Everyone had variations on the theme.
In some instances, such as on my Aunt's farm, the toilet was placed over a deep hole dug for the purpose.
The hole could have been two feet square by six foot deep and the 'lav' remained in situ until the 'level' of the hole necessitated a shift.
A new hole was simply prepared in a new location and the soil that was removed in its creation was used to fill in the old one.
(I had nightmares about falling down that giant hole and sinking to the 'bowels' of the earth, never to be seen again).

At home our toilet featured a flap door at its rear and this apparatus made life easier for the 'Lavvy Man'.

In the 'wee' small hours, this phantom of the night would creep into our yards and exchange the old can through that trap- door in the rear of the construction. He would hoist the used pan to his shoulder that had been covered by a leather cape as it rested against his ear as he left the premises.

In no time the new smelly device became even smellier despite Mum's valiant efforts to scrub the structure around it from top to 'bottom'- if you'll pardon the pun.
'Phenyl' was dispensed in copious amounts and it was always a matter of conjecture as to what constituted the worst odour- the disinfectant or the 'matter' it was trying to mask.
The seat received a thorough scrubbing with scrubbing brush and sand soap.
We were so 'proper' that we had a toilet seat lid!!

I am inclined to think this was designed with the the curtailment of odour in mind.

The entire building was smothered with an unkempt Honeysuckle bush.

As one sat 'cogitating' it was possible to lean forward and reach for the florets which, when sucked from the base, exuded minute amounts of sweet, tasty nectar.

This choice of climber also emitted a very pleasant perfume for months at a time.

Newspaper, cut in uniform squares, was our only source of toilet paper.

Large bundles were held in readiness as a nail was driven through one corner of thirty sheets, then threaded with a piece of string.

The string was tied to form a hoop so the paper could be suspended from a special hook within range.

Ouch!

The snow trail to Ryan's lavatory

PERHAPS when I grow up I will indulge myself with the extravagance of using reams and reams and reams and reams of SOFT toilet tissue ---if it has been invented by then and is readily available!

Dad had made a new, very 'flash' toilet seat that nearly covered an area from wall to wall.

I always felt this addition was for the benefit of the resident spiders.

Resident Spider

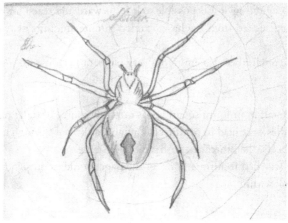

"There's a Redback on my toilet seat la la la!" was a popular song at that time! The toilets being down the bottom of the yards, and used frequently, sometimes had a 'made' path joining it to the main structure.

A disadvantage of the tyranny of distance was we were scared to go 'down the back' after dark because it was like a half day's hike, so you would beg a family member to accompany you.
This was a disadvantage if you happened to be down the pecking order with not much power to trade.
You WENT when ordered, yet your pleas for accompaniment fell on deaf ears.

I devised a method to ensure I was not accosted on my nocturnal journeys.
I would turn off the lights in the kitchen and slowly open the back door and stand until my eyes became accustomed to the dark so I could make out any foreign shapes in the yard then I would 'bolt' in the direction of the toilet so fast I was sure nothing nor no- one could catch me.

We always had a chamber pot under the bed for voiding in on nights of really bad weather.

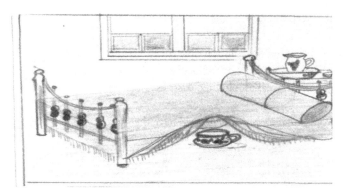

Wednesday was polishing day and all of the floors that were then covered by lino were washed and then covered with a thick layer of floor polish.
They were then rubbed with clean cloths until a shine appeared.

Bread, fruit and veggies, and later milk, were also delivered by their respective specialists with their horse and carts.
We welcomed the baker whose van had double doors at the rear.
When the doors were opened we would be enveloped with the unmistakable smell of freshly baked, hot meat pies.

At threepence a pie they were a rare treat.

The range of cakes was sufficient to tempt the taste buds and on the rare occasion one was allowed I would choose puff pastry' horse- shoes' with bright pink icing on the top.
We loved Bracey's delivery day of groceries on Thursday because a bag of boiled lollies was always included for the kids in the family.
Frequently a bag of broken biscuits was also included.
Braceys had their own truck that they used for the purpose.

Mum kept fine glass mugs in the glass fronted dresser, each one housing the money for the various accounts.
It was strictly a cash economy in those days before credit cards and the like.

My parents believed if you didn't have the money to pay for an article then you couldn't afford to have it and Mum insisted all bills be paid immediately they arrived, especially Bracey's who kept monthly accounts.

The only exception to this rule was the house.

Friday was cooking day and the cake tins were filled to overflowing.
Date cakes, orange cakes, and chocolate and coconut cakes.
Small cakes, large cakes, biscuits, pastries.

If you could imagine them we would have them.

There were no ENDOCHRINOLOGISTS when we were kids!

It is also worth noting that we knew exactly what was likely to be on the men for tea each day.

Monday it was rissoles or cutlets and gravy, veggies and pudding (usually a steamed date, fruit, ginger or jam pudding).

On one occasion Mum had made a jam roly-poly (made from suet, spread with thick jam, then rolling into a log which was either boiled in a pudding cloth or baked in the oven).

Either way the jam tended to escape from the ends of the sweet therefore we preferred the middle section that housed more jam.

Dad mostly served up our sweets and he asked "Who would like a pudding end?"
No one spoke until Fay finally broke the silence. "I suppose I'll have one".

With that Dad cut the roll in half and gave half to Fay and kept the other half for him. Despite Mum's protestations he did not share the pudding ends with the rest of us.

Lesson learned.

Tuesday we might have roasted rabbit or corned beef and boiled veggies of all kinds-carrots, parsnips, turnips, pumpkin, peas, silver beet, cabbage and mashed potatoes flavored with finely chopped onion, jelly and tinned or bottled fruit with lashings of cream.
Wednesday was a casserole of one kind or another or a grill and baked custard, tapioca or blancmange, sago and stewed fruit.

Thursday it was a home-made meat pie or steak, depending on Mum's timetable.
Strips of steak were threaded into the funnel of the mechanical mincer that Mum had screwed to the table edge and as the meat, chunks of onion and bread crusts re-appeared as mince she would place the mixture in a saucepan with stock to cook it.
The juices from the home-minced steak in the pie would be simmered with some veggies to make a soup that was devoured after school soaking through a large chunk of bread.
This was also 'novelty' day and we awaited a special treat of something for sweets Mum bought in town.
This was sometimes fresh fruit we did not see very often like watermelon or grapes or a big bun from the baker's.

Friday was a non-meat day because Catholics weren't permitted to eat meat on that day so it was egg casserole, fish, salmon patties or fish casserole.
The sweet was usually a baked pie-blackberry, apple or apricot, served with jugs of custard and lashings of that delicious scalded cream.
Yum, yum, yum.

Saturday Mum would make a huge boiler of soup that constituted a three course meal!!
It would be brim full of bones, meat, veggies, macaroni, and herbs.
I learned to spell my name with the alphabet macaroni that escaped the big pot.

Sunday was roast lunch day after church and the favorite of mine (and still is) was roast lamb and fresh mint sauce.
Move over Tom Cruise!

The dining room was the centre of our home.
The open fire was ordinary with its metal fender that captured any coals that rolled through the grill, an ornate hob and a blazing fire during most months of the year.
Above was the mantle.
The centre piece was the seven day clock that passed each day reminding us each quarter hour that each minute was precious.
Inside the clock lived the special key that was religiously removed at seven o'clock every Monday night.
Mum would wind the key until it ceased to turn and the key would be returned to its place for another week.
Two crystal vases balanced each other on either side of the clock.
On either side of the fireplace rested two large cane armchairs.
Next to the fireplace was a console radio that commanded the corner.
Reaching nearly four feet in height it was veneered in a rich timber and the sloping upper top was adorned with a fan-like window in which the stations were clearly displayed.
In the back of the wireless a conglomeration of wires and valves could be seen.
Static was common and the slightest adjustment of the dial usually rectified the problem.
The reception of Radio 2LT was crisp and clear.
Next to the wireless was the settee that doubled as my bed for many years.

The wooden table and chairs were part of a set that included a sideboard and Mum's pride and joy, her dresser.
The furniture was kept in pristine condition and polished every Friday.
The table was especially rubbed with brown boot-polish.
Mum would not permit us to do the polishing as we weren't 'fussy' enough.
The upper glass doors of the dresser were kept bright and shining by cleaning them with crumpled newspaper that had been dipped in a mixture of Methylated spirits and soap and warm water.
Dry paper was then used to absorb the mixture before a soft cloth ensured the surface sparkled.

The doors were covered with dainty curtains that bore a pattern like honey-comb in a cream colour.

Behind the curtains, several compartments had been constructed.
In one lived a cream teaset that was decorated with pink flowers.
Hanging on cup-hooks in the same compartment were clear glass mugs featuring a pattern resembling a plant where the 'flowers' had been created by smudging your fingertips.
They were very Art Noveau.
They had been a wedding gift to Mum and Dad from their attendants, Jim and Ilma.
In another compartment six beautiful and elegant long-stemmed, green tumblers rested.
Simply and tastefully embossed with garlands they were my favourites.

The pink fruit dish and Granny's jardiniere rested on crisp, starched doileys.
The doileys were everywhere and were changed every week.
The lower cupboards held tins and bulk items.
The drawers were the home of the family cutlery and the current tablecloth.

The sideboard comprised two cupboards with drawers in the centre.
The biggest top drawer was the home for everyone's socks.

Inside the right hand cupboard could be found any bottles of medicines, sticking plaster, bandages, or other items that had no permanent home like a pretty little pink alabaster clock that didn't work and a lovely little silver jewel box that stood on four elaborate legs.
Next to them were bottles of ink in red and black and blue.
The shallow mirror atop the sideboard reflected the crystal and glass dishes on top of the piece.
The banana shaped dish in the middle was always full of flowers.
If the flowers were gladioli they were shortened each day as the flowers began to wither and by weeks end the arrangement would look very different.

The final piece of furniture was the matching ice chest.
An ice-man delivered a large block of ice twice weekly.
He carried the block in by hoisting it onto a sugar bag that covered his shoulder by means of a large caliper-like tool that had embedded its points in the ice.

He would lift the lid of the enameled top compartment and lower the ice. During the ensuing days the ice would melt and drip to the drip tray found at the base.
This tray was emptied every morning.

Although the food could not be frozen it did manage to keep the butter from melting in the summer.

We always sat at the table for meals and it was a joyous time of communicating the day's events.
There was a lot of chatter and laughter and lots of "Hurry ups" from Mum who hovered over your dirty plate as the last vestige of the meal was taken.

Dad then served the sweets.

Mum dressed the table with a beautifully laundered table-cloth and a range of condiments-tomato sauce in two varieties, (one for David and a home-made variety for the remainder of the family). 'Hot' sauce for Dad, salt and pepper, sugar covered with a crocheted and beaded cover, butter in a lidded dish, jam in a dish, honey jar and mustard, pickles and chutney and a large jar of freshly pickled beetroot, condensed milk and a dainty silver teapot that shone with a polish that suggested it was brand new.
The bread board and breadknife ensured slices of bread that varied in size depending on the freshness of the loaf.

The teapot would be used so much that the handle eventually broke.

Every night every receptacle was emptied and washed so as not to encourage infestation by tiny, black piss ants.
If, on the rare occasion the ants did manage to infiltrate the barriers Mum created the food would taste and smell of very strong urine that was impossible to remove.

We would all leave the table satisfied to the maximum.
It was as well that we were all physically active.

Part of the mealtime ritual involved arguments that took place there.
Dad would ask our opinion on a subject and agree, encouraging further input.

Then he would commence to systematically tear down your argument and force you to defend the stance you had adopted.

Dad maintained it encouraged us to think critically and clearly.

I think it encouraged two already argumentative middle daughters to become even more-so!

I would maintain my love of argument throughout my life and honed my skills by participating in debate teams throughout school and higher education.

All the cooking was done on a fuel stove (in which both wood and coal was burned) in a tiny, weeny kitchen that housed a small table that had a shelf under it for pots and pans.
They were hidden by a checked gingham curtain.
Later we had a porcelain sink put in under the window with a cupboard underneath.

Mum didn't like to wash up in the sink because it was so hard it chipped the china.
She sometimes placed a towel in the sink to protect the china but generally she used the metal wash- up dish that also used much less water and the water, when used, could easily be carried outside and thrown on the garden.

The china 'lived' in the dresser in the dining room, as did the cutlery, so everything was carried from one room to another.
It wasn't until after I left home that the kitchen was made to look like a kitchen.

It was also then that we would purchase a chip heater for use in the bathroom.

Although we had a bathroom (not all houses did) we bathed in a big, round, galvanized tub that was placed in front of the kitchen stove every weekend.

The doors of the firebox and oven would be opened to give out warmth.
Buckets of hot water were carried from the copper in the old laundry and emptied into the bath.
The youngest was bathed first then the tub would be topped up with a kettle full of hot water from the stove top before the next candidate entered.

This procedure took place on Saturday nights and the other nights we washed in the bathroom hand basin or the very shallow water in the bath.

Dad bathed at the mine each day as miners were covered with coal dust and only the whites of their eyes were visible after a working shift.

The scarcity of water was also a serious consideration and the rungs in the tanks were regularly tappedby banging them with an upturned broom to gauge how empty they were.
It was all a matter of priorities and there was not much point in being well and frequently bathed if you died of thirst.
It would be some years before we would get a town supply of water to augment, and eventually replace, the tanks.
That was the way it was living in the bush.

Mum took delivery of a very modern device called an electric washing machine.
It was a Simpson brand and was a green enameled bowl perched on four legs.
On the top was a wringer that turned by itself when you turned a knob.
Inside the bowl was an agitator that went from side to side 'stirring' the clothes to remove the dirt.
This gyration resulted in much movement.

Our neighbors, Mrs White and Mrs Hughes came down to see the new addition.

They stood at the old laundry door very near each other, very unsure of this contraption, and in her broad Scottish accent Mrs Hughes was heard to say "Well, I never, ever."

On very, very, special occasions, usually on Sundays, a block of ice-cream was purchased but this was very rare for several reasons.

Firstly, we had no fridge, just an ice chest that kept food cool but didn't freeze anything.

Secondly we had no car to rush to a shop at the appropriate time and thirdly we had no shop like a supermarket that was open at weekend!

The rare block would have to be purchased by someone who had a car who would pick up the treat for us at one shop in Wallerawang that sold ice-cream and deliver it to our house in a reasonable state.

We couldn't wait to tear the cardboard from the rapidly melting treat that was devoured with ecstasy.

Part of the ritual was to suck the cardboard covering least any tiny morsel be wasted.

It was a red letter day when we had our first fridge delivered.

It was called a' Silent Knight' and it ran on kerosene.

Inside it housed two tiny trays for home-made ice cream.

My favorite was passion fruit and it was made from fresh cream, eggs, condensed milk and fresh passion fruit.

The mixture was frozen then removed and re-beaten at least twice producing a smooth, flavorsome ice that couldn't be surpassed.

Glycerene was sometimes added to stop the mixture from freezing.

As the volume increased during the mixing, it was necessary for someone to slurp the overflow so it was not wasted.

I offered.

See? I really tried to be helpful.

PERHAPS when I grow up I will still think ice-cream to be one of my very favorite foods.

Sunday night's tea was salad, in particular Granny Nolan's Egg Salad, cold meat and a smorgasbord of treats.

Lamingtons, caramel tarts, cream filled sponges with passion fruit icing, fresh scones and home- made jams, butterfly cakes and a variety of slices.

It was an endocrinologist's nightmare and we loved it!

In daylight hours I would run from the corner of our street down to our house pacing myself against cars that came around the corner from Lithgow.

I repeated the process running up.

I tried to reach our gate before the cars passed the top of our street from where I had started.

I was unaware that this training contributed to my athletic successes.

A favored family occupation was to pick blackberries when they were in season.

We often started with the bushes across the road and if they showed signs of snake comings and goings we would set fire to the bush and eliminate the offending reptiles with our waiting shovels as they hastily left their home.

Buckets were filled, (despite the amounts eaten by the pickers,) and there was always enough fruit to be bottled for blackberry pies in the winter and to make jam.

No sprays were used on the fruit so it was safe to eat any we saw.

Huge mushrooms grew in the paddocks shared by the cattle.

We had special 'Mushie' knives to cut the stalks and the old cane baskets were kept just for the purpose of transporting the delectable fungi.

We had competitions to see who could find the biggest ones.

Breakfasts of stewed mushrooms, crunchy bacon and thick buttered toast ensured we were set for the day ahead.

Dad loved to play "Put 'em up".
He would adopt a boxing pose and call to us "Put 'em up" and we would attack him en masse.
Mum would show her disapproval and rouse at Dad accusing him of being too rough with us. "You are too strong and forget they are little girls Jim. Don't do it, you'll hurt them Jim".
"One of these days they will be big enough to give you a dose of your own medicine" she told him prophetically.

Dad would laugh and continue to spar with us, dancing and weaving with considerable skill as he goaded us "Come on, catch me. Hit me, come on hit me here" and he would thrust forward his chin or pat his upper arm as he skipped provocatively in our direction always just out of reach of our feeble efforts to vent our frustrations.
He would lightly tap us with make-believe punches all the while voicing a running commentary.

"Yes. A right to the side of the head, a left uppercut to the chin, a sharp jab to the solar plexus, a right to the body like this, and this".
Mum would intervene. "That's enough Jim". and she would step in front of him and gather us to her skirt despite Dad's howls of protest that it was just a game and no one would ever get hurt.
Well, he wasn't quite right.

Over the years this ritual continued and on one occasion when now teenager Shirley Joyce retaliated when a delivered blow did connect with her, she administered a swift, sharp jab of her own to Dad's upper midriff---and broke two of his ribs!

He was trussed up for weeks in ten inch wide lengths of sticking plaster and through his labored breathing was heard to say he had lost all enthusiasm for pugilistic activities.

And indeed he had!

We always had a very special outfit to wear to church or for very special occasions.

I remember some of those special outfits including a bought, apple green, Georgette dress that had a smocked bodice adorned with pink grub roses.

The matching straw hat had shirred green Georgette under the brim and green satin ties under the chin.

Fay had a similar outfit just a little bit more grown-up than mine.

Many times I received a good scolding for chewing the ends of my ribbons.

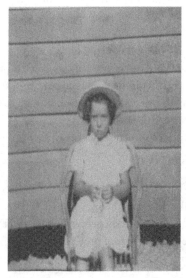 

Bev and Fay resplendant in green georgette

Another dress, was grey linen with a square neck and very full skirt around which Mum had fancy-worked a hemline of pansies in variegated colors.
Mum liked to make me pinafores in different colours and I had a tartan one, pink and lemon ones and a variety of blouses that could be interchanged.

Although I never had straight hair, Mum would insist on 'setting' it.
This demanded a strict ritual.
Firstly the hair was washed with Sunlight or Velvet soap then rinsed in precious tank water to which a spoonful of vinegar had been added.
While still wet my hair was divided into regular sized tufts and as I held one end of a piece of linen above my head Mum would wind the hair around the other end she held then she would take it back up covering the hair until she could tie her end to mine.

The result was a head of 'Shirley Temple' curls that Mum loved.
If she had known how bloody uncomfortable the lumps of trussed hair were to try and sleep on she may not have been so keen.

On one occasion I thought I would be bald when I caught my hair that had been plaited in the branch of a tree while climbing.
I was left dangling, unable to reach the lower branches with my feet or support my body weight to unhook my hair.
While I cried and yelled my Uncle Doug (who had been seated on the toilet) heard me, jumped the back fence and came to the rescue.
That did not stop me from climbing trees of all kinds in the future.
I had a 'cow-lick' and Mum preferred a fringe.
My hair would not sit evenly and Mum even cut my hair on one side to make it 'sit right'.
The trouble was Mum liked to part my hair in the middle and one side was curlier than the other.
I mostly had plaits when I was young for that reason.

There were times when I was cheeky to Mum and if I didn't think an action or punishment was fair I said so.
This mostly involved Fay who told 'whoppers' and derived much pleasure in getting me into strife.
As she was so much older Mum would believe her.
Much of the time she fabricated a story and as punishment I was banned from visiting Nottle's.

On one occasion after a couple of days absence Aunty Glad asked where I'd been and when I told her the story that Fay had told Mum I had been rude to Aunty Glad she displayed the rarest of angry behavior and phoned Mum and in no uncertain terms told Mum what she thought of the punishment AND of Fay.

I think Fay's behavior was partly the reason why I was spoiled by the neighbors. Shirl was also very highly thought of.

We had plenty of fruit (except for oranges that were a rarity.)
If we did happen upon an orange or apple that was a bit on the sour side we simply sprinkled it with salt to make it palatable.
If you don't suffer from high blood pressure try it sometime.
I can still relive the pleasure of swinging on the antiquated rope swing in the old apricot tree at Nottle's as we reached up higher and higher to pluck the delectable, sweet fruit from the uppermost branches.
They were the most delicious apricots I have ever eaten and I recall slurping every morsel of juice from my chin so as not to waste a singledrop.

I felt God had gathered all the sunshine in the world and placed it inside those apricots, they were so special.
In Granny's orchard there were different trees of plum, apples and pears.
And every year there were the tiny sweet apples on our tree that were usually full of coddlin-moth.
As this tree grew in the chook run it was never treated for the invaders, least it poison the valued chooks.
This tree was also a perfect place to hide when Mum was chasing me with a switch off the Pussy Willow tree that lived near our back door.
By the time she stopped to break off the switch I was up the tree and out of reach as far as I could get!

Another favored safety haunt was under the old brick tank stand because it was always full of spiders and cobwebs and there was no way Mum would come in after me.
The much maligned spiders came in handy when anyone cut their hand as the broom handle was employed to gather some spider's web that was placed on the wound to stop the bleeding and aid healing.

I devised a series of special 'languages' that I spoke to Mum when she was cross with me.

We would have been punished if we had indulged in bad language but these funny languages could be delivered with all the expressive intonations of the foulest language I'd ever heard, but she couldn't prove what I was really saying. Because the words I spoke sounded so funny Mum would tell me to stop and I would mock her with incomprehensive words and as much facial expression as I could muster and, invariably, I would make her smile, then laugh at my cunning, and not once did I get a belting when I actually deserved one.

As Mum was the only female in her family not to have a 'flower name' I learned early on how to press one of her buttons.

Mum and I would be engaged in an altercation and Mum would insist I apologies so I would say "Sorry."
Mum, now getting cross would question "And who am I?"
"Pansy" I would shout as I headed for the tank stand, or the apple tree, or the back fence, or the front gate all at GREAT speed!

The only problem with leaving the scene of the crime was I eventually had to go home!

Years before Mum's sister, Aunty Lil, had married Albert Bourke and they had three children, Jim, Ron and Marie.

The marriage broke down in 1942 and Albert went off with his new partner leaving Aunty Lil destitute with the kids in a commission house in St Mary's, an industrial suburb of Sydney.
As there were no pensions or child allowances or childcare of any sort in those days, Aunty Lil was forced to find work in a factory to feed her children.
When school holidays came she had no-one to look after the children and she would lose her job, and only income if she had taken time off, so she asked Mum to help out.

In consequence Mum took Fay and me down to Sydney. (David wasn't born at this time.)
We stayed for two weeks and returned home on the Friday night with Cousin Jimmy who would stay with his grandparents for a couple of weeks.

On Monday morning Mum was brushing Fay's hair as she got ready for school when a most unwelcome guest appeared at the back door.

It was Mrs Bourke who called Mum by name and followed with the news "Lily's dead. Albie telephoned Corneys to tell us. She had a burst appendix and died in the hospital.

You better go and tell your mother and Fay can tell Jimmy to come home from school".

Mum couldn't believe such news and we all began to cry in shock and sorrow.

Mum had to go up to Granny Nolan's to inform her parents.

The family maintained it was the only time Grandfather was ever known to shed a tear.

We were invaded by visitors. Granny Nolan was there and so were some of the neighbors.

Mum was offered a black dress by Mrs Ruby White to wear to the funeral as she had recently given her 'good' black dress to Aunty Lil.

Can you imagine Mum's reaction when she attended the funeral and witnessed Norma Bourke, the wife of Don, and sister-in-law of Lily, wearing THE dress? Mum described the feeling like the one she had when she caught the local bus driven by her former brother-in-law Kevin and sitting next to him on the 'dickie seat' was his new red haired girlfriend wearing Aunty Vi's new maroon shoes!

Vera was not impressed.

I did not know the full story of what happened to Aunty Lil and was fobbed off with the excuse that Mum was too upset to talk about it.

I guessed wrongly that it must have had something to do with having babies.

It would be forty years before I found out the exact details of the tragedy.

Marie, and older brothers Jim and Ron, were left with the paternal grandparents when their father married months after Lily's death. Mum and Dad had offered to take Marie and Granny Nolan wanted Ron, but their father was so anti the family he refused his permission and the three kids were 'given' to their paternal grandparents.

Marie had so much potential.
She was attractive with thick black hair and a round face and dark flashing eyes that reflected her indigenous inheritance.
She was also quite bright and had a lovely singing voice.
She would bear a daughter to her relative at eighteen then meet a very nice man who would adopt both her and her daughter.
She has been married since the mid-fifties.
I kept in touch with her for many years until, tragically, her twin daughters died and she withdrew into herself.
Sadly our correspondence ceased.

She has six remaining children and I was able to trace her for our sixtieth birthdays and send her a copy of the two of us at a few months old seated in my pram.

Marie taught me much in that fate dictates much of the course of your life's journey.
I was aware from a very young age how blessed you can be.

There were eleven houses, a hall and a double tennis courts that constituted our little hamlet which was part of the wider Lidsdale.
The neighbors were all mining families and included some 'personalities'.
We had no immediate neighbours for most of my childhood so the vacant blocks were used as our playground extension.

We spent countless hours lying on our backs identifying shapes in the clouds or collecting stones from the unmade road to make houses-complete with fruit boxes as furniture.
If one of the local cousins came to play you simply collected more stones and made the house bigger.
There was no greater fun than rolling down the hill at the back of our house.
Over and over and over we would tumble with our arms pressed close to our bodies.
Our punishment was having to pick off the numerous grass seeds and bindis from our clothing before we were allowed inside.

Further down the street was one house that changed hands several times.

I stayed with the current German family named Richter when David was born.

Mr Rictor often took us for a walk down the lane after tea on a summer's evening. Invariably he would stop atop an ant's nest and' let go' with the loudest of farts.

He would chuckle loudly and we and the ants would scatter in all directions!

PERHAPS when I grow up I will try to comprehend an attempted eradication of thousands of innocent, living creatures by a strange German man.

1943 saw the arrival of our brother David James.

Shirl David Fay Bev & Dad

Dorothy, Fay, Gordon, Bev and David

David James   *Bev, Shirl, Fay, Mum and Baby David, 1943*

I had not been warned of the impending addition and thought it a treat to be able to stay at the Richter's.

Playing with Gordon Richter I heard Dad calling me so I ran toward the house in time to see him dismount from his bike while it continued toward the wire fence where the now 'strangled' handle bar prevented further travel!

He raised me into the air and began to swirl me around gleefully shouting "I've got a son. I've got a son. We've got a new baby."

Now here I must pose the question.
What, may I ask, was the matter with the old baby?
No one had consulted me as to the wisdom of supplanting me with a newer model. Had they asked me to 'up' my babyish behavior?
No. Not once.
So I did what any obsolete model would do under the circumstances and cried "I don't want a baby. Take it back."
Despite my protestations home came this 'thing' that resembled the skun rabbits and, swaddled with nighties and nappies and singlets and blankets he was placed in his canvas bassinet and left to swing himself to sleep.

This ingenious device was made by crossing two pieces of timber at either end of two substantial lengths of thick dowel that had been threaded through the hemmed square of canvas.
As the baby moved even the tiniest bit, the canvas was 'rocked'.
Another advantage, when space was at a premium, was this bassinet took up so little room, looking as it did like a half sized clothes horse.

There were occasions when Mum would try to unravel the mystery of a strange and unique malady that afflicted this small infant.

It appeared that he was always waking up with the reddest of ears whenever she wasn't watching him.
Certainly no bruising or scratching was visible and the cat was never permitted to share the bassinet and the child was too young to be teething, so what could be the cause? (No account of the symptoms could be found in her Doctor's book that in one of the forbidden front rooms hidden in her wardrobe under the box of reports and papers that we children would not know about. Anyway, you would have had to find the key to the wardrobe door in the second draw of the dressing table before you could open it.
You know. I'm talking about the book with the pictures of a woman getting fatter and fatter with a baby inside her.
Do you know the one I mean?
It was a thick, brown book with a gold snake wound around something on the front cover, the one we never looked at when Mum wasn't there).

This redness happened very, very, very frequently and was the cause of much consternation in the ranks but, alas, despite the thorough investigation by family and family Doctor, Leo Bamber, no cause was ever found.
I know this because I was always fairly close when he awoke!!!

Shortly after the Richters left to live in Sydney, Marie and Roy Dukes came and it was there they raised their family of six while proving to be fantastic neighbors to Mum and Dad long after we had grown and gone.

David played with the Dukes kids and I spent lots of time toting the younsters up and down the lane on my hip.

Marie resides there still.

'Up' the street lived Mr and Mrs Hughes and next to them Mr and Mrs Jack White.

Helen and Jack White

Mrs Hughes, Betty, and Mrs White, Helen, were sisters who had come over from Scotland with their third sister, Davina.

When a shortage of women of marriageable age made immigration of young ladies from the British Isles a priority in the nineteen twenties these brave souls ventured forth across the seas to an unknown land and future.
Helen and Betty Snr. married two country men and built houses next to each other.

On bright sunny days Mrs Hughes and Prince, Mrs White, Mum and we girls would take a picnic blanket, thermos and some nibbles over the lane to have our own special picnic.

Mrs Hughes (Betty) was a lovely knitter and as she had no children she enjoyed making garments for local kids.
Many a pair of gloves kept my fingers from freezing in the extreme cold, all being of the same brown and green flecked wartime wool.
Mrs Hughes doted on her little dog called Prince.
She had a pottery figure of Prince's color and breed near the hearth in her sitting room whose name was' Princess' of course.

The White's had two daughters, Betty and Helen, who were older than Shirl.

Davina married a Sydney man named Edwards and I can remember their children Andrea and Colin.
I thought Andrea was such a pretty name and Colin could play the piano accordion wonderfully well.
His favorite piece was 'The Harry Lyme Theme' and I have recalled his rendition every time I have heard it since.

Next to the Whites lived the Bourkes.
With this elderly couple lived their 'creepy, crawly' adult son in their grubby house.
If a rat was seen around anywhere Mum would be convinced she knew from where it had come.

At the corner of Duncan Street and Mudgee Road was a property owned by a family named Corney.
Several large sheds covered another generous block of land next door in Duncan Street.
On the Mudgee Road side was Corney's Hall.

Years earlier a family named Lane who owned the few local buses had lived there. Lanes had kept their buses and drums of petrol in the sheds.
The Lane's son, Terry, was married to Mum's youngest sister, Aunty Violet, for a short time.
One of the Corney family members, Gladys, was married to Mum's brother Uncle Peter.
Corney's Hall was a structure used as a focal point by the surrounding population for balls, dances, weddings, movies and indoor sports.
Many, many years later it would become a garage before being destroyed by fire.

Cousin Vonnie(Winsome) at Granny's house.

Our very special Granny Nolan lived next to the hall on a double block, and then came 'Braeside' and the Wilsons.

Mrs Wilson had a turned up nose and she had a habit of rubbing her hand up the point of her 'probiscus' so I figured that was how her very pretty nose had been formed.

In consequence I tried to encourage my nose to develop into a similar shape- all to no avail.

Mrs Wilson, the former Lillian Bryant, much later in life hung herself in the family garage.

Over the road from them were the Birds and Ruby and Lionel White.

Wilsons had a daughter named Barbara, (who would marry my cousin Ron Bourke), and the Birds two youngest, 'Dickey' and Shirley, went to school with me.

Duncan Street had been named after Andrew Duncan, a Scotsman, who had owned the surrounding land.

I had heard that the former name of this piece of real estate had been known as' Graham's' and I can only surmise that family could have owned the property before Andrew Duncan's arrival

His daughter, Gladys Linda, married Bernhard Isaac Nottle in Lake Cargelico, NSW.

They settled in 'Braeside' a lovely old home made of local sandstone that Andrew Duncan had renamed in honour of his homeland.

'Braeside' had had a checkered history having once been a butcher's shop, then a Girl's school run by the religious order commenced by Sister Mary McKillop and, before then, the home of my ancestor, and Mum's Grandmother, Granny Sarah(White) Nolan.

Sarah was famous in the family for having her name written up in the local paper when she knocked a number of live bullets from the mantle piece into the fire and one exploded striking her in the thigh.

'Braeside' was a large house consisting of ten rooms and four sizeable verandahs.

But, more of that significant building, later.

Snuggled in our natural valley we were surrounded by virgin bush and I loved the changing landscape in the summer.

The gum trees wore their deep grey-green canopies in contrast to the cleared paddock opposite Granny's that always appeared to be a deep emerald green. I remember talk of a fresh water spring.

It was there Rosie had her cow bail where she milked her cows every morning in rain, hail or shine.

Most often it was rain or hail and VERY cold!

She could be seen each morning shuffling over the road with milk bucket in hand.

She would call to her beloved cows and they would run to the cow bail to greet her.

We simply loved her.

Born <u>ROSE GRACE TOMLINSON</u> to pioneers <u>FRANCIS J IGNATIOUS TOMLINSON</u> and <u>CHARLOTTE BAKER</u> she was the ninth and youngest child in her family.

She was born on February 16th, 1883, in the old homestead at Wolgan Valley.

*The Old Homestead at Wolgan Valley, NSW,(Built in
1832) where Rose Grace Tomlinson was born.*

(Permission to reproduce this photograph was granted by Emerites, Wolgan
Valley Resort.)

In 1868 Charlotte and Francis Tomlinson travelled to their new property in
secluded Wolgan Valley.
With children Charles, Eleanor and Albert and their possessions loaded on a
horse and dray, they traversed the virgin bush tracks.
Upon arrival Francis, a Stonemason, gathered local sandstone and built a
wishing well for his much loved wife.
The homestead had been built in the picturesque Valley cradled by the
magnificent towering escarpments of colourful sandstone.
It can be found 190 kilometres from Sydney located in the Blue Mountains
bordering both the Wolemi and Stone National Parks. (The Wolemi Pine,
believed extinct for thousands of years was rediscovered in this area in the
nineteen nineties).

Charlotte and Francis would add six more children to their family, namely
Francis, James, Marian, Martha, Edith and Rose Grace.

<u>CHARLOTTE BAKER</u>, died when Rosie was only five (cause of death was cancer of the stomach) and her father, <u>FRANCIS</u>, when she was fourteen.

(A copy of the book of the Baker Family, though written, was not available to me when writing this book).
I have reason to believe <u>CHARLOTTE'S</u> father was <u>CHARLES BAKER</u>, the son of <u>MALACHI BAKER</u> of Camden.

<u>FRANCIS, the son of Joseph and Margaret (Tickle)</u> had been born in Princes Street in Sydney on the first of August in 1841, this street having been 'swallowed up' with the construction of the Sydney Harbour Bridge in later years.

This couple had married at Camden, NSW.

Rosie kept house after her father died, and one of the family stories told relates to her insistence of her sister changing her school panties as soon as she alighted from the horse so Granny could wash them and dry them in front of the kitchen stove ready for the next day.
Said panties, I must tell you, had been hand made from unpicked flour bags. The kids remained on this isolated farm in the Wolgan Valley until they married.

Francis   *Charlotte*

107

One of the first people Francis employed to help run the farm was a young man called Tony Luccetti who would go on to serve the constituents of the area in his capacity of long serving Member of Parliament.

FRANK'S MEMORIAL
Toby and Rose had six children.

Their children, to remind you again, were Ernest, Vera, Peter, Lily, Violet and Douglas (An unnamed daughter had been stillborn between Uncle Ernie and Mum).

Granny was prematurely aged and looked one hundred when I saw her for the last time in 1957.
Yet, she was only seventy four.
She had exceptionally wrinkled skin, was small and very bent, had no teeth behind a cheeky grin, had bad cataracts that made her eyes a smoky grey, was deaf and had severe arthritis that crippled her little hands and feet.
Her small feet had huge bunions that protruded from the holes cut in the maroon blue Knights slippers she always wore.
In all seasons she chose a tea-cosy style hat crocheted for her by Mrs Lamb in grey and pink wool and she always had an apron on.

Our Darling Rosie.

In the pocket of her apron Granny gathered dried seeds from plants in her garden.

She would store them in a dish that lived on the old dresser until the promise of spring manifested itself and she would scatter the seed to all corners of her garden that included the vacant block next door.

How delightful it was to wander through the maze of cottage garden favourites from tiny Alyssum to Hollyhocks taller than I was.

Granny Bonnets, Wallflowers (which smelled wonderful), Marigolds, Nasturtums, Corn flowers, Gladiolas, and Asters, Blue Bells, Daffodils and Jonquils grew below old fashioned roses.
The white 'pom-pom' tree was raided annually and huge bunches adorned the teacher's desk as the result.

It was only when I occasionally slept at her house that I got to see Granny's wispy white hair.

As she was illiterate and couldn't even read her mail she relied on us to share the contents of letters, and anything that required an answer was dispatched to my Dad.
Dad would attend to the problem and get Rosie to sign the correspondence with the only two words she could write--her name.

Granny could never have foreseen two of her granddaughters and numerous great grandchildren graduating from University.

Dad and Rosie had a deep and loving relationship and they would often join in a joke.
Rosie would not allow Mum to make a complaint about Dad when they had 'words'.
She would defend Dad always and tell Mum how lucky she was to have him.
Mum would seethe with anger and Dad would point out how discerning Rosie was!

Rosie was a good cook and some of my favorites were her ginger sponge (in octagonal shaped pans), her home-made meat pies made with pastry containing dripping and a casserole she made that was topped with thinly sliced potato that curled and crisped on top.
Yum!
(Dripping was the fat left in the pan after roasting and it was generally kept in a bowl or enamelled container designed for the purpose and used for many forms of cooking).

The old house was devoid of mod-cons and for many years Granny carried the water in a bucket for indoor use.
I guess the house could be described as shabby, dusty and untidy but it certainly didn't influence our opinion of Granny.

I particularly hated the fly papers, a length of exceptionally sticky paper about an inch wide and eighteen inches in length that unfurled from a cardboard capsule and was attached to a nail driven into the ceiling for the purpose. The flies would be attracted to the honey-like surface on the strip where they would become trapped and die while struggling for freedom.

I learned the word 'repulsive' in response to this device.

Granny absolutely refused to have her photo taken and she never quite forgave Aunty Vi's partner, Fred Hollis, for one of her by her garden gate.

Granny's laundry/bathroom was an extension of an old shed out the back that was supported with stout tree trunks, open to the elements and housing wooden wash troughs and a fuel copper.
The uprights had been punctuated with a huge selection of nails and hooks that had previously been considered the ideal place to skin eels and rabbits and chooks that required the removal of feathers.
Across the two stout entrance posts a line of fencing wire was stretched.
Here hung the rabbit skins that had been skun from the animals then pulled over a piece of fencing wire bent to form a deep 'V' shape.
When thoroughly dried out they were sold to a travelling fur dealer who appeared spasmodically in his horse and dray.

The numerous metal rabbit traps not then in use hung on another line.

Granny did the best she could with the little she had.
She loved her chooks and her pigeons, her cows and her many Grandchildren.
Each evening she would open the aviary door and allow the pigeons to exercise
They would perform a variety of acrobatics as they soared overhead, higher and higher.
After an hour or so the flock would re-appear and find their way back home.
Occasionally some made their way into a pigeon pie!
If the chooks tried to emulate the pigeons and fly the coop Granny would clip one of their wings by chopping their feathers off.

Granny also loved her 'Cocky'.

Uncles Peter and Doug taught the Cocky every swear word in the book (and a couple that hadn't been entered yet) and the responsive bird would give forth with a tirade of bad language if you mentioned the name "George".

It was no co-incidence that Grandfather's name was the same!

Being deaf, Granny wasn't aware of the trigger-but we kids were.

Cocky resided in a large cage made of timber with a wire netting front resting against the Braeside side fence.

At night, and during times of inclement weather, a curtain made from wheat bags was lowered, rendering the cage dark.

We would call the magic word and the performance would begin, then we would run to the old house and tell Granny what the bird was saying being careful not to omit one single syllable.

Fearing the bird would corrupt our young, innocent minds, Granny would order us to lower the curtain and tell 'Cocky' he was very naughty indeed.

We would follow Granny's directions.

The bird would complain telling us to 'put that ....curtain up or he would peck our ....noses off'.

Then he would shriek in the ensuing darkness.

'Rosie. Help me Rosie. Those little..............are telling .... lies".

Rosie's Cocky

Despite her lack of education Rosie was a wise lady who was very highly regarded in the district.

I never once heard a bad word about her though I once overheard some neighbors say she was too 'soft' and generous and her children took advantage of her.

One lady actually said the family members were like boomerangs- always coming back!

They were pretty right too.

Uncle Ernie and Mum would have been the only two not to have lived at home at some time after their marriage.

One of Granny's most ardent admirers was her brother-in-law, Uncle Bill.

Uncle Bill owned a string of bakery shops up through the western country towns.

He was such a sweet old gentleman noted for his gentlemanly behavior at all times and, despite his wealth, (he had won the lottery at one stage) and the number of staff he employed he insisted on personally making two Christmas cakes and puddings for Rosie every year.

He took numerous overseas trips and would always call to see Granny when he returned. (Many years later she would inherit his wealth--and refuse to spend a penny of it).

A story about Uncle Bill relates to him visiting Granny on her birthday.

Fay called in on her way to the Post Office to see if Granny wanted anything and Granny asked her to collect the mail.

This she did and there found a parcel from our Aunty Gladys in Sydney who was married to Uncle Peter.

It was a container of powder.

Granny took the top off to smell the talc and withdrew her nose with disgust and made the announcement she had never smelt anything 'quite like it'.

She handed it to Uncle Bill and asked if he could suggest anything to do with it.

Uncle Bill leaned forward near Granny's good ear and said "Perhaps you could make it into a sandwich and eat if hoping it will sweeten your terrible farts today Rosie."

Fay was shocked to hear Uncle Bill's 'rude words' and ran home to tell Mum what he had said.

In latter years I have questioned if perhaps our Uncle Bill may have been gay.

The buses to school or Lithgow stopped in front of Granny's house and we all stood on her verandah out of the weather.
If we were early we could sit on the old school form (seat) and read the pile of comics found there.
Comics were forbidden at home so this was a treat.
It was here I learned of Superman, Mandrake the Magician, Ginger Meggs, Popeye the Sailor man, Flash Gordon etc.

The buses had ladders attached to the rear and the driver would climb up the structure to place any luggage in a metal rectangle on the roof of the vehicle.

I loved school and found it easy.
As I also loved to sing I was always in the school concerts.

My first concert at the end of my first year at school is memorable.

Another little student named Billy Cripps was chosen to sing a duet with me.
It was a well-known war song called 'The Quartermaster's Store' and we sang the words:-
"There was jam, jam, mixed up with the ham, at the store, at the store
There was jam, jam, mixed up with the ham at the Quartermaster's store
My eyes are dim I cannot see, I have not brought my specs with me
I have not brought my specs with me."

As we sang Miss Mugeridge stood on the side of the stage at Corney's Hall and indicated for me to move closer to Billy.

Every time I took a step nearer him, he stepped away.

I would look at the teacher and she would flail around her hands indicating I should take another step.

This I did with the same result as before.

Not once did Billy Cripps look at Miss Mugeridge.

Meanwhile the audience was in stitches and when we finished they clapped and clapped although Billie could no longer be seen!
(Billy's older brother, Jerold, would one day become a High Court Judge in NSW).

I will never chase a boy again- PERHAPS!

Now my Nellie Mugeridge was a very rare lady because she smoked.
I, and a number of my brave peers, had peeked through the classroom's keyhole and witnessed this activity with our own eyes.
As smoking was strictly forbidden in our house it really was a novelty.
It should be noted that Mum had particular reason to hate smoking as the old family home situated between Corney's Hall and the old miners cottage I knew as Granny's had been destroyed by fire when a boarder fell asleep smoking in bed.
Mum was only a child and Granny was over the road milking.
Mum had to drag her younger siblings to safety.
She was deeply traumatized by the event and even though Dad smoked all of their fifty years together he was never allowed to smoke inside the house.

One autumn day, as I approached my fifth birthday, I assembled my dolls on boxes and made a 'classroom'.
Out front I placed a fruit box as a desk and seated myself on a tiny cane chair from where I could instruct my 'class' of pupils.

I read my charges a story and ask appropriate questions just like Miss Mugeridge.
I placed my feet on the desk and leaned back in the comfy chair as I lit up one of Dad's cigarettes.
Enter Mum who couldn't believe her eyes.

To say she was not amused would constitute an understatement.

I was the recipient of a substantial paddling which I must confess did not deter me from smoking in later years.
The day following that smoking incident I was very surprised to receive the birthday present I wanted, namely a little iron of my own.

I still have that iron.

Many, many times it was heated on the hob of the fire to allow me to iron the hankies. (I'm sure Mum would have done them a second time after I'd gone).

My iron

No tissues in those days my children.
Such things were not dreamt of.
(A hob is a round of iron the size of a bread and butter plate that had an iron spike that fitted a hole on the front of the open fire).

Wallerawang Public School 1947 Our class after a sleepover.

Beverley 2nd row-middle

Some years before I commenced school a new Headmaster, Mr Fred Daley, was appointed and his ideas of running the school and the School committee were very different and not at all well received by the locals.

After several altercations several of the parents threatened to remove their kids from the school and send them to Cooerwell School in Lithgow.

Shirl and Fay were part of the boycott.

By taking the numbers from the school at "Wang" the status would be altered and a teacher of a different grade would be needed to run it.

The parents followed through with their threat and the students began attending school in Lithgow having been transported on the tray of Mr Bulkley's truck.

Mr Daley was duly sent to another post.

(Fred Daley later became a much respected and long serving Member of the Federal Parliament).

Dad was an outstanding sportsman who represented the district in tennis, football, cricket and his first love, golf.

He excelled at everything he did but the fact that he played off a scratch handicap for seventeen years bears testament to his golfing prowess.

He was Blue Mountains and the District champion for many years.

He was presented with a miniature of the Perpetual Trophy because he had claimed that prize so often.

Dad the Golfer   *Perpetual Trophy*

Dad always took the time to encourage young golfers though he didn't insist we girls learn from him.

PERHAPS one such youngster, one Airforce member, Jack Potts, will play an important role in our destinies in later years and introduce me to a fellow Air Force member whose name many of you bear.

Dad had devised a practice game which involved us girls.
He would walk about 100 yards up the hill situated at the back of our house with a bucket of golf balls.
Before he left he would mark an area about eight feet wide on the fence with a couple of bits of timber.
He would insert his tees and systematically hit every ball towards the designated area, and rarely did they go awry.
In consequence, his promise of three pence for every ten balls outside the area was rarely paid.
We were engaged in collecting said golf balls and struggling up the hills with them to where the exercise was repeated.

Closer to home there were jam tins, inserted at ground level for putting practice that he was happy to share with us.

I could hit the golf ball quite some distance left handed yet my brain never felt comfortable doing so.

I comfortably played all other sports left handed, even tennis at which I was ambidextrous.

I could not play golf right handed at all, despite Dad's encouragement.

A small, but good looking man, Dad sported a small, well clipped moustache and half a gold tooth.

He was also regarded as a smart dresser and he wore brightly colored shirts long before they were readily available in the shops.

The sleeves of the shirts were always too long and Dad had several pairs of sleeve links to wear on his upper arm over which he folded the excess material.

I well remember him going off to golf on a Saturday afternoon dressed in hand knitted sleeveless jumper and matching socks that complimented his plus-fours.

PERHAPS when I grow up and marry I'll choose a man of good taste?????
Who.................

One of Dad's important accessories was his shoes which he kept in pristine condition by polishing them for ages as he sat listening to the radio.

(He would also polish ours to a sheen).

His very special new golf shoes at this particular time were two-toned with brown patterned leather on the lower section and crisp white on the upper.

As Mum insisted such messy items as shoe polish be kept down the yard in the detached laundry, Dad's shoes were relegated to that building during the week.

Being a people pleaser, and a deft hand at making a mess, I decided one Saturday morning to make my Dad the happiest of men by cleaning, or should I say endeavoring to clean, Dad's beautiful, new, fashionable, very expensive, two toned, leather golf shoes.

This experiment did not go as planned and not a small amount of brown polish appeared on the white part of the shoes and an equal amount of white polish seemed to find its way to the once brown area.

I didn't think this looked right so I found some water and proceeded to wash the offending white polish from the brown bits and vice-versa.

Enter Mum who screamed a blood curdling scream of "What have you done? Your father will kill you. Look what you have done to your father's new shoes. You've ruined them. All of that money and you've ruined them. You naughty, naughty girl. Your father will kill you" she repeated often as she whacked me hard and fast.

And on and on she went, broadcasting to the birds that I was about to be put to death for the dastardly crime of ruining my Father's beautiful, new, very expensive, specially made golf shoes.

My loud protestations did nothing to alley Mum's fears of the cost of an unscheduled family funeral as she rehearsed my eulogy. "Why?" she asked skywards to the now curious birds.

"How could this happen? So lovely SO lovely." she wailed. "All the things I went without and now ruined! Ruined! Admired and envied by everyone and now gone. Boo hoo"!!!!

She continued raving like a demented banshee.

I could comprehend her sadness at my imminent demise because I was feeling a bit that way myself.

My muffled sobs masked the arrival of the execu..,I mean Dad.

Mum lit straight in and told him the whole mournful story.

Dad was fairly quiet at first and then he suggested Mum stop blubbering.

He pondered for what seemed a very long time and then said to Mum "It's pretty crook when the little bloke only tried to do something special and she ends up with a bloody good belting instead. Where is she"?

"Under the tank stand where no one can reach her" was the reply.

And then a miracle happened.

My Dad, who wasn't on as friendly terms with the resident spiders as I was, crawled in under the tank stand and brought me out, all the time assuring me he wasn't cross and I would not be sacrificed that particular day.

"But your shoes Jim?" Mum reminded him. "What will you say at the Golf Club"?

"I'll tell them my little mate here cleaned them for me." he replied, "And, if I win any trophies today, they are yours young Bevie Ryan."

Picture of vase won by Dad for me

It was probably ten o'clock that night when Dad shook me awake to show me the vase trimmed with gold bands. "It's for you Bill. Joe Cook offered me five quid and I said no that's been promised to my little boot cleaner at home."

PERHAPS Mum will let me take it to my own home in thirty- seven years' time after my Dad dies and I can tell my children, and grandchildren, and their children about a day in my life when I felt very loved and very special---and very sore!!

Weeks before in 1942, and just a few days after Granny's birthday, the Japanese Army bombed Darwin.
My Granny paid us one of her very rare visits with the newspaper tucked under her arm.
She had heard the news and wanted Mum to read the paper to her because she thought the danger must be very close.

121

Mum sent me out to our 'lane' to collect stones.

She then placed ten stones on the verandah and explained to Granny they represented the distance from our house to Lithgow--- the furthest distance my Granny had travelled!

Then Mum had me count out and line up one hundred stones to present the distance, in miles, from our house to Sydney.

Mum noted this distance with my skipping rope and we measured distances to the bottom of the yard to represent the number of miles to Darwin, thus reassuring dear Rosie that we were safe.

Satisfied, Granny returned home.

Most family have rituals and sayings perculiar to them.

Often sayings are inherited from original families.

Such was the case in our house.

If someone suffered from flatulence Mum would ask in a horrified voice "Did you 'blow off'?"

I would giggle in response to this odd question.

Granny was the recipient of so many boxes of hankerchiefs that she could have started a hanky shop.

Invariably we received a cake of Cashmere Bouquet soap and a box of Granny's gifted hankerchiefs for our birthdays and Christmas yet the shelf in the old cupboard in the middle verandah was never empty.

I was soon old enough to be included in the annual holiday ritual of catching yabbies in the local dam.

A chunk of steak was tied to a six foot length of string and the other end tethered to a stick that could withstand the muddy edge.

Pretty soon the stick would begin to move and a game of tug-a-war was undertaken with the yabbies who were determined not to let go of this unexpected banquet.

Gradually the crustacean would be raised to the surface where an old tennis racquet frame, covered with fine, loose wire, would be employed as a net.

Being careful not to be nipped by the menacing claws the animal was transferred into a waiting bucket.

When a substantial feed was gathered, with no room remained in the bucket, we would head for home.

Mum would boil the kettle and the life expectancy of the victims would be reached.

They would be boiled in the boiler until their color changed to bright red, then peeled and eaten with salt and pepper, some vinegar and fresh bread and butter.

Such, wondrous spoils.

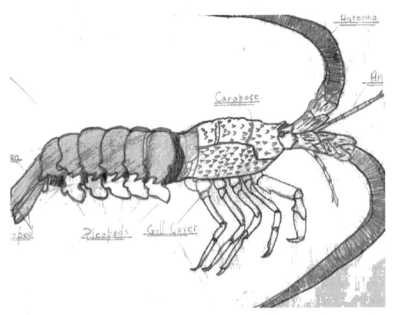

Big Cousin of a Yabbie A Spiny Lobster (Drawn when I was twelve.)

Even as a very young child David had a distinctive palette.

He was repulsed by the texture of vegetables and no matter how many combinations of different vegetables Mum tried to feed him he would protest and refused to open his mouth.

If she managed to force a tiny morsel into his mouth when he cried, he would vomit.

This daily procedure was stopped by Dad who had a few well chosen words to say and from then on David was permitted to eat what he liked.

David's eating habits have never improved and his pre-deliction for smothering the few foods he does like with copious amounts of Fountain brand tomato sauce is legendary within the family.

Uncle Doug had ferrets and he would take me rabbiting to teach me how it was done. He also showed me how to set a rabbit trap using a cigarette paper to hold the first covering of soil.

I thought the traps were so cruel the way they caught the rabbits and didn't like having to break the necks of the rabbits by placing the foot on the head and tugging it until the neck snapped.
Still I ate and enjoyed the meat.
Rabbits had become a scourge in Australia after just twenty-four were allowed to escape from a property near Winchelsea in Victoria owned by the Austin family.
The gamekeeper, a man named Warner, who had been brought out from England especially for that purpose, would ultimately share some of my descendants.

Digger Nottle arrived home to Braeside after serving in the Air Force in New Guinea and with him came boxes of souvenirs.
He gave me beads in bright red and black and a choice of carved boats with coconut palm sails.
The boat sat on the tiled hearth in the front lounge room for as long as I could remember until Mum decided it was making a mess.
He gave Mum one of the 'Sweetheart' necklaces made by servicemen from damaged perspex windows found in unserviceable aeroplanes.
It bears the Airforce logo of Wings and crown.

What novelties!

Christmas1946 BevDavidRickHollisJanice&gift of a Bunny soap

Dad's disbelief in the commercialization of Christmas, together with rationing, certainly curtailed any Christmas extravagance yet we were so happy with our lot.

A few nuts, a bag of lollies, a hanky, a special cake of soap and, if you were very lucky, a book would be found in our stockings.

As the school awarded books as prizes at the end of each year I was always trying to be amongst the winners and I cannot recall a year without a book. I still have 'Joanna from Little Meadow' from 3rd class and 'The Templeton Twins' from 6th class when I won the writing prize again.

There were several classics like 'Alice in Wonderland' that were so well worn they disintegrated over time.

Christmas was a special time despite the lack of gifts.
We traditionally went to midnight Mass on Christmas Eve if the weather permitted and then tumbled into bed after the hike of several miles.

A hot lunch of free range roast chicken, ham and piles of veggies smothered with gravy was the usual fare.
Then would come the plum pudding Vera had made the first week in November.

She would scour the copper until it resembled a copper mirror and boil it up just for the many puddings she made.
As each pudding was threaded onto the copper stick and lowered into the boiling water we were allowed to make a wish.

There would often be a dozen puddings for Granny and other family members bobbing up and down emitting a wondrous smell that made us impatient to try them and add some hidden sixpences and three-pences to our wealth.
The money had been collected and scrubbed and distributed evenly throughout the mixture to ensure everyone had an equal opportunity of sharing the booty.
The boiled puddings were then hung up to dry from the rafters of the old wash house.

Then on Christmas day there would be custard, sweet white sauce and lashings of cream as accompaniments.

After an afternoon rest we would collect up all the food that was left and head for tea at Granny's where all of our Aunties and Uncles and cousins who were talking at the time would gather.
There would be huge bowls of trifle and cakes and mince pies, shortbread, salads and meat bought with collective coupons, Uncle Bill's special Christmas cake and pudding and even lemonade and home-made raspberry cordial would be offered.

We would play chasing and try to outrun the mozzies who wrongly believed they had been invited to the celebrations.
Everyone would have a great time--except 'Toby' who was always grumpy.

Rosie and Toby barely spoke as he couldn't be bothered shouting at her and she, being deaf, was unaware of the niggling asides he directed her way.

They had not shared a bedroom in my living memory.
They simply co-existed.

PERHAPS I should study this relationship so I don't make the same mistakes.

As I was sometimes allowed to attend the little Methodist church up on the hill, St Cuthberts, I looked forward to the nearest Christmas Sunday service and the presentation of yet another book.
No such goodies were distributed at the Catholic Church

The Church on the hill

A double rainbow over St Cuthbert's

Then, before we knew it, we repeated all the Christmas fare for New Year.

At about seven I instigated a conversation with Mum regarding wedding rings and the reason why they were worn.

She succinctly explained the reasons why a woman wore a wedding ring as "It's just traditional."

During a visit to Granny's when I was eight I took my favorite doll, named Veronica May, and as Granny examined her new clothes I had tried to make I noticed she didn't wear a ring so I queried if she was really married at all.

She laughed and told me she definitely was and to prove it she took me into her bedroom and told me to fetch a chair in.

She then directed me to climb up and reach for an 'Old Gold' chocolate box hidden there on top of her wardrobe.

I handed it down and she opened it.

It was filled with face powder and smelled good.

She ran her fingers through the powder then wiped her hands on her apron.

There in her hand were two rings.

"Can I have one please Gran"? I asked.

"Well" she replied "I'll make a promise with you. If you never tell anyone where the rings are hidden they will still be here and you can have one when you grow up.

How would that be"?

It certainly seemed a good deal to me.

The time came when I was forced to follow the family tradition of making my First Holy Communion in the Catholic Church.

Not even the prospect of a new white dress and lavish morning tea afterwards could engender enthusiasm.

I should clarify the then unusual circumstances of my situation.

My mother was not a Catholic.

In fact, when my parents married in the Catholic Church the service had to be held behind the alter, rather than in front of it, because Mum was not one of the fold and she had no intention of becoming one.

She did however agree to bring up any children of the union as Catholics.

And that she conscientiously did.

It was Mum who drug us out of bed on cold and frosty mornings to walk the miles for Church.

It was Mum who made the decision to send three of her four children to Catholic schools.

It was Mum who reminded us to say our prayers each night and to abstain from eating meat on Fridays and Holy days of Obligation.

First Holy Communion 1946 Aged 9

When Peace was declared following the dropping of the Atomic bomb on two cities in Japan in 1945 the whole country celebrated with "V" for Victory parades.

Each town or city held their own celebrations.

I was chosen to lead the local parade.

Mum made me a long white dress out of mosquito netting adorned with "V's" of red and blue ribbon.

The same trim was repeated on the matching bonnet and I carried a basket that Shirl had carried years before when she was flower girl.

The gold painted basket on this occasion was filled with red, white and blue flowers.

I couldn't understand why everyone was so happy and I really didn't know why they were all clapping and yelling and waving new flags when so many had died.

V for Victory

Because I was singled out for the honour I had access to adults ready to answer questions and I was horrified to learn that more people than I had even seen on trips to Sydney were killed as a result of the bomb.

Since Aunty Lil had so recently died I didn't much care for death and so, for many years afterwards I tried to comprehend why the people of Wallerawang and district were so joyous that evening.

The more the people waved and shouted and cheered and smiled the sadder I became until the tears began to flow for all of the Japanese boys and girls who had nothing to do with the decision to engage in war and who would never be able to grow up and go to school and marry and have babies.

"She's overwhelmed with the occasion" my teacher said of me.
And in a way he was right though he would never know what a profound effect it would have on my opinion of war and the politics that led to this state of affairs long into my old age.

PERHAPS when I grow up I will be better able to express those thoughts in a poem.

August 6th.
In a city across the sea of which I'd then not heard
Every living organism-flower, person, bird
Had vanished in an instant, they were simply vapourised
Quite beyond my comprehension was the number there who died
I asked questions how this gruesome act could happen in our world
Weren't people slain a lot like us families of boys and girls?
"Oh, no" they said "You have to know at war they've killed our kin
That little bomb we dropped that day ensures this war we win
Now wear your cutest, brightest smile and put your mind at ease
Those people there are not just like us for they are Japanese
Now eat your special dinner and don your dress of white
To head the celebrations we will celebrate this night".
Well I wore that dress, heard speeches made folk waved and cheered our fate
But I knew well I hated war, and I was only eight.
Time passes, smaller grows our world
And many years have passed
The horrors of Hiroshima and what took place still lasts

Beverley Ann Farmer

I've learned how high the temperature of the surface of the sun
Enclosed within that mushroom cloud by scientist was done
Still victims die from illnesses they live on mounds of bones
Recalling charred remains of kids, of pain, of burns, of groans
Haunted by those agonies when on that Autumn day
Two hundred thousand human souls freed by Inola Gay
That Atomic bomb at Truman's wish not once, but twice released
They justified this obscene act because the war would cease
Dear God please let my children see that wars for which boys train
Can never have a winner true just sadness, death and pain
Our world consists of people, some are evil, some are good
But each one has a right to life, clean water, love and food
Why can't we live together, let us look beyond our skin
Put aside our fears, our greed our pride
In that way we all could win
Let us ponder simple positives,
Put aside our tools of war, stop the current nuclear testing
Make World Peace our right by law.
We can each one make a difference
And set free our own white dove.
Join hands with all our fellow man
And create a world of love.

Copyright. Greenbank Queensland 1993.

When the Priest came out from Lithgow every second Wednesday to take a small group of Catholic kids at our school for Religious Instruction, it was often to the Ryan's he later went to enjoy a sumptuous afternoon tea.
One of the Priests who came was Father Madden who loved onion sandwiches. He would overlook all of the cream cakes and leave the sandwich plate clean. Another Priest who came was Father Prendegast who always spruiked to us the importance of honesty, and he forever assured us that if we ever had a problem we could go to him and he would guarantee us confidentiality, and assistance, wherever he could give it.
Now I had a very big problem at the time so I took him at his word and confided in him this tale. "You see Father I have a problem. When I stay at Nottle's they take me to their Methodist church where we sing lovely songs

and the minister tells stories in our own language and everyone is happy and you don't have to tell the minister about your sins and all that.
So Father I want to ask you for help to change my religion."
His opened mouth was not a pretty sight.
"You would have to seek permission from your parents" he lied. "I'll see what I can do."

Well I'll share with you what he did.
He headed straight for Mum's laden table and, over a cup of tea taken in one of the best cups he spilled MY beans adding that he thought I should be 'taken into hand' at the earliest opportunity.
Mum and strap were waiting for me when I arrived home.
She said I could never change my religion and that I was a disgrace to the family and I wouldn't go to Heaven for thinking such 'wicked' thoughts.

The strap spoke a different language but the results were the same and I vowed I would never trust another Priest ever again and I was not going to share make believe sins with anyone.

And I haven't.

PERHAPS I will change my religion after all.

An absolute thrill was the arrival twice a year of the catalogues from the big stores of Grace Brothers and Farmers and DJs in Sydney.
They were lavish productions that contained information on the latest fashions, household items and most importantly for me, jewellery.
It was these publications that really formulated my deep interest in jewelery, both old and new.
I spent hours cutting and pasting pictures of rings comprising the band of one and setting of another or creating colored stones from the pictures of fashion to match a design I'd created.
Even as a young person I could recognize gemstones and would often comment on rings I saw being worn by adults.
Never once has anyone objected to this practice in seventy odd years.
Thus I was to become somewhat of a ring 'fanatic' and even if I couldn't remember the name of a person I could describe the ring they wore.
I vividly recall Mum's three diamond 'milgrane' setting engagement ring that she later had remodelled, Ruth Nottle's 1940's single diamond and the

two diamond heart setting of her sister, Linda, their mother's, (Aunty Glad's) unusual two diamonds in an oval ring setting, and the huge diamonds of Shirl's first boss, Mrs Porges, the Chemist's wife.

Later I would drool over the huge sapphire surrounded by diamonds chosen by my favorite matron, Pam Schultz and the emerald set in a similar setting worn by Maureen Sullivan at RAAF Richmond, Fay's pretty diamond solitaire with square ruby shoulders, Shirl's lovely oblong Ceylonese sapphire in that unusual setting across her finger, the red of the Argyle diamond of a student in Bunbury and so on.

I would be VERY disappointed at not being able to choose a ring I liked as my own engagement ring and hope this disappointment was conveyed to my sons who were encouraged to show sensitivity to the taste and likes and feelings of their partners at such an important time in their relationships.

PERHAPS, many years later when I visit Granny for the last time to introduce her to my new baby daughter, she will remind me of our conversation of rings and offer me the choice of the plain gold wedding ring or embellished 'keeper' featuring tiny rubies.

PERHAPS I will choose the wedding ring and love it well into my old age.

A typical winter's day would be to wake to the call of the kookaburra family who resided in the dead gum tree over the lane and jump out of bed quickly to get dressed before you froze to death.

Then, after dipping your fingers in the freezing water in the bathroom if the pipes weren't frozen, you washed your eyes and made for the dining room and a giant breakfast.

Coat, hat, gloves and schoolbag full of tasty lunch and off up the lane to Granny's via every puddle found on the unmade road.

The pleasure of cracking the ice was immeasurable despite the aftermath of sitting in damp, cold shoes and stockings for the rest of the day.

Woollen stockings were kept up with garters made of pieces of elastic. Panties with elasticized legs fitted over the garters and kept the breezes at bay.

Shirley and Fay, Beverley and David 1945

Onto Granny's verandah or, if it was sleeting and windy, we could stand inside the front room door.

On the dresser in this 'front room' was a cloth runner under which money multiplied.

It didn't matter how often, or seldom you, 'took a look', there remained the same number of halfpennies there.

It also didn't matter if you took an occasional one for I can guarantee the space would be filled the next time you looked.

That stolen half penny bought an entire packet of 'Wriggley's' or 'Juicy Fruit' chewing gum.

On the cedar Chiffonaire rested two jardinières that had been made at the renowned Lithgow pottery by Granny's oldest brother, Charles.

He had especially designed the one that featured a kookaburra just for his little sister.
One was predominately a rich, dark blue and the other deep green trimmed.

If the garden happened to be dry Granny would pick a bunch of flowers for me to take to the teacher.
A particular favorite of mine was her lilac.
I so loved the mauve colour and shape and the way the tiny flowers grouped together and hung down when drenched with rain.

The rickety old bus driven by Claude Bridges from Portland took us to Wallerawang Public School.
On cold days we went straight inside to rooms heated inefficiently by a single coal burning fire.
With so many coal mines around there was no shortage of the fossil fuel.
One of the 'big boys' would be responsible for keeping the coal shuttles filled from the huge piles delivered in the yard.
The same boys would have the job of mixing the ink powder with water and filling the china inkwells that lived in the holes drilled in our desks.

The giant school bell was mounted atop a stout column and it was an honour to be chosen to ring it by pulling the attached rope.
Lunch usually had to be eaten in the rooms when conditions were extreme.
The door of the heater would be opened and you could take it in turns to thread your sandwiches onto the wire toasting fork which you held to the opened door by the long handle until the bread turned to a golden brown.
The kids with home-made pies placed their lunch on the in-built hearth and the smell of the slowly cooking pies (and the brown paper bags that held them) would pervade the air.
We could play Ludo or Snakes and Ladders or sometimes listen to a story read to us.
One I recall is Kenneth Graham's 'Wind In The Willows'.

It was often so cold that writing was difficult and many of us had fingerless gloves for that reason.
Then it would be time to catch the bus home.
A couple of hot drinks and changes of clothes and off up to Nottle's.

Sometimes I would visit the Post Office for the mail while holding tightly to the borrowed umbrella least it would pick me up and convey me to places unknown.

Back at Nottle's I would help with the preparations for the evening meal by shelling the peas and if invited to stay for tea I would run home and ask Mum for permission.

Aunty Glad put a pinch of carb soda in the peas and beans so they would 'keep their colour'.

Sometimes if I really liked the meal at home as well I have been known to have both!

As we always ate much later than Nottles this was indeed possible to organize!

After tea we would listen to the radio.

Firstly, there was the death notices played each evening at six o'clock after the playing of 'Abide With Me'.

As the local paper, The Lithgow Mercury, was only sent out by mail it was always out of date before you got it.

Then there would be the news.

Depending on the night there was Radio Theatre or Pick a Box with 'Yank' Bob Dyer and his Australian wife, Dolly, or Jack Davey or Roy Rene Mo to entertain us.

We all loved the Amateur Hour and many well-known Australians would get their start in their singing careers because of their debut on this program.

I loved that you could listen to the drama programs called 'Lux Radio Theatre' and allow your imagination to fill the gaps, much like you can with reading.

On nights when the cricket was 'on' Dad would wake us up and wrap us in a blanket and seat us around the blazing fire.

We would sip huge mugs of milk coffee with sugar that Dad had prepared before we went to bed.

He would tie freshly ground Harris coffee grains in muslin and suspend the little parcel in a saucepan of half milk and half water.

The saucepan was placed on the hob of the open fire where it would slowly simmer until required.

Dad would clap his hands at the many successes of Don Bradman. "A true champion of the game" he would tell us "His name will still be revered when you are old women".

I awoke with severe pain in my very swollen neck and Mum informed me I had Mumps and it would only be uncomfortable for a day or two.

After the day or two had past and there were no signs of improvement Mum went up to Nottle's to phone the Doctor in Lithgow.

Doctor Bamber said to phone back in a few more days, to keep me warm and give me an aspirin once a day until the swelling subsided.

Well, after two weeks I still had pain and swelling and I was still bawling about lunchtime each day Mum made the trek to the only phone in the area, to Nottles, and phoned Dr Bamber.

Doctor Bamber was very surprised and suggested he best come out to see if it really was Mumps.

It certainly was and he was convinced I must have had a 'light' dose followed by a 'severe' dose.

How true.

Mum made me a hood to keep my face warm by folding one of Dad's scarfs in half and sewing it together for eight inches.

I wore that garment long after the mumps had subsided.

It was royal blue in colour and I never un-picked it to return it to its original form.

Bev astride Peter The Horse

We were a very healthy family and it would never have occured to me to ask if I could have a day home from school.

In fact the mumps were responsible for me having my very first day away from school though there were days when I needed a day at home to recover from eating green apples before they had time to ripen.

Mum worried about Fay who was very thin.
In an effort to 'build her up' Mum administered a daily dose of Cornwall's Malt.
Many, many years later Mum was heard to proudly state how conscientious she has been in buying the malt to encourage Fay weight gain.
Fay let Mum finish then looked at her somewhat 'rotund' figure and said "Yes. And you could say it bloody well worked"!

David was due to commence school the following year.
Considerable discussion took place about my going to Lithgow for High School and Mum mounted the arguments that I was too young at eleven to travel in by myself and I should stay at 'Wang for an extra year at Public school to 'look after' David.
Dad was opposed and felt it was pretty stupid to hold me back when I was doing so well.
Mum won the argument and I sadly bid farewell to my peers and faced being a member of a new class the next year with forty-five other kids.
Dad bought me a Fountain Pen and a bottle of Swan ink as a consolation gift. I was the only kid in the class to own such a modern device.

Shortly after the new year began I came to realized I had a big job on my hands.
David was the victim of terrible bullying.
The 'big boys', some of whom were dullards approaching leaving age, would snatch his glasses and throw them away and heckle him as he stumbled into buildings or other obstacles.
As much as he cried and cowed, they laughed and ridiculed him.
I complained long and loudly to them and teachers with no results.
It was all too much for me so I took it upon myself to punish the perpertrators.
Although I could outrun many of them, the problem was my reach was very short when I drew near.
The solution was that I would tie my shoes together and holding one I could 'clock' the offending bully with the other.

The 'taunting' diminished as my reputation grew.

I felt no need to report my activities to my parents and probably wouldn't have if I had not returned home twice without my shoes.

The older boys I had so punished decided to curb my efforts by snatching my shoes and throwing them into the open toilet pans in the boy's toilets!!

Oh shit!

Bev 2 nd row 4 th from the right, 6 th class

Dad had the highest regard for the owners of Wallerawang House, namely Miss Loveday and Mr Lionel Barton.

They were the local landed gentry and their influence and affluence in the district was considerable.

They even had their own private cemetery where a collection of relatives and servants both black and white were rested.

One headstone I recall was 'HERE LIES JACKY THE FAITHFUL SERVANT OF THE BARTON FAMILY'.

I don't believe there would have been too many Aboriginals buried in consecrated ground anywhere at that time, let alone in the private grounds of an influential family.

Aboriginals were not even counted in the census as they were considered as non-human.

The Bartons had been original local land owners from the early years following the crossing of the Blue Mountains and the allocation of Land Grants.
It was this family who built the lovely old St John's Church on the road to 'Wang.

I was to draw this church many, many times during my school years and win lots of prizes as a result.

During the Great Depression Mum, who since her marriage had regularly cleaned the aforementioned church for a very small amount, was informed by Miss Loveday that her services were no longer required as Miss Loveday believed the position should go to a member of that particular congregation. Mum was furious as she had walked the distance with small children in the pram to carry out her duties 'religiously' for years and the small amount of money was worth a great deal at that time of no employment.
In consequence whenever we were walking anywhere and Miss Loveday drove past Mum would comment "Bloody snob, I don't know who she thinks she is".

I was sure she knew.

Miss Barton wore men's overalls and had her hair in a severe bun at the back of her head.
She wore no make-up even on Sundays when she would dress up for church in her tweed skirts and twin sets and beautiful pearls.

One Sunday afternoon Dad asked Mum to tidy me up and he took me to the Barton's mansion on his trusty bike

I had never been close enough to see the huge garden impeccably kept by the ground staff.
It was a grand occasion for me.
Dad knocked on the huge front door which was answered by Miss Loveday who greeted Dad warmly.
"And who have we here"? she questioned.
Having been formally introduced I was greeted with a charming smile and led upstairs to the kitchen where I was served a glass of buttermilk and two home-cooked jam drop biscuits.
The 'snob' turned out to be a charming hostess.

She led me downstairs to a room with huge doors and as I entered I saw Dad and Mr Lionel browsing through some papers that I learned were the property of the local Golf Club.

I was directed to a miniature armchair where I remained twirling my hankie until Dad made ready to leave.

Once a year Dad would take us to Sydney for a week where he participated in Country Week Golf and Mum would allow David and me to choose a special treat.

David would always want to go to the zoo and I would want to go to the pictures in the State Theatre.

We stayed right in the city at a place called The People's Palace in Pitt Street.

Mum liked it because it was run by the Salvation Army and no alcohol was permitted on the premises.

It was also cheap and offered special deals for country folk.

We loved it when Mum took us for lunch at the big city Coles store where I ordered meat pie served with peas and mashed potato.

One year in the late forties Dad went to golf as he always did on Sundays with the promise that he would be home at a reasonable time to lend a hand in packing for our annual holiday.

As no buses ran on Sunday he relied on a lift from someone travelling our way.

While he waited he had more than a few beers and by the time he eventually did get home he was very merry.

Mum on the other hand was not.

Dad knocked on the back door which Mum had locked and gleefully asked for the door to be opened.

Mum yelled at him for breaking his promise and he apologized and she yelled some more and said she wasn't going to Sydney with a drunkard and so on and so on.

With that she opened the door and Dad handed her a crystal bowl he had won that day "There you are love. It's a special Peace offering" he stammered.

Mum took the bowl and hurled it down the back yard. "You can't crawl to me you mongrel" she cried and she turned around and started to throw all of the beautifully ironed and starched clothes out of the suitcase and flung them across the room.

As fast as she threw them out Dad rescued them and threw them back into the case.

After a time they decided they had to get up so early in the morning to catch the train that they should go to bed.
And they did.
Dad must have woven his magic as they were very pleasant to each other in the morning when the one local taxi, owned and operated by 'Dutchy' Holland came to take us to the train which in turn took us to Sydney.

Dad looked spiffing in his beautifully pressed suit, shirt and tie and his fedora hat that he wore at a jaunty angle.
Mum wore her tweed coat and that small, perky red hat was even worn to the pictures.

Everyone was happy and affectionate, and smiling and pleasant.
We were even allowed to get off the train at Katoomba and get a home-cooked morning tea of sandwiches and freshly baked pikelets and a mug of steaming hot tea!

David had his trip to Taronga Park Zoo and Mum had her treat on a ferry ride to Manly.
I was intrigued to see the beautiful birds that swooped down from the sky to share our chips or sandwiches.
Mum explained they were called 'gulls' and were only found near coastal waters.
Today was my turn to see my first colored movie called 'National Beauty' featuring a young girl named Elizabeth Taylor.
We had enjoyed an ice-cream sold to us by an ice-cream boy who carried a tray of the buckets of confection around the theatre, just like the cigarette boy.
Smoking was permitted in the theatres and it was common to view the picture through a smoky haze.

Bev Dad Mum and David Sydney 1949

The revolving stage had appeared during interval and a gentleman dressed in tails played a magnificent Hammond organ. We were mesmerized.

When the afternoon show ended we were met by Dad who intended taking us for a meal.

As we walked down the street a paper boy shouted "Double murder at Wollerawong. Read all about it. Double murder at Wollerawong".

"I think he means Wallerawang. Stay here while I get a paper" Dad said.

Mum started to cry and gathered us close.

Born and bred near the little town she knew every single family.

My sisters were the fifth generation to be born in Lidsdale.

Dad returned ashen faced. "It's Lionel and Loveday Barton" he whispered.

"They've been shot by their farmhand and he's taken Loveday's car. The police are looking for him. Mrs Moon found them when she went to do the housework this morning.

They were shot when they returned from church yesterday morning".

Then he began to cry softly into his hanky as we walked towards The People's Palace.

He looked at Mum and noticed her emotional state. "Vera? Are you alright? Would you like to go home? Are you worried about the girls"?

"What do you think" cried Mum.

We caught the night train.

William Harvey Bugg was duly captured and tried.

He was sentenced for the murder of Miss Loveday but received a much lighter sentence for the murder of Mr Lionel.

The locals were shocked when evidence was given that their highly respected Mr Lionel had an 'appetite' for young men.

The general consensus was that he had shown 'extreme kindness' in taking in so many young boys over the years.

Oh yeah, he did that alright.

Mr Bugg joined the Sydney Smphony Orchestra following the completion of his sentence and became a valued and respected member of society.

Mum was always warning us about talking to Gypsies who appeared a couple of times each year with their horses and brightly painted caravans.

The caravans were drawn by beautifully cared for horses and were painted in bright coloured designs with rounded roof and small metal chimney.

They were so individual, yet the same.

I was somewhat surprised that Mum would show such a lack of respect for these travelers.

I may not have made friends with the adults but I certainly did with the kids.

Mum was adamant, none of the adults enter the yard so I used to take out the scissors, axes and knives to the gate for sharpening by the male of the species.

I was too short to ride Dad's bike in the orthodox way though I tried often.

About that time I mastered riding Dad's bike 'through' the frame.

The bike had to be ridden on a peculiar angle but the thrill was the same.

I would wait at the corner of the lane for Dad to arrive home from work and he would either dink me home or hop off the bike and let me ride as he carried his crib bag.(Crib was the term coined to describe food).

I still carry scars on my knees to remind me of that learning situation.

Beverley Ann Farmer

I was also allowed now to borrow Ruth Nottle's red Arrow bike to ride to the Post Office to pick up the mail and buy any goods needed.

The Post Office was the only shop in Lidsdale and the variety of goods sold included bread and cold meat.

It was not unusual for my Granny to want a half loaf of bread (equivalent to a quarter in Victoria) and three pence worth of Devon (Fritz or Beef German in other states) for the men's lunches.

Uncle Peter only liked Devon and tomato sauce sandwiches while Uncle Doug only liked fresh bread.

I am ashamed to confess that not once did Granny get her full three pence worth of meat home despite the careful wrapping, and that high tin shaped bread really didn't have a big whole where the soft, delicious bread had been separated before I left the shop.

Granny would give me a penny most weeks to spend as I wished.

She also gave Shirl a shilling several times each year 'for good deeds'.

The Post Office was owned and operated by Mr and Mrs Young Senior when I first visited.

They sold the business to a family called Johns who had a young family.

One such child was a beautiful and very friendly little girl named Sylvia.

Sylvia had blonde bouncy curls and was really the prettiest of children.

The residence was attached to the shop and sported a shared driveway with the next door neighbors Mr and Mrs Young Junior.

One afternoon Mr Young Senior backed out of the driveway as Sylvia ran out to say Hello to him.

She slipped under the wheels and was killed instantly.

The township was shocked and saddened.

Occasionally our paternal Granny came to visit and the longer she stayed the thicker the air became. Mum really disliked her Mother-in-law who years before had been overheard to say that Mum, not being a Catholic, was not 'good enough' for Dad.

Dad on the other hand really loved and admired his mother and he defended her behavior with tremendous loyalty whenever Granny Ryan's name was mentioned.

You may recall that Sarah Jane was the eldest child of William and Annie Dowdell and had been born on February 9th, 1868 at Off Flats, via Hampton. She had married George Bernard Ryan Jnr. at Bathurst in 1892.

Dad told us how Sarah cooked on an outside camp oven as her mother had done and, with absolutely no income after Barney left her she had really struggled to feed her children.

Jenolan Caves were located some distance from Hartley and it was common for the old cars taking tourists to that venue to stop at Wilson's Half-Way House.

Meals were provided for the house guests and a supply of beautifully laundered linen was required for the dining room.

It was Granny Ryan who laundered all of that table linen.

Granny walked or rode the old horse to and from Wilson's and in an outside copper open to the elements she laundered the linen then starched it and ironed it with a flat iron heated on the stove.

She would return the laundered linen every few days and collect the next lot. This small amount of money thus earned was her only source of income to keep six children.

Granny was a most talented lady with handwork of any kind, but particularly with crochet.

I loved the tablecloth she made.

It was square white linen piece with the corners removed.

Where the corners were missing they were replaced by triangles of crochet featuring a dove holding a rose in its mouth.

The tiny matching serviettes simply featured a rose.

She was also admired for the wavy 'hairpin crochet' that adorned the edges of our best pillow shams.

One of her special pieces I inherited from Aunty Doll is an afternoon tea cloth with a crocheted edge featuring a tea-pot, sugar bowl, tea cups and sugar tongs (used for blocks of sugar).

Aunty also gave me small cloths she had in her Glory Box, one that is much used.

It has cut-work butterflies in each corner and Granny's crochet around the edge.

147

Granny always told us she had made a special parcel for each of her grand-daughters that were to be distributed when we married.

She maintained they were in safe keeping at an Aunty who only had sons but we Ryan girls never received any such parcel.

Granny Ryan's Crocheting.

I had never seen my Grandfather Ryan and his name were rarely mentioned. Another reason Mum objected to Granny was because of her favoritism displayed to Shirl.

Granny simply adored this friendly, vivacious little pet but couldn't abide Fay in any measure.

All of her life Granny acknowledged Shirl (and sometimes me) and completely ignored Fay.

Mum related a story of how Granny took a piece of apple from Fay and gave it to Shirl.

Aunty Doll had another version of the same story told to her by Granny who maintained Fay had snatched the piece of apple from Shirl and she, Granny, had returned the apple to the rightful owner.

I am inclined to believe Granny's version of events.

Depending on who you spoke to Granny had a reputation of being 'different and difficult' at times.

Even placid Uncle Paddy was heard to voice his critical opinion of her.

Although I didn't see her often she was always pleasant to me.

Mum often showed her bias towards Fay throughout the years and when I questioned her behavior in my adult years she told me it was 'natural for a mother to defend her weakest child'.
Think of that statement what you may.

My Granny Ryan took a dislike to Fay, because she had refused to acquaint Mum with the truth of what happened with the apple.
I always thought it ironic that Fay was actually much like Granny and shared many of Granny's unattractive attributes I had heard about including her moodiness, laziness, inability to forgive others, judgemental opinions, difficulty organizing, maintaining social relationships and plain, straight out rudeness.
As I have grown older, and a little wiser, I ponder if my relatives may have suffered from some mental illness of some kind that had been handed down the generations.
Observations of current generations lead me to believe this may be the case.

Granny's cleanliness was brought into question by Mum when she found her cleaning her false teeth in the wash-up dish.
Mum was furious and discarded the dish by hoisting it over the back fence and catching the next bus to Lithgow to buy a new one.
Granny was appalled at this display of extravagance and took Mum to task for wasting Dad's money.
Mum was also unforgiving of Granny who went through the receipts and bills kept in the dresser as she again admonished Mum for being a spendthrift who wasted 'her son's money'.
After Dad and Uncle Arthur had purchased the house in Blackheath for Granny Uncle Art met Aunty Trix and married.
They all lived together.
Over a period of time Granny was forced out of her home and became homeless.

Many years past before Dad looked into the legitimacy of Sarah's being evicted from her own home, half of which had been purchased by him.
He learned that by occupying the house for a length of time Uncle Art had been granted legal ownership and there was nothing Dad could do to recoup any monies, or claim anything on behalf of Granny.

Homeless and poor Sarah engineered a scheme whereby she visitited each of her children in turn until she 'wore out her welcome'.

She would then move on to the next child's home.

Come Mum and Dad's turn and Granny contacted Dad to make the necessary arrangements.

Only problem was that Dad didn't tell Mum.

Unaware of the the impending visitor's arrival Mum was very surprised to see our neighbor, Mr Ernie Hughes, pull up at our front gate, jump out of the truck, open the gate and drive into the yard.

On board were several pieces of furniture.

Not surprisingly Mum questioned his mental state and cheerily questioned. "Ern? What are you up to? Have you forgotten where you have to go? Ha, Ha". "Oh, no Vera. This is Mrs Ryan's stuff. She's coming to live with you."

"Like hell she is" responded Vera "I have kids and I don't have any room for her and I won't have her back here and that's that.

You can take her furniture back where it came from. How dare she just show up like that"?

"But, Vera. Jim made the arrangements and paid me to bring the furniture here, and unload it, and that's what I'm obliged to do."

"You unload one piece of that woman's furniture and I'll chop it up with the bloody axe" threatened Mum.

Ernie laughed and unloaded a fine set of cedar drawers.

He did not unload another piece however as Mum, true to her word, wielded the axe and proceeded to make kindling of the piece of furniture.

Now we didn't have close neighbors to hear of Dad's homecoming that day and psychologists had not yet warned of the inadvisability of fighting in front of your kids, and there were no tape recorders to record for posterity the transcript of any 'slight misunderstanding' that may have taken place between my parents BUT, I can tell you that my Granny Ryan never came to stay at our house ever again.

On warm summer evenings while trying to dodge the irritating mosquitoes who left me with large, red, itchy lumps, we would take a walk down the lane and dabble our feet in Cox's River where it crossed the road.

We were well versed in the local knowledge that the Blue Mountains had first been crossed by explorers, Blaxland, Lawson and Wentworth in 1813.

No acknowledgement of the aboriginals who led the men over the impassable mountains is to be found in historic papers, yet it was actually those men who opened up this country enabling settlers to graze and live far from the confines of the Sydney area alone.

Local historians credited a chap called Evans with the first crossing as far as Mt Wilson.

Another explorer was named Cox and it was after him the River was named, or so the story went. (You may remember earlier I told you of the brother of Gregory Blaxland the explorer was John from 'Newington' east of Parramatta who employed as an assigned servant my ancestor, convict William O'Neill).

The water in the river was completely free of any signs of pollution and was clear and sparkling allowing us to see the variety of pretty, colored stones that formed the river bed.

We all loved to play 'skimming' and we would count aloud the number of times the stones skipped over the surface of the river before reaching the other side.

We all had collections of pretty stones and we would frequently wander down and augment our collection especially when our Sydney cousins, Dorothy and Barry, came up to stay at Granny Nolan's and we were sent down the lane to collect loose coal that fell from the loaded train trucks.

The train tracks followed the route of the river for a distance before crossing over at a height of about twenty feet.

The rails were mounted on railway sleepers to form a bridge which was supported in turn by timbers resembling telegraph poles.

We devised a game, may I say a very dangerous game, whereby Barry and I, at about nine or ten, would wait for a train and then climb down between the sleepers and hang on to one of them while the train steamed inches away overhead.

If the train was a long one every muscle in our arms would be screaming as they supported our bodies and we would pray for the train to end so we could pull ourselves up through the sleepers onto the track.

The alternative of letting go the sleeper and falling to our death didn't really appeal either.

With eyes full of black coal dust and not a few bumps and bruises caused from falling, bouncing coal we would load the sugar bags of coal into the old wheelbarrow and head home to Granny's.

Perhaps this particular cousin was practicing to commit suicide in later life.

The Joint Coal Board announced a holiday camp for children of miners and names were submitted for the draw.

When I was lucky enough to be chosen one of the local families complained that Dad's position as Deputy should exclude me because he would earn more money.

Dad was very cross and he wrote a letter to the JCB and the family saying they could come and tell me to my face why I couldn't go.

We never heard another word and I packed to travel to Port Macquarie in northern NSW.

Living one hundred miles from the sea you wouldn't be surprised to learn I did not own a swimming costume and as one was 'on the list' of what to take, I really wanted one.

Linda Nottle came to the rescue and gave me a three piece set of beachwear consisting of a two piece costume with matching jacket.

I was thrilled and felt very grown up when wearing the outfit.

We caught a train to Sydney and then another to Wyong.

There a bus waited to take us to a National Fitness Camp on the shore of Lake Macquarie and we couldn't wait to settle in to this new experience.

We were housed in bunk houses that had eight beds per dwelling and we shared ablution blocks conveniently located nearby.

The wide verandahs became the favoured spot for recreational activities.

What fun we had learning camp-fire songs and indulging in sporting activities we could only have dreamed of like canoeing and water volley ball, flying fox competition and the like.

So keen was I to catch the first fish I ventured out on a fallen log to rescue my line and slipped and fell tearing off my toenail in the process.

There was so much fresh air, sporting fun and an abundance of food that we relished.

Miss Bowen and 'Scotty' were our favored leaders and we 'Wang kids were determined to accrue the points required to win the Macquarie Shield for their sakes.

Fay Bush had taken her guitar and she serenaded us with tunes from her country and western repertoire like 'The Overlander Trail' and 'Old Shep.'

We learned fun songs like 'Sambo' and 'The Baby Has Gone Down the Plughole' that I would sing to my own children in years to come.

Fun days at Pt Wolsterncraft

On the return journey we stopped at Wyong for a meal of fish and chips and when I counted my remaining few pennies I worked out I could afford a jar of oysters for Dad if I went without my marvelous smelling treat and that's what I did.

The only disappointment I had was that Dad didn't seem near as excited about the 'oysters' as I was and the jar sat in the cupboard for quite a while until Uncle Doug was skiting about his muscles one day and Dad gave him my gift!!.

When we arrived in Sydney we were whisked off by bus to one of the pylons of the Harbour Bridge where a huge microscope enabled us to view the magnificent views of that most wondrous harbour.

As if that wasn't exciting enough we had our photos taken by the Daily Telegraph, a copy of which appeared in the following day's edition.

I cannot describe how exciting that was for country kids to experience.

Mum kept the cutting for years before it was taken along with Mum's papers.

Perhaps one day I will comprehend why Dad would choose to give away the most expensive gift I had ever purchased.

Uncle Ben owned Corney's Hall. Over a period of time the verandah at the front was closed in and he built a projection-room in the corner of the new structure.

He then began to show movies twice per week on Saturday, and Wednesday nights.

Shirl, together with Linda Nottle, acted as Usherettes to show patrons to their seats and collect the tickets.

I was also employed with my very first job to take the posters for the upcoming shows to Wallerawang and attach them, with drawing pins, to the specially erected poster board outside the brand new Hamburger shop owned and operated by Joe Young.

How I enjoyed my brief encounter with Bette Davis, Henry Fonda, Rita Hayworth, Tyronne Power and many others.

I decided my favorite was an actress, named Marta Toran, who was absolutely beautiful in an oriental way, but her acting ability left a lot to be desired and she faded from the screen.

She was quickly replaced by Irene Dunn, Bette Davis, Vivian Leigh, Ingrid Bergman, to name but a few.

For this errand I received one shilling (ten cents) per week and free entry to the movies.

I was in movie heaven.

At interval I would rush out to the old supper room where a shop had been organized to satisfy the hungry patrons.

Lollies, chocolates, soft drinks at three pence a bottle and one penny glasses of home-made raspberry cordial for the kids were served.

My job was to wash the glasses, firstly in hot water, then rinsing them in cold. With no sink or hot, running water, the kettles would have to be carried down from Nottle's.
The now sparkling glassware would be left to dry on pristine tea towels.

For this service I received a bottle of drink and my choice of a box of Marella Jubes or Fantales or Jaffas or everyone's favourite-Gobstoppers.......

PERHAPS I will be the first in the family to require a filling for a tooth!

As the movies were very old (therefore very cheap) releases very frequently 'broke down'.
A hole would appear on the film on the screen and grow larger by the second.

The accompanying soundtrack would 'whirr' to a crackle before ceasing altogether.
The hall lights would be turned up and the audience would begin to clap, then stamp their feet and become quite vocal.

Uncle Ben would find the offending piece of film, 'fix' it by taking the two ends of the damaged film (that had now been spliced in a small, hinged device), join it with an acetate adhesive, hold the mend for a minute or two until adhered, then rewind the reel and re-thread the film into the projector and try again.

In the meantime the audience would become even more restless and start to whistle and grate their movable chairs until the now 'blurry' film began to run normally again.

I would gather the tiny slivers of film that had found their way to the cutting room floor to add to my growing box of 'stills' and posters from the glass cases where they were held to promote each new program.

There were also the promotional books and programs that would be sent to the proprietor and I built an enviable collection of memorabilia on the industry.

I still recall the thick, exquisitely presented books of the Zigfield Follies and the underwater pictures in beautiful color of Esther Williams.

After the show Uncle Ben would rewind the reels and place them into their special flat, round tins and stack them in a metal drum that was collected the next morning by the bus driver who delivered them to the railway station where they would be returned to Sydney.

The boxes of my collection were destroyed when Mum heard that the pieces of film were capable of spontaneous combustion and she wasn't taking any chances.

The picture theatre was not the success it might have been and it would be many years later that I discovered the reason why.

In 1949 a huge strike occurred across the entire mining industry in NSW.
Although considered an essential service the conditions under which the miners worked were appalling.
The mining union was led by communists and even the word Communism engendered great fear in the people of this country.
It was a widely held view that the Russians were planning to invade our shores at any time.
The strike meant less electricity was being generated.
Electricity was therefore rationed to two hours a day for each household in the early spring.
The union was seen to be holding the government to ransom and the entire economy was at risk of collapsing as the country was literally run on coal.
Two union bosses were taken to court and jailed.
The new leaders then issued the government with a log of claims.
To their surprise the government agreed to their demands.
The union tried for more concessions.

When the Government, then led by Prime Minister, Ben Chifley, refused to negotiate with the men they retaliated by refusing to return to work.
Dad said of Chifley he was a 'pimple on the bum of society'.

The government then brought in the Army to operate the machinery in the open cut mines and there was very wide resentment as a result.

A couple of local men refused to join their fellow miners and continued to go to work thus breaking the 'one hundred percent black-ban' in the Lithgow and district mines.

They consequently were branded 'scabs'.

One of those men was Uncle Ben Nottle and the locals despised him thereafter to the extent that no miner, or his family, would patronize the movie theatre-and none would attend his funeral many years later.

The other local lived to see his centenary which was treated with indifference and he, too, was ultimately 'farewelled' in a neighboring town where only family attended.

Although I was just a kid I can still recall the mini drama that took place at home. When the soldiers arrived they were housed at nearby Marrangaroo, an Army facility.
They quickly 'sussed out' where they were most likely to find girls and they walked miles to attend the local dance in Corney's Hall.
One of the boys called 'Darkie' attached himself to Shirl and Fay and they invited him home for Sunday night's tea, but warned him not to come in his uniform.
The panto that followed with Dad unknowingly entertaining a 'strike breaker' at his table on Sunday, and then rallying the miners on Monday, was really quite humorous.

Dad became very suspicious when luxury items began to appear in sugar bags after Darkie's visits and we were served extra sugar and tinned asparagus and so on.

The remarkable co-incidence was that Darkie was in charge of stores at the army base!
Quite a few heated discussions took place when the entire story was told.

Another interest of Dad's was horse racing.
Approaching a local race day at Wallerawang Dad would place me on the trusty old bike dressed in my yard clothes and take me to the race course where I was given a large paint brush and a tin containing some white paint.

He, with his even bigger brush and huge tin of paint, would commence painting the white posts that surrounded the track.

I would move the opposite way.

It was such fun to be given a job that would inevitably result in a permissible messy end.

Dad had purchased a metropolitan horse named 'Royal Routine' and as the owners planned to keep the name our horse was re-named 'Kelty Chap'.

Kelty Chap had built for him a most elaborate stable in the backyard of our neighbor, Jack White.

This arrangement permitted Jack to indulge in pampering the animal to his heart's content as he acted as a strapper.

Kelty Chap

Kelty Chap suffered from a condition called 'Greasy Heels' and Dad would mix up Vaseline and bright yellow sulpher bought in a powdered form, to treat the complaint.

Of course 'Kelty Chap' had to have his own silks for his jockey to wear and Dad chose royal blue and gold-mainly because there were some old satin curtains being removed from Corney's hall ---and they just happened to be--royal blue and gold!

The jockey employed to wear the silks was Cec Young from out Hampton way.

Race day was a picnic day for the community and the number of visitors from surrounding areas would greatly increase the local population.

The overflow from the two local pubs would patronize the many tents erected on course around the perimeter of the rails.

There was much color and noise and excitement as we, dressed in our Sunday best, would crawl through the rails to spook the horses and join in the vocal encouragement given to the horses as they charged down the straight.

Dad, being a friendly chap, would greet the bookies with a cheery "G' day mate" as he shook their hands and proved how well he could count as he mumbled multiplications like "Five in the fifth" and the bookies, understanding the language Dad was trying to teach them would answer "Two to one Jim" and Dad would shake their hands again and off we'd go so he could say "G'day" to someone else!.

'Kelty Chap' never did make Dad a fortune, rather I suspect the balance sheet was decidedly lop- sided the other way, but that horse did give us all much pleasure.

Our interest in horse racing grew and we got to know the names of the famous jockeys of the day like Neville Sellwood, Scobie Breazley and Athol Mulley as they rode home the champions racing in the city races that Dad listened to.

If Dad wanted to bet on a race he would send Shirl up to 'Wang with the money for Mrs Francis.

The day that the champion Bernborough, ridden by Athol Mulley, fell at a big race in Sydney breaking his leg was one I remember.

Dad cried openly as they announced, Bernborough had been put down as a result of the fall. As he held his head in his hands we cried in sympathy.

I was particularly distressed to see Dad in such a state, but then he did love these animals.

Many years later I would recall this incident with Shirl. "Wasn't Dad distraught that day? I have never forgotten how much he cried for that wonderful horse. He loved all horses but he must have loved Bernborough most of all to have cried so much."

"Yes" agreed Shirl, "He certainly did cry but then so would have you if you had known how much he bet on him that day".

I was horrified to be one of the kids who caught Chicken Pox and the watery blisters were so itchy that no amount of threatening from Mum would prevent the occasional scratch.

I still bear the 'pock' mark hidden amongst the wrinkles on my face.

I dreaded the repeat of the discomfort I had experienced with the mumps.
That pain invariably arrived at the same time as Mum's favourite radio seriel called 'Blue Hills".
At one o'clock as the announcement was made of Gwen Merediths long running saga I would begin to wail with the throbbing pain in my neck.
Mum thought I WAS a pain in the neck and was not very sympathetic to my discomfort!

I also started getting occasional pains in the tummy and Dr Bamber warned Mum not to give me any Castor oil as this aperient would aggravate my 'grumbling appendix.'
This suited me fine as I hated the taste of Castor oil that Mum administered every month and I did occasionally have a little smile when my poor sisters gagged and swallowed while being subjected to what Mum referred to as 'a good clean out.'
There were also regular users of some home-grown cures.
If we had a head cold we were subjected to a Fry's Balsom inhalation.
A large mixing basin was kept for the purpose and it would be filled with boiling water to which the Balsom was added by the spoonful.
We would have our head completely covered with a towel as we inhaled the resulting fumes.
If we had a sore throat Mum made up a mixture of honey and vinegar that was usually administered after a coughing fit.
If the cough persisted we were sometimes able to purchase a packet of Irish Moss Gum Drops.
They were black, licorice tasting, made of sea-weed and delicious!

We had pets of various kinds and one was a family dog with the very ordinary name of Laddie.
Laddie was no ordinary dog.
David was already displaying a profound rapport with animals and wherever he toddled Laddie was by his side.
If his steps faltered Laddie would crouch down so David could clutch his coat and he would slowly stand up so David could again steady his gait.

David was not at all adventurous.

One of his favorite past-times was to drive his little trucks in the sand-pit Dad had made him.

One morning as David played happily in the yard and Mum did the morning dishes Laddie went crazy and kept barking and jumping and crying at the back kitchen door. Mum scolded him but he just became even more agitated. Eventually Mum opened the wire door to show him just how cross she was and the dog grabbed her by the apron and tried to pull her to the sandpit. There, basking in the sunlight within inches of where David played was a large, black, red bellied snake.

Mum snatched David up into her arms and the brave little Laddie attacked the neck of the sizeable snake and hung on tenaciously as the creature writhed and thrashed until life left it.

Mum, who viewed this little drama from a safe distance inside the wire door of the kitchen was sure the small dog would have been harmed and it was with great relief when she saw the little hero appear at the house steps with the snake in his mouth.

He then returned to the sandpit where he frequently sat, fully alert.

On another occasion the Dukes kids pedaled their new tip tray car up to our house and we pushed the miniature vehicle back to their house with the baby of the family in the tray which had been tied with string so it wouldn't tip up. Mum came with us to ensure the baby was safe and when we arrived at Dukes we were invited inside for a drink.

The baby was removed and the car 'parked' under the sunroom windows. When we went outside one of the kids shouted "Snake" and in the tray of the car where a short time before the Dukes' baby had been was a large reptile that had curled itself in the hot metal rectangle.

Mum ordered us all inside and she boiled the kettle, opened the window and poured the water onto the snake.

When we were sure it was dead we carried it up to the ants nest across from our house.

All that remained the next morning was the skeleton.

Grandfather Nolan called in one morning on his way down the lane to catch some eels.

He invited me to accompany him which was a most unusual gesture on his part.

161

When we reached the river (Cox's) he detoured off the road and folloiwed the bend of the river for a distance of two hundred yards.

He positioned himself close to the bank and bending down he swept back the overhanging foliage and beckoned me closer.

There before me in the crystal clear water were several platypus.

As they glided and cavorted one burrowed between the pebbles at the bottom of the pond and emerged with litter in her bill that she deposited in a nest constructed on the bank.

Her industry was impressive.

I stood mesmerised at the scene.

Grandfather waited patiently until I'd had my fill.

Then he said "I hope you'll keep our little secret under your hat."

And I did.

Many years later I would choose to study the journeys of Charles Darwin who in his publication of 'Darwin and the Beagle' described how he watched 'the amazing platypus cavorting in the Cox's River when visiting Wallerawang'.

One hundred years before I was born Charles Darwin had studied the ancestors of MY platypus.

I was to develop a lifelong dislike for cats arising from the behavior of one of our succession of snowy white cats given us by Aunty Doll who bore the original name of 'Snowy'.

I had been given a rabbit kitten by my Uncle Doug and her name was Veronica. Veronica was regularly patted and pampered and I loved her dearly.

She lived in a wire sided fruit box and needed little care.

Enter Snowy who thought her need for rabbit company was greater than mine and she burrowed under the box and demolished my pet.

Shortly after that Snowy gave birth to a litter of kittens.

This was not an unexpected event and follow up plans for the birth had already been hatched.

Dad insisted the kittens be destroyed as soon as they were born before Snowy took them over the lane and hid them in the bush until they grew into fluffy kittens.

The kittens were to be drowned immediately.

Mum summoned me to catch the kittens and place them in a bucket. I, suspecting what was about to happen, refused to obey.

After some contact counselling I collected the kittens whose cries couldn't be heard over my bawling.

The tiny fluffy babies scrambled over each other trying to escape the container as though they knew their fate.
I was ordered to place the bucket under the tap at the old tank stand as the Mother cat screamed and struggled within the confines of the deceased rabbit's fruit box.
"Turn on the tap at once" Mum insisted.
Reluctantly I did as I was told and as the water level rose the kittens one by one ceased crying.

I sat on the ground crying and refusing to take further part in digging a hole in which to bury the bodies.
Mum poured the water from the bucket and I couldn't avoid seeing the tiny faces some of which were exuding vomited milk.

I began to shake and cry and vomit uncontrollably and to this day I cannot abide a cat's vomit or the smell of cat's food without feeling nauseous.

'This' and 'That' Cat

Perhaps I should not consider becoming a farmer's wife!!!!!!!!.

When I played 'houses' by myself, or with visiting kids, I loved to bring out my special canteen of cutlery made from a new product, called 'plastic'.
The tiny knives, forks, and spoons were in a range of colors but all matched the turquoise tea set that was kept for special occasions.
These treasured possessions had been a gift from Fay's friend, Pat Adams, who would marry Digger Nottle in later years.

I attended school with the nicest group of kids you could imagine.
Most of them were the offspring of miners and a few had Dads who were employed to work on the railway.

A couple of fathers were farmers and very few were tradesmen who may have had their own business.
On reflection I can only name one boy I really disliked and I may even have to mention him, and share with you the reason why, at a later stage.
Weather permitting we would commence each day lining up in front of the main building of the school when the bell rang.

Then came the exercises where we marched on the spot and placed our arms in a variety of positions in time with the music played, before the march into school.
On Monday morning we would have a long assembly and follow the ritual of pledging ourselves with the words:-
I honor my King, I serve my country, I salute my flag.
We would then sing God Save the King, our national anthem at the time.

Some of the poorer kids had jam sandwiches wrapped in newspaper while others had beautiful planned lunches that were sometimes shared.
One girl, Josephine Cook, had a beautiful, long, lunch tin that featured a scene from the French Riviera and it always contained tiny trimmed sandwiches, home-made cake, vita-wheat biscuits with butter and Vegemite (that created little worms when squeezed together) and a piece of fresh fruit with the skin first removed then replaced.
Fancy or not we made no difference and often swapped our luxury treats for a plum jam sandwich with no butter.
On reflection it is little wonder that so many kids had to have time off school due to infections of boils and carbuncles with such restrictions of food-and bathing water.
The range of treatments for such maladies included poultices of bread and soap, soap and Epsom salts, Sulphur and molasses, linseed oil soaked flannel and other odd concoctions made from readily available ingredients like starch.
Carbuncles resembled a collection of boils grouped together and were known to be an extremely painful 'Staph' infection.

There were some school rules that did not meet with Dad's approval.

One was that the teachers were not permitted to go through my hair with a fine tooth comb dipped in kerosene when there was an outbreak of nits (lice).

If any of the girls with long plaits had nits the boys liked to sit behind the girls and pretend to stab the nits with their pen nibs as they 'marched' down the plait onto the desk behind.

As Dad routinely brushed my hair of an evening after my plaits had been undone he would have been the second to know if my head was infected!

Secondly, we were not to be included in an 'emu drop' when all of the kids went around the vast school yard picking up paper and conveying them to the incinerators that were lit daily.

Dad made us promised we would never drop papers, so we didn't.

That way he could justify his insistence that we were not to pick up rubbish dropped by others.

On very rare occasions we had an overnight sleep at school.

We slept in our clothes on the hard floor with only our personal pillows and blankets brought from home to comfort us.

The fire was 'banked' up and we were allowed sit around and drink the soup provided by the Headmaster's wife.

For supper we ate large chunks of 'Ration Cake' (that was cheaply made without rationed eggs and butter) washed down with mugs of cocoa.

After lunch each day we played rounder's with a tennis racquet and ball.

It was necessary to hit the ball through the pine trees from the top playground.

I loved being the captain of my team and if for any reason anyone couldn't run then I was your girl.

We all practiced running to the back fence to watch the trains rush past.

We had great respect for train drivers as one named Ben Chiffley had, that decade, become Australia's Prime Minister.

The gravel topped tennis court attracted onlookers and I thought it an opportunity to show off how good I was at jumping and so I jumped the tennis net with monotony.

I begged Mum to put more material in the dresses she made me and less in the legs of the matching knickers, or even to buy me some 'shop knickers'.

To add more insult to injury she refused to put tight elastic in the legs of the home-made variety as we might get varicose veins when older, so the legs would tend to 'hang' down.

Whenever I ran, the knickers felt as though they were falling right down and I tended to hold them at the waist just in case.

As a result the boys nicknamed me 'Hitch-em-up'.

Although a school uniform was not compulsory several of the girls wore tunics and blazers.

In summer fine, straw, Panama hats were sometimes worn.

They were colored off-white on the outside and olive green underneath and were very effective in sheltering one from the summer sun's rays.

Many, many years after we had left school I met up with June Connely and she said as a kid she often wondered if I wore my big sisters knickers to school! We laughed so much at the visual image it evoked- tiny Bev in large, loose, adult knickers.

One of the activities at school, weather permitting, was the Maypole dancing. If anyone missed a step invariably Miss Mugeridge would insist the offending student watch me and copy exactly what I did.

You could say I was the Maypole Champion.

Now I should explain a little more about the Maypole for your edification.

The Maypole is a tall pole mounted on crossed beams to ensure it remained upright.

On the top of the pole were found metal clips.

In special little boxes in the storeroom were different colored ribbons six inches wide and ten feet long.

One box had yellow Georgette ribbons and another one had red taffeta ones. Rolled up after use the ribbons were returned to their boxes.

Periodically I would be given the ribbons to take home for laundering.

The purpose of the exercise was to have ten people, five clutching red and the same number choosing yellow, evenly spaced around the pole who would dance and weave around, under and over while holding the ribbon, so that attractive patterns were formed around the pole.

When the ribbons became so short the participants were close to the upright the dancers changed hands and reversed direction, thus unwinding the patterns formed.

All of this stepping (usually to a polka dancing step) was accompanied by a scratchy old record playing on an antiquated record player.

Many, many years later I would learn that the tradition of the Maypole dance went back to medieval times when it was employed as the MOST powerful fertility dance of all.
Now they tell me!

PERHAPS I practices too hard do you think?

At school we were taught Geography.
The Teachers all seem to have a map of the world stamp that covered an entire page of our exercise books.
We were encouraged to colour around the edges of countries in blue to denote coastlines.
Our studies centred around only the countries belonging to the British Empire.
We knew about Trade routes, the West Indian Trading Company,the timber industry in Canada, diamond mining in South Africa.

Everywhere we learned about those countries had been colonized by the British.
Although we were instructed on the foundation of our own country there were no references to Aboriginals except in relation to them spearing 'whites'.
Then, in August 1947, India became Independent.
Our teacher was appalled and broke the news to us with a tremor in his voice.
One of the students asked if he thought South Africa would follow suit.

Mr F looked aghast and answered "God forbid."
I related this conversation to Dad.
Dad chuckled. "We'll see." He commented.
I related the contents of the geography lesson to Dad that evening and I wondered why he smiled when I told him I'd also heard a song on the school radio about 'The Vulgar Boatmen' in a place called Russia.

Joan Samuels had a sister who was deaf. Her name was Maureen.
Joan taught us the entire signing alphabet and I have shared this lesson with hundreds of my students over the years.

During a game of basketball I inadvertently scratched Joan's beautiful face and for years I was haunted by the possibility that she may have remained scarred. After a school reunion attended by my sisters, I was able to contact Joan and learn no such disfigurement had resulted from the accident.
Yet I had carried the scars of this event for all of those years.

Shirley Conelly had dreadful scars from a scalding accident when she had climbed up on the side of a boiling copper and been badly burned.
Shirley would marry a second cousin of mine.
Shirley Faber had lost her big toe by chopping wood with an axe but it certainly didn't retard her running ability.

Margaret Woods and I stole some cigarettes and hid them in a hollow log down the lane.
Occasionally we would return to the scene of the crime and thrust our hands into the cavity that could have housed anything.
In later years we would learn that this log had very significant meaning to the Aboriginal tribe who had frequented this area.
It was believed to have been the burial place of 'King Billy', their leader of the tribe.
A bushfire would eventually destroy all evidence of our hiding place.

Margaret & Lindsay Dukes & the extension of Duncan St (Down the lane)

My cousin, Marie, had the quickest reflexes I had ever seen.

She was the only person who could outsmart a fly and never failed to swat one that came near her person.

How could we have guessed that Lynette and Joan would become sisters-in-law, attractive Val Littler would be a very young child bride, Merle Quince would dedicate her life to church work and Josephine, Lynette and I would undertake nursing studies?
Could it possibly be more than seventy years since I first met those kids at Wallerawang Public School?

Perhaps we will continue to be nice to one and other as we remember each other as being forever young.

I here reflect on my sister's schooling.

Shirl had attended Lithgow High School for two years and when it was time for Fay to go to secondary school some changes were afoot. I was then about eight years old.

A girl Fay went to school with had an Uncle who was a high ranking official in the Church and he planned to send Margaret to a 'posh' Girl's School in Bathurst where she would be educated by the nuns of the order of St Joseph. Mum figured if it was good enough for Margaret Warren it was good enough for Fay.
Shirl would also go for company and support of Fay.
Mum spent hours dyeing and making the many uniforms required on school lists as she could not afford the real uniforms only sold at exclusive shops in Sydney, as well as the very expensive fees for boarders.
Although the girls were fully aware of our family circumstances when compared with the families of other students they made friends with staff and students that endured for many years.
Shirl, always an outstanding all-round student, embraced the opportunities Perthville provided.
She excelled at her singing, debating, acting, academic subjects and sport.
Fay, on the other hand, suffered terribly from home sickness and did not appear to gain the same benefits.(It should be said that Fay was no dill either and she would continue her language studies by correspondence after she returned to the Catholic School in Lithgow after a couple of years away).

A new family ritual was born as soon as the girls wrote to Mum and mentioned they were sometimes hungry because food access was limited after hours. Mum was appalled to think her girls may fade away to shadows.

Solution? We would send up a cardboard carton of cakes every week on the Bathurst train that stopped at Perthville Station.
Resembling the goodies that appeared at Sunday night's tea the box would contain cream sponges full of mock cream (made by beating together butter and castor sugar until the sugar dissolved), fairy cakes, moist chocolate cake ("It keeps well Jim"), 'Mushrooms' (small pastry cases filled with jam and cream and dusted with cinnamon and decorated with tiny pastry stalks) and caramel tarts (made from boiled condensed milk) and everyone's favorite, lamingtons.
The box, and most times me to hold the box steady, were placed on the bike and off up to Wallerawang we would go.
And guess who got to lick the spoons and clean out the basins without any competition?
A-h-h-h, life was s-o-o-o good and I want you to know just how enthusiastic a supporter of my sisters getting a good education at a famous college I was.

No longer did this kid have to share a bed with two big sisters or wait in line for the shank off the Sunday roast or get drug down the backyard in all weathers at my sisters' whim!!

There was just so much to be said for a good education I would humbly suggest, and I would recommend it to all big sisters even though their little sisters may never learn Latin roots and be able to spell as well as they can she may benefit in other ways.
A-h-h-h, life was S-O-O-O good!

I slept in the big double bed on the 'back' room and I even had room for my clothes in the lovely old wardrobe with its oval mirror and inlaid bows found adorning the outer panels.
I didn't have a sister present who pulled my hair because it was curly or who told big fibs to impress Mum.

In the girl's final year the school put on a full production of Shakespeare's "The Merchant of Venice" and we journeyed up to Bathurst to see it.

No expense was spared and what lavish costumes that weren't hired from 'Buttons and Bows,' the huge costume hiring company in Sydney, were made by the nuns.

Shylock was played by Shirl and Fay was a Prince.

The staging was exceptional and even the programs were memorable adorned as they were with wispy, delicately hand-painted pink butterflies edged with gold, complementing the mauve ribbon bows that held the double pages together.

I was never to forget this special, special introduction to Shakespeare.

PERHAPS one day I can go to University and study Shakespeare, Theatre and Drama.

I may even have the opportunity in old age to visit The Globe Theatre and Shakespeare's home in England.

It was on that particular day that my religious fate was sealed.

Having travelled up to Bathurst on the 'cake train' in the afternoon we arrived early enough to visit the two most important stars of the show before they partook of the evening meal.

As I was considered too young to enter the inner sanctum of the girl's dorms I was relegated to a chair in a room near the front entrance with a nun called Sister Mark.

She had been utterly charming to Mum since we arrived and I could see just how impressed Mum was with this quiet, serene 'presence'.

She gave Mum serene direction to where the girls could be found and waved her off with a serene smile.

Then she turned to me and glowered and snarled "Get over there and sit on that chair and do not utter one single word you sniffling little frog.

We'll straighten you out when we get our hands on you".

"But".

"I said not one word" she yelled.

"But..." I tried again "I need to..."

"YOU WILL REMAIN SILENT" she shouted and she grabbed me by the coat collar with both hands and began to shake me so violently I thought my head would fall off.

I felt my life was in danger and I fought with all my might to break free of this assassin as I shouted loudly "You let me go you bloody black and white magpie."
And she did!
I found my own way to the toilet and returned to sit quietly and comfortably (as any little lady should) in the entrance to Perthville Catholic Ladies College.

Shirl expressed a wish to join the church as a Nun but as she was under-age and needed the permission of my parents her desire was thwarted by their refusal.
I was very relieved that she wouldn't have access to find out about my altercation with that awful Sister Mark.

Sitting in the sunshine that streamed over the kitchen steps where I sat, I pulled up my top and fingered my navel.
"Mum. Why do we have a belly button?"
Mum gasped in horror and in one stride was smacking my curious hand.
"You must NEVER touch that" she said sternly. "You will find out all about that when you become a woman and I don't want to hear you talk about it ever again."
The conversation was over.

PERHAPS she should have been just a little forthcoming at the time.

I loved to sing and dance on my back verandah stage.
As if my prayers were heard a notice came home from school announcing that a recent graduate of the Lithgow Dance Academy, and star pupil, Val Malcolm, was considering taking dancing classes out at 'Wang if sufficient students could be found.

Mum and Dad discussed the investment of two shillings (i.e. twenty cents) and I was allowed join the troupe.

I thought the opportunity wonderful and I couldn't wait for each Thursday to arrive to learn new steps and practice old ones.
New ballet shoes were ordered and a pair of toe dancing shoes bought from a school friend's sister.
'Taps' were nailed loosely to a 'good' pair of shoes.

I asked how the names we used had come about as we added to our vocabulary passé, barre, pas de deux, positions 1st, 2nd, 3rd etc., plea, demi, pirouette, the 'step of the horse' and others.

My question remained unanswered as not even Dad knew the answers.

Many years later, whilst undertaking an assignment on the subject of dance at Uni, I would learn that the names had been bestowed on the moves by a Frenchman named Beauchamp who had been the fencing teacher of Louis X1V.

In 1661 Louis had directed his instructor to give names to the moves of the 'pretty steps' which would ultimately become ballet.

A few kids dropped out of dance classes during the first six months mainly due to the difficulty of getting to the venue without transport.

I walked all the way, even in winter weather, and Miss Malcolm gave me a lift to the Lithgow corner in her new car when we had finished.

Towards the end of the year Miss Malcolm announced she thought we should undertake preparation for the British Ballet Organization (Australian Branch) Examination.

This was to be the culmination of our years' work and Miss Malcolm warned us that she would be making great demands on presentationln what was supposer to be the "spontaneous" section though Miss Malcolm promised she would 'tweak' our presentation just to make the 'spontaneity' even better!

In consequence, we prepared two different mimes and Miss Malcolm chose the one she thought best and most likely to earn the highest marks.

We were also versed on the oral introduction of our 'piece'.

When Miss Malcolm suggested lots of changes to both my pieces I became quite downhearted.

Then I had a brainwave of combining the better of the two pieces I'd prepared and so a third 'piece' emerged.

I did my own 'tweaking' and my excitement grew.

I said nothing to Miss Malcolm who would get a really big surprise when she saw it at the exams.

Twinkle Toes

Appropriately dressed in a beautiful white satin and tulle tutu with a pink rose (removed from Mum's big black hat) pinned at my waist and delicate satin ballet shoes whose ribbon ends floated up my shins, I waited to be summoned.

My name was called and I faced the examiners.

Clearly and precisely I introduced my original masterpiece.
"This piece is entirely my own creation" I announced. "It was inspired by my habit of performing in front of my audience of dolls on our back verandah. The scene is a toy shop in Magic Land.
A bad doll-maker tried to make a doll into a real girl.
I shall now begin" I told the stony faced, Sydney Examiner.
I felt so confident I wanted to add 'I may be just a kid from the bush but I sure can surprise you stuffy old ladies'.

And so I mimed my mime with exaggerated facial expressions and flamboyant gestures.
"This is going so well" I said to myself.
I glanced at Miss Malcolm.
She held her brow with her hand as though she had developed a sudden bad headache and there was no longer any sign of her lovely smile.
I finished my act and remained in position for what seemed an age before being dismissed.
A long, long time followed before the next candidate was called in.
Eventually Miss Malcolm appeared and instead of taking me in her arms and giving me a big hug like I expected she embarked on a tirade using unfamiliar words like ops' and 'peels' and 'ias' and such things- whatever they were.
"You certainly won't get in the nineties now Beverley" she said as she hurried away.

I felt I'd been robbed and not enough credit had been given to my genius.

I was none too pleased in later years to learn that an old man by the name of Hoffman had many years before I was born pre-empted my 'original' idea and created a ballet called "Coppelia".
The examiners from Sydney AND Miss Malcolm had obviously learned it also.

Apart from my lovely tutu, there were other costumes I loved.
My 'rainbow' dress was made from layers of different colored tulle the predominant color of my dress was mauve.
Four other girls had the same frock but different 'main' colors of lemon, green, pink and blue for a group ballet number.

A national Spanish dance featured a long black skirt lined with flounces of bright red on the inside.

A tiny black lace mantilla was worn, held in place with a large, intricately carved, black comb that belonged to the teacher.

Then there was the white tulle with red crepe paper trin that allowed my 'Hitch-em'up' nickers to be clearly seen!

I was none too comfortable in the grass skirt and two coconut shell halves tied together, then around my neck and around my back implying I had 'boobs' where in fact there was nothing.

The shells chafed and moved of their own accord as we swayed our hips to the strains of the Hula-Hula Lullaby.

Perhaps I will still recall the steps to the songs of 'Strawberry Lane' and 'By the Side of the Zeider Zee' or 'On the Good Ship Lollipop', the 'Dance of the Swans' and 'The Highland Fling" well into old age.

There would probably have been a few more if I hadn't wagged a couple of sessions and spent the two bob (20 cents) on treats.

Mr Bill Ford was the worst of my Primary teachers though I greatly admired his proficiency at playing the flute and his love of poetry.

He had a nasty habit of 'putting you down' and his game with me was to make comments about my much loved Shirl.

If I sang with too much gusto during our School of the Air Music lessons every Tuesday afternoon he would say things like "Think you are your big sister coming second at the eisteddfod do you Beverley?"

Shirl never came second.

The same couldn't be said for his sister, Heather, who was consistently beaten by Shirl.

Mr Ford had many rules and the punishment for breaking these rules was that he would whack your hands by administering the cane.

The cane was a substantial piece of bamboo.

The punishments only varied by the number of blows registered.

A popular one stroke was given if you used the word 'got' in a composition.

Mr Ford hated the word.

We were only permitted to use the word 'nice' in relation to food.

One of Mr Ford's rules was that if you were caught eating in class and you didn't have enough to share with the entire class you received the cane.

Not a few had fallen foul of this rule and none of us relished the hissing sound made as the bamboo cane came travelling through the air and connected with the flesh of an outstretched hand.

With such large classes if one intended eating you needed to be clever, cunning and careful.

I thought I was all three.

I had a big 'pig out' when I walked to 'Wang to spend my dancing money.

I bought a pie for three pence, a bottle of drink for three pence, a McNiven's Ice Cream for three pence, two cakes for one and a halfpenny each and three penny worth of lollies.

As it was my intention to devour the lollies during the course of the afternoon I also purchased something for every kid in the class in the form of a packet of hundreds and thousands.

I still had money left over to indulge in an afternoon splurge.

As anticipated I commenced to eat the lollies in class.

As anticipated I got caught.

"Beverley Ryan? You are chewing in class. Get out the front" Mr Ford said as he reached towards the top of the chalk board for the cane.

"But Sir" I protested "I have some for everyone" and I produced the cellophane packet from my pocket and hurriedly attempted to tear the end with my teeth.

The tiny colorful confectionery balls began to tumble everywhere and the look on Mr Ford's face warned me I was in BIG trouble.

He grabbed the remains of the packet from my grasp and threw them in the direction of the waste paper bin.

He then proceeded to administer six of his 'best' cuts to my small hands.

The lesson learned by me that day still lingers.

PERHAPS Mr Ford did not like hundreds and thousands!

On the rare occasions I skipped dancing classes or when the slower students bored us to tears we would abscond.

The little church hall where we met was some distance from the school up at 'Wang.

We would walk up through the township and cross the railway bridge then follow the road up and around towards the back of the town.

Situated on the Great Western Highway was a large saw-mill that serviced the surrounding pine forests.

Huge mountains of sawdust some twenty or thirty foot high covered the area and there were so many of them, once inside, detection was difficult.

We, Valerie Littler and I, and occasionally some other brave souls who were not members of the dancing troupe extraordinaire, would seek out old pieces of corrugated iron, bend one third of it to form a forty-five degree angle and use the resultant item as a toboggan.

We would hold on to the rusty old edges and slide, at considerable pace, down the saw-dust mountains with no fear, no brakes, no presentment of danger, no thought of decapitation and no bloody sense!

In the New Year Miss Malcolm became engaged and later married.

We were left with no teacher when she moved away but not before she spoke to Mum and suggested I should continue my studies every Saturday morning at Lorna Hart's Academy in Lithgow.

Dad had a routine for scratching his back in the manner used by horses.

He would sidle up to the open hallway door and position himself so that the protruding lock came in direct contact with his itch.

He would then gyrate his body until the itch subsided.

It was as well that he was short in stature.

Some Saturdays Dad would come into town on the same bus and conduct his business at the bank or solicitor or whatever.

He would call for me when my lesson had finished and it was not unusual for him to give me sixpence to buy myself a treat--usually some trinket from Woolworths or Selfridges, but more often food.

My favorite was fish and chips.

This particular day the sixpence was a bit slow in coming so I asked Dad for it.

He was decidedly unimpressed by my forwardness and said no.

Then, as we walked up the street in silence towards the top bus stop Dad stopped and knelt down to attend to a filthy, old, intoxicated hobo who was lying in the gutter near one of the hotels.

Dad wiped the old man's mouth with his own scrupulous white hanky and after a few words took out his wallet and gave the man money.

Meanwhile I was wailing loudly begging Dad to get away from the disgusting creature.

The old man pushed Dad away and crawled back towards the Pub door.

Dad looked at me with tears in his eyes and said gently. "You know that old man once owned an entire suburb of Lithgow called Sunnybank and now it's all gone on drink.

(Sigh) There was no need for you to be scared Bill. He's my Daddy-

--and he's your Grandfather".

He offered me sixpence but I refused to take it.

Not even the joy of entering Mr Jones' fish shop and hearing his cheery greeting of "Hello. Hello. I do believe it's Smiler Ryan's little sister" could make me feel good that day.

Perhaps as a result of that experience I will very, very rarely ever have a drink of alcohol.

Not long after that incident I learned Grandfather had died in Lithgow Hospital.

I well remember Aunty telling me how some members of the family dug up his backyard to recover the biscuit tins full of bank notes that the old man had 'planted'.

Sister Writer took me aside one night on night duty at Lithgow Hospital and told me Grandfather was the 'finest looking elderly gentleman' she had ever nursed.

We collected wood for the fires from local fallen trees in the horse and dray. It was a competition to sit up the front on the duck board with Dad.

Dad would usually let us take it in turns to sit on the duck board though it was not unusual for me to be squeezed between one of my sisters and Dad.

Visiting the Annual Lithgow Show was a highlight.

We would dress up in our Sunday finery and all catch the bus to town.

I loved to visit the livestock with Dad while Mum headed for the handwork and cooking pavilions.

The fabulous show bags were brimming with good value.

Dad & David Lithgow Show

There were sample sized tins of beans and spaghetti, fruits and jams, cereals, tiny boxes of lollies and a range of groceries, toys and hankies, brooches and skipping ropes.

We would here meet my Granny Ryan and Dad would give her large amounts of money- then offer me much smaller amounts to bribe me so I wouldn't mention the transaction to Mum.

We would also catch up with Aunty Doll and Uncle Paddy at the livestock pavilion.

Uncle Paddy was renowned for accurately guessing the live weight of cattle and not a few old farmers would gather around and challenge him if they dared.

Invariably I would be invited out for a holiday but Mum didn't seem too keen on me going, though occasionally Fay and Shirl went.

On one occasion when Unc returned the girls after a weekend at the farm he came inside for a cup of tea and suggested I throw some clothes in a bag and return with him.

It was school holiday time and after some resistance Mum gave her blessing. She took me aside and quietly said "Find out why Doll is mad with Fay while you are there will you?"
Of course I would.

I took the YoYo that I had won at the show when Unc had given me sixpence to spend on the sideshow.

Perhaps when I am much older I will travel with a sideshow family and see just how they work.

We travelled out to Lowther by way of River Lette.

As we drove along Uncle kept calling me 'Youngin' and when I asked him why he said it was because I was so special being the youngest girl in the entire family.
I asked him if I could give him a special name and he said I could if I could spell the new name.
From that day he was forever 'Unc'.
As we approached the Lowther sign three huge pines came into view marking the Curran's farm.
The trees looked enormous as we grew closer sheltering as they did the extensive sale yards below.
I was surprised to see a tethered sheep in the front garden and Unc, observing my curious look, anticipated my question by simply nodding in the animal's direction and saying "Resident lawn-mower. Name of "Baaaaarbra."

"Baaaaarbra" and triplets

181

The old verandah was edged with blooming Wisteria the racemes of which hung down in clusters of mauve.

Aunty Doll was another member of the family who had the reputation of being a 'difficult' personality.
She spoke quickly in a high pitched voice.
I particularly recall her melodious address of Unc when she summoned him with a three note call of "Da-r-ls."

Uncle Paddy, in contrast, had a true ocker drawl.
He was very calm and jovial with a large bulbous nose.
He had the ability to time his few words perfectly giving them considerable impact when expressed.
His favourite word was "Ghost".
He very, very rarely swore and was shocked if anyone blasphemed.
He simply used "Ghost."
His sizeable paunch rumbled when he laughed and his mirth was infectious.
Aunty would never admit to being wrong on any subject and she became extra cross when Unc and I joined forces to argue a point.
This we did often.

Shortly after I examined my room, checked the kapok mattress to see if it would be as comfortable as the one at home and unpacked my clothes, I thought I had been there long enough to ask Mum's question so I approached Aunt.
She and Unc laughed and looking at each other, nodded, and said together "Vera".
Aunt then told me how Fay borrowed her precious Prayer Book and deciding the color had faded from the page edges she painted them with ordinary gold paint!
As the pages were now all stuck together, and the little pages were unable to be opened, Aunt had not been impressed. I examined the book and had to agree. I know this is so because not only did I look at it then but I inherited said treasure.

Unc and Bonnie and dogs

Many new experiences awaited me at this much loved venue.
I could not believe that you had to strain the water you drank through muslin to catch the wrigglers.
These were actually immature mosquitos that made their homes in the old tanks.

At the edge of the road a large drum was mounted atop a pole. This was the mail box in which a locked, large canvas bag was delivered in the morning and collected in the afternoon.
Curran's mail (and paper) was addressed to Road Mail Box (RMB) and was sorted at Hartley prior to delivery.

The day after my arrival Unc saddled up horses Josephine and Bonnie and with a substantial lunch in our saddle bags we headed out to Black Ridge to bring in some cattle for the upcoming sales.
He untied six or seven dogs and invited them to follow us.

I was amazed to see the enormous number of rabbit warrens that riddled the paddocks.
From the elevated height on horseback it was possible to steer the mount towards solid ground.
The rabbits of all sizes ran from one burrow to the next visiting their rabbit neighbours.

There were dozens of them giving the illusion that the land was moving in some areas.

The dogs would go crazy catching one rabbit after another.

Unc would alight from Bonnie and inspect the rabbit for visible signs of Myxomotosis, a virus that had been engineered by the south Americans and introduced to Australia in an effort to curb the rising population.

If the eyes were clear he would attach the furry creature to his saddle and continue on his way with the dogs baying at his heels.

The infected animals were left to die a slow, lingering death.

It was not just the paddocks that were over-run but any structure around the farm.

Cow-bails, tank-stands, sheds, dog kennels-all bore signs of the plague and it was not unusual to find an out-building collapsed when their foundations had been undermined by the invading hordes.

Young local men were often invited to hone their shooting skills in an endeavor to eradicate the scourge yet nothing decreased the mounting numbers.

The rabbits continued to multiply like rabbits do.

The country found itself with a major problem.

On tree stumps and fence posts numerous skulls with horns of both sheep and cattle were strategically placed.

Lady and friends

Bev, Josephine, dairy& old shed.

The Garden Gate

Gwen, Win, Paddy, William and Susan Jane

On the way I was intrigued to see the cattle 'interacting' like the ones I had noticed in the paddock at home and in Granny's paddock where her cow bails were.

"Look at the cows playing leap frog" I said. Unc said nothing.

When we rounded up the cows and calves I asked Unc where the cows had 'found' the calves.

"I think you had best ask Aunty Doll" he answered as he pointed out some unusual plants, skilfully re- directing my attention.

The plants were bright purple Scotch thistles and the horses strained to munch them on their way home.

I observed Aunty Doll's nightly ritual.

Following supper she would take a bowl of warm water to the laundry and wash her face with a face washer. She then splashed her face with very cold water before applying copious amounts of a lotion called 'Ol Olive,' a pale green concoction that came in an unusual round bottle.

Aunt had beautiful skin even in her advancing years and I wondered if this was due to her consistent toilette.

That night after we retired and both Aunt and Uncle mumbled through the Rosary I heard Unc tell Aunty Doll of the day's events.

"I think you had best have a talk to her about the birds and bees" he suggested.

Perhaps

I lay there thinking I may not know much about bees but my knowledge of birds was pretty good judging by the birds egg collection I had in those cotton wool lined shoe boxes at home!

During a very recent chat with Dad he had requested I not take anymore Plover eggs because we wouldn't have any birds to tell us when the rain was coming. It was also the day he told me about Cirrus clouds.
He told me they had been called 'High' cloud when he was a kid and he recognized them because they reminded him of bird's feathers.

I instigated a session whereby I would have my first lesson on bees.
"Unc. When will you be taking the honey from the hives?" I questioned.
"Might happen this week, 'Youngin' "he answered.

And it did.

We donned overalls and long sleeved shirts and gloves and a hat draped with netting so that not one single bee could come in contact with our skin.
Unc primed a blow torch with some charcoal, moistened with a drop of methylated spirits, and gathered a bucket for what he called 'the scraps' and a new, unused kerosene tin that would house the honey.
Unc sprayed the hive to make the bees so drowsy they were incapable of attacking us invaders.
He lifted a square frame from the box and it was bulging with honeycomb and covered with a film of wax.
With a sharp spatula that he heated with the blow torch, he removed the thin film and placed that wax in the bucket, then tilted the frame to allow the honey to flow freely into the 'kero' tin.
Once drained the resultant honeycomb was broken into pieces and added to that in the bucket.

The procedure was repeated until all six frames were drained and returned to their position within the hive.
I enjoyed the large mouthful of genuine honeycomb which consisting of the wax that had now melded into a firm globule surrounded by succulent, virgin honey.

What a wonderful, natural treat.

After an evening of cards the honeycomb pieces would re-appear and they would be 'drowned' with thick, thick cream and slurped in ecstasy.

I recalled learning about the Ancient Egyptians revering honey and I thought I knew why.

I told Unc I would really like a bike of my own to keep at the farm. Unc pointed out that as I wasn't allowed out on the road to the Caves I would have nowhere to ride it.

I hadn't thought that far ahead and was still trying to convince him otherwise when I hit upon an idea.

I again broached the subject and told Unc I had solved the problem.

I could, I told him, ride a bike to the old 'Lav' way down the back yard!

I didn't get the bike but some months later an old friend of the family asked me if I still rode to the 'dunny' these days.

Obviously Unc had shared my solution!

In the afternoon Unc challenged me to a game of marbles, and he produced a calico flour bag of marbles he had when a boy.

There were 'Tom bowlers', 'Goobers', very old original stone spheres, variegated glass marbles in a multitude of colors and design.

We drew a circle and started off with ten mini globes.

This became a ritual each time I went to the farm until one day Unc challenged me believing I had 'fudged' and I was so angry that he would believe me capable of such dishonesty I threw his marbles on the cement verandah, breaking three in the process.

He calmly picked the remaining marbles up and placed them in the bag saying as he did so "It will be a long time before you get to see them again 'Youngin'".

And it was.

In fact he would leave them to me in his will.

I have wondered if this gesture was made to say sorry for accusing me incorrectly or to remind me of the need to curb my temper.

PERHAPS it was a little of both.

Aunty Doll purchased a doiley and some embroidery cottons with the sole purpose of teaching me how to fancy-work.

The shapes of pansies looked easy enough and I began the task full of confidence and concentrated on one petal.

I was happy to show Aunt my handiwork which she examined and expressed her opinion that the sewing was 'too tight'.

Without warning, she took the scissors and sliced through the stitches, then removed them completely. "Try again" she said.

I was NOT impressed but began all over again.

The process was repeated and again subjected to scrutiny.

This time my efforts were deemed respectable and Aunt suggested I may like to take my handiwork up to show Uncle Patsy.

I held out the doily for inspection as Unc put down the paper and looked over the top of his glasses.

"Hmmm. Very neat and natty Youngin" he said in his bush drawl. "Reminds me of a bull's arse drawn up with a drag-chain".

One of my evening duties was to bring in the cows.

If you have been up close to a cow you will know that they have beautiful eyes like brown velvet.

Those eyes are framed by long, full eyelashes and when they blink it is like watching a ballet in slow motion.

The cows soon got to know me and would come to meet me when I called their names.

We would walk through the paddocks together with me chattering to my companions as we went.

On occasions one of the beasts would come to me and rub a nose or neck against my small frame as though I was a scratching post. I would move away in order to remain standing and avoid the protruding horns.

I was permitted to name a new calf and I suggested we call her 'Moover" or 'Moo' for short.

Beverley Ann Farmer

"Moover" The Cow

Now that we had the phone connected at Duncan Street we no longer had to walk up to Nottle's to use theirs in emergencies.
Their district number was Wallerawang 9.
The Ryan's new number was Wallerawang 80.

Nottle's telephone consisted of a large box that was mounted on the wall.
On the side of the box lived a removable hearing piece hanging from a hook.
In the front of the box a funneled mouthpiece and metal dial with finger-holes that exposed numbers were attached.
On top of the box two mounted bells sat waiting to vibrate.
Ryan's new device was much more modern and consisted of a small bakelite handset that fitted nicely onto a cradle on a small box that lived on the tall occasional table next to the settee.
The telephone system worked from the 'Wang exchange and was run manually by a lady who operated the calls.

Every number had its own 'socket' on a large board.
We would lift the mouthpiece and turn the handle and wait.

The operator would answer and we would indicate the number we desired.
The operator would take our connection plug (much like a computer's speaker connection) and plug it into that of the desired number.
She would turn the bell handle and the call would be heard at the source of the receiver.
When they answered the operator would tell us to 'go ahead'.

190

The system worked well with the only impediment being the actual lack of privacy and it was an indisputable fact that the exchange operator was the best informed person in the district!

As I loved to draw, the tiny sandstone church on the hill named St Cuthberts, was a favored subject.
St John's in Wallerawang, where my Granny Nolan had been Christened in the 1880's, was another favourite.

This church was close to my Primary School and could be sketched from every angle.
When the weather was really lousy I drew still life composition, especially Mum's pink fruit dish that rested on a pedestal of the same glass.
I would pile it high with fruit, or sometimes flowers, and happily wile away the hours.
Although I've owned the dish for numerous years now I have never drawn it in adulthood.

Every Christmas I would be sent on a Christmas message for Granny Nolan to an old sandstone house near the church on the hill that I saw every day of my young life.
The house belonged to Mrs Lamb who lived there with her single son Roy.
This was never viewed as a chore but rather a highlight of my year.
It was akin to a child today visiting Disneyland.
Every child should be able to visit a house like Mrs Lamb's.
It was a truly magical place.

Immediately you entered the closed-in back verandah bathed in bright summer sunlight your eyes feasted on the hundreds of little miracles before you.

Just like her daughter Mrs Fitzpatrick from Lithgow, Mrs Lamb was a small, plump, snowy headed lady with a gentle voice and lovely hands.

With these hands and her remarkable talents she created untold works of art.
The house was simply chock-a-block full of treasures on every surface.

There were the pieces of furniture, flowers, ornaments, toys, pictures, paintings.

There were bright curtains throughout the house with gay cushions, tablecloths, hand painted vases and breadboards, tins, whistles, yo yos, tiny pretty brooches, highly painted whirligigs, kaleidoscopes made from scraps of old glass and mirrors that somehow produced myriads of patterns in different colors when turned, fairies, farmers, angels, golliwogs, Snow White and her dwarves, Red Riding Hood, bears of every shape and size accessorized with reading glasses, hats, aprons, wee shoes in different hues sitting on tiny tables and chairs set with delicate miniature tea sets and painted miniatures of faux foods-bowls of porridge, eggs, bacon, fruits of all kinds, vegetables, cakes and pies.

In the front bedroom lived a cedar chest of drawers that housed Mrs Lamb's doll collection.
Old porcelain dolls, celluloid dolls, boudoire dolls, rag dolls, dolls from France, from Germany, from Russia and my favorite dolls made from wax, which so resembled a delicate, sleeping child.

Each doll was exquisitely dress in ancient finery of silk, satin and lace so fragile you daren't not touch them.
One visit Mrs Lamb gave me a tiny square pin dish on which she had attached a spray of little pink roses and leaves she had fashioned from bread dough.
I thought it the most beautiful treasure I had ever owned.

PERHAPS over time the spray of bread flowers will deteriorate but the much loved dish, with its delicate scalloped edge, will withstand the test of time.
It is my belief that every child should have a visit to a house like Mrs Lamb's.

Joe Shirl Fay Peter Mrs Lamb's Hill

Sunday afternoons when the weather was lousy we would sometimes gather at Corney's Hall and play indoor Shuttlecock.

On other Sundays we would go to the hall and push back all of the seats left in situ from the Pictures and with giant brooms we would sweep the floor with sawdust and kerosene.

Having no car ourselves it was rarely we saw our extended family, especially those in Blackheath.

Dad's sister, Aunty Win, not only owned and ran the kiosk at the pool in Blackheath- the only one outside of Sydney in those days-but she owned a shop in the main street.

It appeared Uncle Burwood and Aunty Win Rolfe were in the habit of sharing all of the household goods with the staff at the pool and they had numerous arguments about who was the worst offender and where the items should live permanently.

If something couldn't be found it was because the other party had taken it to the pool.

Once when their dog was small and was prone to stealing clothes that had been hung around to 'air off' the dog jumped up and took a pair of Aunty's panties and ran---all the way to the pool kiosk!

193

Uncle Burwood told everyone this story to make his point insisting even the dog was taught the ritual.

They were a really lovely couple who had two kids much older than we were, namely Ray and Gwen.

Uncle Burwood had a wooden leg and a huge car that seated nine people.

He transported tourists from the train at Hartley to the Jenolan Caves and back and could have been seen as a pioneer in the tourist industry.

Uncle Burwood in his nine seater (Dad centre front)

A tall, elegant lady Aunty Win had a wonderful dress sense.

After Uncle Burwood died she would retire to a unit near to her beloved Randwick Race Course in Sydney which she would frequent until she died aged in her nineties.

PERHAPS Aunty Win will share with me her Diabetes when I grow up.

Dad was always busy around Tax return time completing forms for several of the local miners who couldn't read or write.

The men would come and sit at our dining room table and Dad would write on the forms with great flourish, shake hands and off the men would go.

One regular was a local policeman who would take his farewell while bowing and scraping promising to buy Dad a bottle of Whiskey when the Tax return came back.

He never did.

Years later at my Dad's funeral said policeman stood stiffly to attention as the cortege passed by. "I think he has a smile on his face" commented the driver. "Probably has" said Mum. "He just saved himself a bottle of Whiskey."

At school whenever a teacher was away Joan Wilson and I would be sent to supervise the kids in that teacher's class.
We both loved this task and would take it in turns to read stories and the like.
It figured that the staff thought we could miss formal lessons without suffering the effects too much.

About this time I noticed there were two sexes and to catch the eye of one young boy, I thought I would impress him by jumping over the tennis net during a game when we swapped ends.
I hit the ball that finished the game and casually ran and jumped the net somewhat unsuccessfully.
Down I went and, clutching my shoulder, I wailed loud and long for someone to get a teacher.
Fortunately one of the teachers owned a car and I was bundled off to Lithgow to have my broken collarbone attended to.

I had successfully jumped the net dozens of times before, but such was not the case on my 'show off' day.

Pat Adams brought down a pink knitted frock her mother had made for me to wear over the sling.

Many years later while dancing with the same young man I had hoped to impress, I confessed how mortified I had been to have fallen in front of him. He laughed and told me how funny he thought it was at the time to see me bawling, dribbling like a baby with my dress above my head, and wearing panties with purple flowers on them.
I did not accept his offer of another dance!

I spent countless hours at Nottle's and I really loved the entire family and their beautiful old house.

Originally I called the lady of the house 'Gag' as I couldn't say 'Glad'. As I grew up a bit I began to call her Mrs Nottle as the rest of my family did and it was she who suggested I, alone, call her 'Aunty Glad'.

So 'Aunty Glad' it was.

Uncle Ben' worked at a local mine.

Aunty Glad

I would later learn from a census document that he had been an engine driver and that was how he had come to the district.

He was a very large man who could 'turn his hand to anything'.

There were four kids who were much older than we were.

The youngest, Linda, was a very young child when Mum and Dad married and shifted into the front rooms of Braeside.

The eldest was Edna who was a couple of years older than 'Digger '(real name Andrew George) who was a couple of years older than Ruth.

Then came Linda.

I remember Edna's wedding to Jim Slater.

The neighbours saved their clothes coupons and gave them to Edna so she could buy enough material for her wedding dress.

I was most truly miffed that I wasn't invited to the wedding but Mum took me up to the house to see the bride dressed in her finery before she left for the church.

I was about five at the time.

What annoyed me most was that the daughter of the groom's boss was invited and I figured I had priority over her because I loved Edna more.

I spent the remainder of the afternoon swinging on Granny Nolan's gate as I watched the invited guests arrive next-door to join the Wedding feast held in the front room of Braeside.

Then it was Ruth's turn to marry Bob Legge in the same church with the reception at the same venue.

'Digger' had married a Sydney-sider named Verna but after he went away to war as a member of the Air Force the marriage faltered.

He would later marry Fay's friend, Pat Adams, and Fay would be the bridesmaid.

All of the Nottle girls had undertaken a dressmaker's course at the Lithgow Tech and they were exceptional sewers.

There was always a kettle simmering away on the fuel stove which burned both summer and winter.

This stove was unusual in that the fire box was very wide. I would never again see one like it.

Above the stove hung a genuine' cat and nine tails' made from leather.

A strip of leather a foot in width had been cut to form numerous narrow strips about eight inches in length.

The leather was then rolled up tightly so the uncut end formed a handle.

On the loose end of the thin strips small, sharp chunks of metal were attached.

These whips were widely used as a method of punishment of the convicts and I have often pondered how such a revolting device came to live in a lovely old country house with a kind, caring country family.

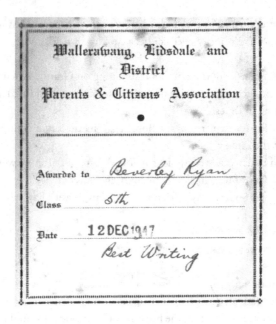

Wallerawang, Lidsdale and
District
Parents & Citizens' Association

•

Awarded to *Beverley Ryan*

Class *5th*

Date **1 2 DEC 1947**
Best Writing

As I got older I was trusted with more difficult tasks.

I knew I had arrived when I was able to clean the Coolgardie safe.

This important piece of equipment was the forerunner of the ice- chest and ultimately the fridge.

The safe was constructed with an oblong wooden frame like a cupboard.

The hinged door that opened wide had as its handle a half wooden cotton reel and inside it housed two spacious shelves.

The entire structure was covered with Hessian.

On the top of the frame was a tin tray with upturned sides to the height of about three inches just like the sand trays we had at school.

The bottom of the frame was supported on four stout legs that sat in a slightly bigger tray which contained a plug and plughole.

The entire device was supported on a heavy wooden frame like a mini tankstand.

Cold water was poured into the top tray.

Woollen socks that had been cut into three inch strips were draped into the water in this tray and then folded over the edge onto the upper Hessian walls.

The water in the upper tray was soaked up by the woollen strips and as the volume of water increased the water began to drip and spread down the Hessian creating a cool interior for keeping the perishables fresh.

The water would soak down to the bottom where it was collected in the lower, bigger tray.

When nearing the capacity of the lower tray the plug was removed and the water allowed to cascade into the bucket.

The bucket full of water was recycled by emptying it into the upper tray again and the process repeated after any slime in the bottom had been removed.

Other duties included sweeping the verandahs--all four of them that encircled the local sandstone structure.

Each one had a specific function.

The back verandah housed the big wood box that fed the hungry stove

On the left end the laundry could be found and on the other the 'verandah room' which housed an eclectic range of items including the old tennis racquets, large raincoats, umbrellas and the like.

The front verandah sheltered the big front room with its French windows and huge front door.

The side verandah, that was always covered with leaves from the surrounding trees sheltered the side door and sewing room where, too, the ironing was done.

As I swept I tried to envisage my great-grandmother, Sarah White/ Nolan sweeping the same area and I would daydream how she would be dressed and what her next duty would be.

The middle verandah joined the higher 'front rooms' of the house with the 'downstairs' rooms of sewing room, Aunty Glad's and Uncle Ben's bedroom and the true centre of the home, the kitchen.

I was allowed dust the furniture in the front rooms, a treat for a kid who wasn't allowed do any helping at home.

My reward was to be able to play the beautiful old Beale piano found in the huge front room.
A strict routine was adhered to on these occasions.
I would first have to wash my hands and dry them then hold them up for inspection by an adult.
If I passed muster I would be able to remove the piece of pale blue flannelette that kept the keys free of dust and I would then be able to play to my heart's content dreaming of the day I would commence to play and the sounds made would resemble a concert pianist like those I had seen in the movies.

I forever felt there was a 'barrier' at the piano that kept me from displaying my true musical genius as I was sure that at some time in the past, even before I was born, that I had been a competent pianist.
Dad described a 'piano playing machine' that had been invented in the nineteen twenties and no matter how hard I tried I couldn't comprehend how it would work.

Finally I gathered it would work like a vacuum cleaner.
You would turn it on and touch it and you could go away and play beautifully.

As I haven't heard of it since I don't think it was all that successful.
I did, however, love to play the pianola at Corney's Hall.
By sliding the panels behind the music stand you would find a machine in which you placed a piano roll wound around a bakelite reel.
The rolls were one foot in width and sported a thin cord loop that attached to the machine.
This waxed paper roll was perforated with hundreds of tiny squares that corresponded with tiny pins like those found on a music box.
As you pumped the foot pedals the rolls produced a melody as the appropriate keys also 'played'.

PERHAPS I will buy myself a piano one day just in case that lost ability is suddenly restored.

In Braeside's enormous back yard lived giant ivy which had a partly concealed opening that hid a leafless 'room' within.

This space was the castle, the cubby, the witches' mansion, the draw bridge, a car or boat depending on the game we played.

It was within this space I would experience my very first kiss.

There also lived there a giant oak tree with its leaves of bright green and its numerous acorns that seasonally fell covering the dimensions of the tree canopy.

I wondered if this ancient relic of the past had been planted by my ancestor, Sarah White.

The huge sheds down the bottom of the yard housed a very old stationary car and the most wonderful model steam train village you have ever seen.

'Digger' and his Dad had built their model railway to include tiny people and streams and trees and hills and valleys and houses and fences and roads.

The many miniature engines belched smoke as they steamed along the tracks avoiding each other as they crossed over and under the little bridges on their way to the tiny signals and railway stations where they would sound their shrill little whistles.

It was incongruous to imagine these two huge men creating these tiny treasures.

Part of the shed housed the cow bails that were so sturdily built they are probably there still.

Behind the sheds was the orchard full of lovely old, but productive trees that would give untold pleasure to many of us throughout the years.

Pretty soon the Nottle's became grandparents and their eldest grandson, James, would go through school with my brother, David.

James would have a Downs Syndrome brother, Keith, who would be my very first encounter with a person with any disability.

Ruth had two girls, Margaret and Christine and years later Eric would join the family.

It was the family ritual to visit Braeside every Sunday afternoon and I loved to play with the youngsters.

Margaret Legge Bruce and Bev at Braeside

*Ruth dressed her girls in pleated tartan skirts and red
jumpers and they always looked so cute. Perhaps I will dress
daughters of my own in similar outfits in the future.*

Fay thought she wanted to go nursing and as only Intermediate was needed
she applied for a position at Katoomba and was accepted.
Her nursing career lasted for three weeks of the four trial weeks and she left
suddenly and returned home.
Matron, who was a friend of Aunty Doll, had commented that Fay 'would
not take orders' and she was 'a danger to the patients'.

I could certainly believe the bit about not taking orders.

Fay's first real job was working for a couple, Beryl and Joe, who owned a fruit
shop in Mort Street in Lithgow and Fay was employed to help Beryl with the
kids and do some housework.
She was not at all happy in this post.
After a few months she gained a job in a box making factory and later changed
to another factory that made neat little boxes for fountain pens and jewellery.
It was here she met Merleen Hasler who would introduce her to her brother,
Mervyn.
The rest is history.

(Fay had previously become engaged for a very brief time to Mal Souter, despite Mum and Dad's strong objections.

He was considered too old for her AND he was divorced!!!

When Fay was sixteen Mal came down to collect her to take her for a weekend in Woollongong.

Dad nearly had a seizure and flatly refused permission for her to go.

Mal threatened Dad and Dad retaliated.

The visits of Mal ended with fisticuffs in our tiny kitchen.

We never saw Mal again).

Shirl and I hugged each other in the back bedroom as the shouting was heard (In later years Fay told me Mal's mother had promised to buy her a house if she would marry Mal after her other son had committed suicide in Lithgow).

Fay bought a dress pattern and made herself a frock that really suited her. She duplicated that pattern so often she could cut it out without using the actual pattern varying the neckline but always keeping the same skirt with its two un-pressed pleats at the front.

Shirl had a position in Mr Porges' Chemist shop arranged for her by Mr John Bracey.

I wondered how she could bear to work with Mrs Porges who had the reputation of being the epitome of a snob.

Because David had been found to have very limited vision it took Mum some time to accept that her one and only son was not just quiet and pliable and perfect.

He had to have glasses, the lens of which resembled the base of a lemonade bottle.

They did nothing to improve his looks and he was exceedingly shy as the result.

I figured if I did regular eye exercise I wouldn't have to ever wear glasses.

Every single day I rolled my eyes this way and that whenever I remembered.

PERHAPS I will be wrong again.

Mum and Dad were much more supportive of Shirl's choice of fiancé, namely Ken Eckersley, a Victorian, whom she had met in Lithgow at a dance.

203

Ken worked in the shale/oil industry in Glen Davis and he had been estranged from his Victorian family for many years.

Ken was very generous with his gift giving and he bought Shirl beautiful silverware and perfume.

One perfume I particularly recall was a much desired bottle of Chanel Number 5, complete with delicate stopper.

A beautiful engagement ring of an oblong sapphire set across the finger, was chosen by the happy couple after a fairly lengthy courtship.

Everyone was delighted with the union with the exception of yours truly.

I had reason to dislike Ken who would bring a big bag of lollies and make such a display of presenting them to Mum and Dad, then put them up on the top of the dresser so it couldn't be reached.

I just didn't feel he was the genuine article and I couldn't imagine life without my special big sister when she moved so far away to Victoria.

Following their long engagement Shirl begged Ken to contact his estranged family and finally he did.

He returned home to the property near Ballarat and was welcomed back into the fold.

Shirl visited at Christmastime.

Her departure was of such significance it was noted in the local paper as very few flights interstate were then undertaken.

She returned home sad and dejected, pining for her fiancé as she began plans for her Easter wedding.

There was much interest in any dances that were held locally though they were intermittent.

A meeting of interested parties was called and the subject of a weekly dance was suggested.

Thus the Lidsdale/ Wallerawang Social Club was born.

Shirl was delegated the treasurer of the club and she collected the two shillings (twenty cents) entry fee each week.

It was decided to hold a concert that would showcase the local talent in 1950.

Not one, but three Ryan girls would feature on the program, each singing her song of choice.

Mum became involved also and she organized and made much of the sumptuous supper.

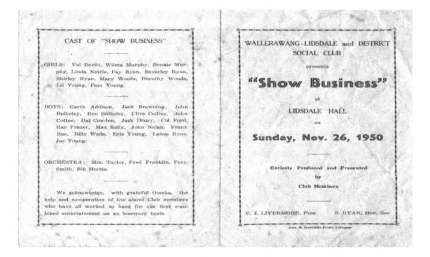

One year it was decided to hold a mock wedding and a hilarious evening resulted.

The biggest men in the district Norm Eaton and 'Digger' Nottle, were flower girls and the smallest adult, i.e. Shirl, was the father of the bride.

Fay, who was the Parson, read from the currently banned book called "Love Me Sailor" dressed in one of Dad's suits and back-the-front collar.

Our neighbor, Roy Hubbard, was the bride and Mrs Eaton was the groom.

Jacky Browning looked his cutest in his bridesmaid's bonnet.

Several of the boys dressed up in ballet dresses to dance their version of "Swan Lake."

A proper wedding breakfast followed with cake made and donated by Mr Orchard and magnificent country cooking.

It was an evening spoken about for years.

The costuming was arranged by Shirl who budgeted the two-shilling entrance costs to cover the cost of the bill from 'Buttons and Bows' hiring company in Sydney.

Mrs Eaton, Roy, Jack Browning, Norm Eaton, ?, Fay, Digger Nottle

Mrs Eaton, Roy, Fay

At school it was announced that we would audition for a part in a musical. We were all so excited at the prospect and I lined up with the other kids the casting took place.

I was shocked to learn I had a 'too deep a voice' and I could only be considered for a boy's role.

I had always had a leading role in each and every school production. I didn't feel too confident competing with the boys for a boy's role but did manage to land a role.

I practiced the main girl's role in case my voice changed overnight, but it never did.

I still find myself humming that tune and singing the words "A little girl's heart is breaking and all for the love of you" etc. and then the chorus of "Shine little moonbeam, shine soft and bright" and so on.

My cousin Marie won a role and she was able to attend school every day to attend practice up to the actual presentation night.

On the day the Operetta was performed I had my first filling of gold on my front tooth.

I really felt like Dad's daughter now with a miniature lump of gold in my mouth as well.

Wallerawang school held an annual sports day and I was very competitive, especially in the races that were age related.

Just after this momentous occasion we began serious practice for the big combined district sports day to be held in Lithgow.

In 1949 we had a crack tunnel ball team using both a medicine ball and a basketball.

There were four different games we played and all four were entered in the competition.

We were delighted to win the blue ribbon and be declared the champions.

In the age championship I came second.

It was an auspicious occasion as for the first time the Joint Coal Board, who sponsored the day, made available colored ribbons to present to the winners and place getters.

The ribbons were and are cherished possessions.

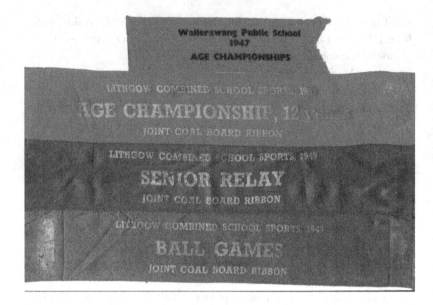

Sewing classes were compulsory and we were directed to purchase some material to make a garment we could wear.

The teacher was to be the wife of the headmaster.
Her name was Corrie McGrath who had a severe limp- the result from an earlier bout of infantile paralysis.

As I felt I had enough clothes I requested some pale green flannelette to make a roomy nightdress that would wrap around my feet when the winter came. It would have a draw string neck.
I had no idea how long the garment would take to make by hand, but I struggled on in the knowledge that the nightie would not be needed for several months.

Mum allowed me to pick the beautiful mauve sweet peas that grew annually around the side of the house. I would take them to Mrs McGrath.

Occasionally I would add a deep red 'Black-boy' rose that smelled like a rose should.

On May 24th each year we celebrated Empire Day when homage was paid to King, Country and the British Empire.

The main activity of the day was the lighting of a bonfire in the evening.

For months before the big day dead logs and sapling trees were collected by the local kids who chopped and carried the timber to the top of the hill above Granny's cow bail so that on the appointed night the residents of nearby Wallerawang could clearly see our handwork.

The results of our labors would form a huge structure and with it our anticipation would also grow.

Each of us would scrounge a few potatoes from our homes in preparation for a feast.

"Gran. One of your chooks appears to be sick. It's coughing and spluttering and sounds awful. I sure hope the other chooks don't get sick too."

"Oh, dear. And Grandfather not at home either. Now I wonder what I should do."

"I know Gran. What about I chop its head off and take it up the hill and bury it for you?"

"Now that's a good girl" Granny would say as she patted you on the head. "You'd best hurry".

And indeed I would as I chopped off the chook's head thereby extracting the bent pin threaded onto a piece of softened wheat that had been the cause of the bird's demise.

Then I would trudge up the hill to meet my cohorts.

"Here she is. Here's Bev with the chook. It will be my turn next year. Do you think Granny suspected anything?'

"No. She hasn't any idea".

Having chopped the head off the chook and before being cleaned out of entrails the chook needed to be dunked in boiling water and plucked free of feathers.

The carcass was then threaded onto a substantial green stick that would be slowly turned to cook the bird over the coals that were created at the outer edge of the fire.

Perhaps our Granny was much more aware of our deception than we thought.

I found it unusual that Dad, and a handful of locals, always met the following Sunday after Empire Day and congregated in the makeshift cubby up the hill. They would throw around pennies on sticks like children and shout strange jargon. We were never allowed at these rituals.

One afternoon our school bus broke down and we had to walk home.
We Ryan's were pretty lucky in that we didn't have that far to go.
As we passed over the rickety old bridge that crossed Cox's River some of the boys climbed onto the railings to simulate riding a horse.
One boy in particular was one of the group who tormented my little brother and I felt some justice should be metered out.
I ran to where he perched and with all of my might I pushed him off the bridge to the banks below.
I didn't wait around but headed as quickly as I could towards home.
I was found to be most co-operative for the remainder of the evening and brought in the kindling for the fire and set the table for tea as soon as I was asked.
All went well until about seven o'clock and a knock on the door was heard.
Dad answered and spoke in a low tone before bellowing"Beverley. Come here."

Now for my Dad to use my full name I knew I was in BIG trouble. "Mr J tells me you pushed his boy off the bridge and broke his arm. What have you got to say young lady"? Dad asked sternly.

"I wish it had been his neck" I told him honestly.
Dad took me to the bathroom after our visitor left and took down his razor strop that hung behind the bathroom door. He told me I had no right to administer justice and how disappointed he was in me. He gave me one light whack and, despite his cross words, I sensed he was actually a little bit proud of my gumption.
The matter was never mentioned again.

I had been riding Dad's bike one afternoon when Mum called me in for tea.
I washed my hands in the bathroom and noticed some blood on my leg.
I called out to Mum that I had bumped myself on the bar of Dad's bike and I had blood on my clothes.
There was much consternation in the ranks and Mum rushed around and brought in a change of clothes and in whispered tones told me to take a piece of elastic, two safety pins and a piece of folded sheeting explaining that I was to put this strange assortment of articles 'on' as I was 'now a woman'.
Relying on my memory I recalled a conversation years before when I enquired about my navel and Mum's explanation that I would find out the reason why we had one 'when I became a woman'.

Thus I placed the sheeting over my navel and pinned it to the folded elastic. The following morning my pale green nightdress bore the results of my ignorance. My much older sisters told me nothing though Shirl was heard to say "Poor little kid".
Much later in life I would learn that it was Dad who took the time to explain the facts of life to Shirl at a very young age.
She did not, however, share this knowledge with her little sister.

My curiosity got the best of me and I asked Aunty Vi what was going on and I couldn't believe what she told me, even though she only told me the bare details.

She informed me this monthly occurrence would continue well into 'old age' and I couldn't believe it may still be happening when I was twenty- five or so! When I started to cry she asked Mum to let me go down to Wolgan with her and Fred for a few days.

Fred grew the best and biggest onions I had ever tasted and we would make sandwiches from fresh bread and butter and cover the bread with one thick slice of odorless onion sprinkled with salt and pepper and vinegar.
Aunty Vi had a lovely singing voice and she would happily sing while pegging out the washing or washing the dishes.
We didn't have a lot to do with Aunty Vi, I think because she was divorced.

Her marriage to Terry Lane had ended years before and though she and Fred Hollis had several kids I do not know if they were ever married.

Aunty Vi's first son died at birth and her second son, Dennis, was reared by his Lane grandparents after Aunty Vi left Kevin, following a belting.

Aunty Vi and Fred later shifted further up Wolgan Rd to live in Connely's house in Lidsdale.

A bad accident occurred at the corner where the Lithgow road forked into the Mudgee road where Mrs. Wright from Wolgan Road and her two sons, Kevin and Alan, waited for the bus from Portland.
The weather was foul and the roads icy and slippery.
As the bus approached Mrs Wright took the hand of the younger boy and in an instant Alan, the older lad, slipped into the path of the oncoming bus.

His injuries were extensive and miraculously he eventually recovered with nothing more than very badly scarred legs.

I can still remember Mrs Wright's screams and Mum running faster than an Olympic champion to lend her help.

Toward the end of the year we prepared for our final Primary School exams. We would sit for exams in History, Geography, Mathematics, English, Spelling, Composition, Reading and Writing.

Our Headmaster and teacher was Mr Appleby who managed a large class of forty-one students with strict discipline.

Prior to each subject exam he would read out the rules

"No talking until your papers have been collected or you will forfeit twenty marks". We were very familiar with the procedure by the time the final exam arrived.

On this occasion it was Geography.

We were seated so that a bright student was next to a less bright student.

The student next to me was a red-headed oaf by the name of Bruce.

He was not one of my favorite people before the exam and was even less so after.

We completed the exam and Mr Appleby came around and collected our papers.

With a huge sigh of relief I turned to the girl behind and said I thought I had done OK and I thought I would hold my first place and be Dux of the school.

"Dad will be so pleased" I enthused.

"Mr Appleby. Beverley Ryan and Joan Wilson are talking and all the papers haven't been collected" said Bruce.

"Mr Appleby said we couldn't talk until OUR papers were collected and OURS have been STUPID" I blurted out.

"I believe I said ALL papers" said Mr Appleby.

"No Sir" chorused Joan, Beverley and several other students.

Mr Appleby exerted his power.

"Beverley Ryan and Joan Wilson you are penalized twenty marks"

"That's not fair sir. Joan wasn't talking at all and Bruce is lying and you said.............."

Walberunang Public School

Report Form.

Beverley Ryan.   Class 6 th.
No. in Class : 41   Position in Class : 3

Subject	Marks	Remarks.
Reading	93	
Composition	75	
English	99	
Writing	86	
Spelling	95	
Arithmetic	78	
History	100	
Geography	68	Penalised 20 marks.
	694.	

Good work. Beverley

K. Appleby

Teacher :   Headmaster

"One more word and it will be doubled" roared the Headmaster.
I shut up all the time seething with rage at the injustice I was experiencing.
And thus I was robbed of the honor of being Dux of my school.
David Pinkerton and Michael Pevitt beat me by eleven and three marks
respectively and innocent Joan slipped from second to fourth.

Many years later the same red-haired 'oaf' had the gall to invite me to dance
with him at a dance in Lithgow.

It was one of the very few times in my youth I was found wanting for something to say- momentarily that is- and I will not repeat it here, but, suffice to say, even this 'oaf' fully comprehended the contents of the ensuing conversation and meaning thus conveyed!

Perhaps I will still be angered by a child's lack of power long into old age.

Dad in mining gear

I begged Mum to buy me a pair of white, ankle strap, wedge heeled shoes I had seen advertised in the Christmas edition of the David Jones catalogue.
They were so grown up and smart.
I don't think I had ever wanted anything so much as those shoes.
For Christmas I not only got the longed for shoes, but received a beautiful gold locket in the shape of a heart.
Around it was another thin heart consisting of tiny gold flowers and leaves.
It was the daintiest of pieces and I absolutely adored it.
As well as wearing the locket to Church I was allowed to wear it to Barbara Wilson's birthday party the following February- and that was the last day I ever saw it.

For years, whenever I visited Wilson's yard, I would search for my much loved treasure without success.

Aunty Doll suggested a trip to Orange to visit Aunty Mary, the baby sister of Granny Ryan who was the Godmother to both of us.
Aunty Mary and Uncle Pat Kirwin had their family close by and we saw lots of Vera and Molly and their children.

I had reason to remember this holiday for two reasons.

The first was Aunty Mary asked me to think of a special gift I would like to receive from her and I requested she let me have my hair cut at a hairdresser's.
I had been begging Mum for permission to have my hair cut for ages and she flatly refused.
Aunty Doll was aware of Mum's resistance and warned Aunty Mary that she didn't think it a good idea.
Both Aunties tried to tempt me with other suggestions of a bracelet or new dress but I remained stubborn.
In the end Aunty Mary reluctantly gave permission and Molly took me to have my plaits removed.
I seemed to be the only one happy with the result.
When I was taken home Mum, as expected, exploded and started in on Aunty Doll but was quickly subdued when she heard it was a gift from Aunty Mary.
As Aunty Mary was a special favorite of both my parents she was immediately forgiven.

The second major event was when Aunty Mary's grandson Ron, who was my age, started teasing me about my 'jiggling' bosom!
I was so self-conscious I refused to play outside until Aunty Mary 'twigged' and took me to town and bought me my first bra!

Beverley 1ˢᵗ row 3ʳᵈ from right.

Although we enjoyed tremendous freedom there were some places that were out of bounds. Such a place was Rocky Water Hole on the Cox's river.

One, Sunday afternoon, during a rare school holiday when I wasn't out at Curran's, Barbara Wilson and I rode our bikes the back way to the forbidden spot.

Several kids were swimming and cavorting in the cool, clear water and swinging on a thick rope that had been anchored to an overhanging tree.

We cooled our feet and engaged in a splashing game with some of the kids.

Barbara was anxious that we head for home and not overstay our curfew, so we reluctantly said our farewells and headed for home.

Later that evening when preparing for tea, Mum turned on the radio to hear the funeral notices for the weekend and the name of one of the boys we had been splashing with was pronounced as being dead.

I couldn't, and wouldn't, believe what I heard and I couldn't stop crying.

Mum scolded me for "over-reacting" about Adrian and I wasn't able to tell her I was actually in shock because we had been with him less than an hour before he swung out on the rope and dived into the pool-and broke his neck-at that forbidden venue.

Adrian.

I still clearly remember what a nice person you were and all of these years later it will still make me very sad that you did not have the opportunity to grow up like the rest of us kids who had so much fun on that Sunday afternoon. PERHAPS I will never be able to return to that venue ever again.

It was time to commence High School and I was enrolled at Lithgow High School.
I was surprised I didn't have to go to St Patrick's but as it wasn't discussed I kept quiet.

As a special gift for me Aunt and Uncle had a leather satchel made from a piece of leather Unc had put aside.

My New Friend Robyn   *First year at HIGH SCHOOL*

It is still usable after all this time.
On the very first day of school we were directed to classes from A to D according to the courses we had chosen.
The students who studied two languages, namely French and Latin, were in the A class, students with one language, French, in B class, Commercial stream in C and Domestic stream in D class.
I was in 1B and as we entered the rooms allocated the teacher told us to sit anywhere until she 'sorted us out'.
I sat next to a girl named Robyn Mitchell and after I introduced myself and had a little chat I thought to myself 'what a nice person this is' and all of these years later I have not had reason to change my mind.

To this day we remain friends having shared our lives and ups and downs as our life's journeys have progressed.

One of the unexpected joys of travelling by bus to High School was that I frequently met Ilma White and her daughter, Lee who was the same age as David.
Ilma would place Lee on her knee so I could share the seat.
She would gently quizz me about the family and tell me about her family, especially Coral.
Coral was Ilma's youngest sister who had been born with a heart condition that left her weak and sickly.
Ilma reminded me that Mum had been present at Coral's birth in Hill's old house.
I was never game to enquire why Mum and Ilma abandoned their lifelong friendship.

Whenever we were bored in class we would cast our eyes up the mountain behind the school to where the Zigzag railway could be seen.
We were unaware just how amazing this engineering feat was until much later when we grew up.
Due to its significance in the town our School magazine had been named the 'Zigzag'.
A sketch of the sight that adorned the cover of that publication had been drawn by a visiting art teacher named E.J. McKenzie.

A relic from Mr McKenzie's Art Class

Mr McKenzie invited me to join a small group of students for an art class he held on Saturday afternoon.

I wasn't sure how I'd go with Mr McKenzie's classical approach that did not allow for personal divergence or artistic license, but I was prepared to have a go.

Mr McKenzie taught us that Art wasn't just what you could see but was also what you felt.

I would forever judge art pieces by applying his teachings.

One of his favorite exercises was to have us verbally describe a scene we had enjoyed.

With a piece of charcoal he would sketch our 'description' with uncanny accuracy.

He taught us to do the same.

The purpose of this exercise was to train us to observe and commit to memory details sufficient to complete an entire picture.

Shirl displayed great excitement when it was announced that the Opera, 'Tosca' would be coming to Lithgow.

We purchased tickets, which included one for me.

On the appointed evening we made our way down to the corner of the Mudgee Rd, 'Wang and Lithgow turnoff and waited for the bus.

After a reasonable time Mum began to get anxious.

There was no sign of a bus.

Finally we walked home as we knew even if the bus came we would be too late for the show.

With no way of finding out why the bus hadn't come at the appointed time we had to be content to wait until our old school bus driver told Mum that the bus that particular evening had gone 'a few minutes earlier' because more people would be expected to catch it!.

Vera was NOT impressed.

Nor was I as it would be many more years before I would get to see my first Opera.

After much begging Shirl allowed me to ride her bike to High School and I pedalled my way towards Lithgow with great enthusiasm, coasting down Tunnel Hill with the wind in my hair and not a care in the world.

On the return trip a heavy afternoon downpour saw me drenched before I reached Dunn's corner and the trip home became the most exhausting escapade I had ever undertaken.

Mum was really worried that I was so late home and suggested I not undertake that mode of transport again.

She described my appearance as resembling a 'drown rat'.

It was quite some time before I repeated this exercise again.

I negotiated with Mum and Dad after they voiced their objection to my being in Lithgow all day on Saturday and they gave me the choice between dancing lessons in the morning or art lessons in the afternoon.

I chose the art lessons and attended enthusiastically until the choice had to be made between art and sport on Saturdays afternoon.

There was no contest. I chose sport.

Our English teacher planned to have us enter the Annual Drama contest and a boy named Robbie Burns and I were chosen for the lead roles in "The Swineherd".

Mum made me a long white tulle gown suitable for a Princess to wear and I borrowed a beautiful, long, purple satin train edged with white swans-down to complete the ensemble.

Dad made me a coronet from twisted gold wire that I thought bettered the diamond ones worn by Princess Margaret, the Queen's sister.

After our particular item had finished, we hurriedly undressed and packed up our costumes and stored them in a designated spot before leaving the dressing rooms.

We then hastened to resume our seats before the next item commenced.

After the concert had finished we filed through the rear of the stage and collected our belongings. My problem was that Nottle's beautiful purple train had been collected by someone else on their way out and despite an offer of a reward it was never seen again.

How any parent couldn't be aware of an eight foot lump of purple satin arriving in their home, and not returning, it is beyond me.

I can still feel the emotions of that time.

I felt I had let down the Nottle's who had entrusted the train to my keeping and though they were understanding and forgave me, I could not forgive myself.

Mr Nichols, the Music teacher, came around all of the classes and asked us to sing.

He then invited some students to join his School Choir.

When he chose me I showed surprise explaining to him that my Primary teacher had overlooked me for a girl's role in a musical because my voice was too deep.

He assured me he was very short of Contralto voices and he would have lots of special jobs for my voice.

He commented on my breathing and insisted I'd had singing lessons and I again had reason to thank my biggest sister for sharing her talents.

A very enjoyable relationship was forged as Mr Nichols found many duets and solos suitable for my contralto voice that took me to competitions to Sydney, Mudgee and Bathurst for State competitions.

A fellow soloist, Delores Ryles, went on to become a member of the Australian Opera Company.

Lithgow High School Choir
Beverley 3rd from left top row. Robyn top far right
Delores middle row 2nd from right

I also tried out for the Basketball team hoping to gain a place in the 'C' or even the 'B' sides.
I was elated to be named in the 'A' side alongside the big fifth year students and I remained in the side until I left school..

BASKETBALL "A"

Back Row: Shirley Lloyd, Beverley Ryan, Joan Rogers, Val Lenehan.
Front Row: Doreen Rodham, Mrs D. Yates, Veronica King (Capt.), Beryl Jackson.

Beverley Back row 2ⁿᵈ from left.

I was a member in the 'A' Softball team and was Girls Tennis Champion in '52-53 and ran in the Athletics Team.

I was always on the sidelines during the Swimming sports carnivals and it would be my fiftieth year before I learned to swim.

AthleticTeam Bev 3rd row 5th from right

Shirl celebrated her 21st Birthday with a big party in Corney's hall. For the special occasion she had Mrs Beecroft make her a silver lace frock mounted on a blue slip.

She received some beautiful gifts of silverware and scarves, pretty face powder compacts, jewellery and things for her 'box' and my favorite a huge tin of chocolates the likes of which I had never seen.

Now as I have never been a chocolate lover how come I chose to eat every caramel chocolate I was offered and to this day I could go a year without thinking of chocolate-until I saw a hard caramel covered in milk chocolate.

To add to the conundrum I positively loathed the giver of the chocolates and you would think that would curtail my gluttony, but such was not the case.

I vividly recall that black round tin on which gladiolus 'Bloomed' and the three layers of delectable confectionary.

Fay was sporting a lovely marcasite watch that featured four rubies on each side of the face, a special Christmas gift from Mervyn.

My friendship with the Taylor Family grew stronger and for concerts or any night activities that took place in conjunction with school I was usually allowed stay at their house as no evening buses travelled to Lidsdale.

I loved all of the family which consisted of Dad Fred, Mum Jean, sister Robyn and my special friend Leslie.

It was Les who introduced me to classical music which he played so beautifully on the piano. He tried to teach me Mozart's Sonata in 'C' but to no avail.

I have learned it in later years as a mark of respect to him.

We could always talk about absolutely anything and he would save his pocket money and give it to me to buy the current girlfriend a birthday or Christmas gift.

Ours was a very special, platonic friendship, the likes of which I have never had with another human being.

I have oft tried to analyze the uniqueness of that relationship and have come to believe that its basis was of a spiritual nature.

How fortunate I was to have experienced it.

Bev 2nd Year Gigh School 1st row far right

During the winter months we participated in the Women's Co-op Basketball Competition on Saturday afternoons.

Alan Taylor, (my soon to become 'boyfriend,') and a group of his friends would be waiting at the bus-stop and they would walk with us to the Rec and watch the games, often shouting encouragement.

If I had an early game I could go to the Pictures afterwards and still be finished in time to catch the bus home.

The routine at the pictures never deviated.

The program would commence with the playing of the National Anthem.

Then the Cine sound Newsreel would inform us of National and World events. On reflection much of what we saw was pure propaganda.

Then followed the cartoons, which for reasons best left for a psychiatrist to fathom, I did not like.

I have found many cartoons to be full of violence whereas other people find the same actions humorous.

Then we would see the main film with an interval half way through to allow a restocking of Jaffas, drinks and the like.

One Saturday afternoon one of the nicer boys asked if he could sit with me.

I thought nothing of it until he began to act like an octopus and I had to move and sit right up the back of the theatre.

He would often try to engage me in conversation after that time but I managed to maintain an aloof silence.

I played in the High School basketball team against my much older sisters who played for St Patrick's in the district competition.

A team-mate of mine, Beryl Jackson, played against her famous sister, Marj Jackson, the Olympic Champion who played in a team named Glengaries.

Marj was my heroine.

Marj Jackson

In 1952 the Olympic Games were to be held in Helsinki and Marj was chosen to run for Australia in the one hundred and two hundred yards and the relay. The previous year, at a state athletics meeting in Sydney, Marj had beaten the world Champion, Fanny Blankers Cohen, in an invitation race.

Fanny's husband, who was also her coach, insisted that there were potholes in the track that caused the upset, but those who knew Marj also knew she was the real thing.

Marj trained diligently under coach Norm Monaghan and as Lithgow didn't have a cinders running track, or any lighting for evening activities, Marj enlisted the aid of friends who had cars.

They would shine their lights on the track at the Rec Reserve so she could see where she was going.

The townsfolk contributed to the building of a cinders track for Marj.

I contributed any spare pennies I had.

The High School held a half-penny drive for Marj and for a week the students added their donation to the ever increasing line that zig-zagged the asphalt playground.

When the week was up the money was collected and a very fashionable overnight bag was purchased and presented to Marj to use on her trip.

As the athletes were only issued with one outfit and one tracksuit, large luggage was superfluous.

Marj did us proud and won both the one hundred and two hundred yards and then dropped the baton in the relay final.

She recovered and ran the quickest ever leg of a relay to register second place.

The thrill of listening to the broadcast of those races is with me still.

Marj would later tell the Lithgow Mercury "I knew no one had won a gold medal in track and field since 1896 and felt all of Australia was on my back: especially those wonderful people at home who had saved up their money to build me a cinders track and everyone who helped me."

My very modest pocket money had helped create a champion.

Marj added "It's great that I am part of history for the sake of the grandchildren."

Well Marj, you are also part of my grandchildren's story.

I recall the hive of activity the day you married fellow Olympian, Peter Nelson from Adelaide.

The Press climbed the trees at Hoskin's memorable Church to get a better look.
I had never seen so much traffic in Lithgow at the one time.

After the wedding Beryl would get me to convert her lemon over pink bridesmaid's dress into a halter necked style suitable to wear to a ball.

Such was the impact of Marj's achievements I promised myself that if ever the opportunity came my way I would attend an Olympic Games.

At the same time that Marj beat Fanny-Blankers Cohan Fay had married Mervyn Hasler in a winter wedding.

The year before Fay had seen the illustration of her engagement ring on the front page of the Daily Telegraph and she cut it out to show Mervyn.
She refused to go to Sydney to Angus and Cootes as she didn't know how much Mervyn wanted to pay for a ring so she left it to him to decide.
She was delighted with the result.
She began to make arrangements for the wedding.

I was the only family member not included in the wedding party as Shirl was to be bridesmaid and David, the page-boy.
I had been very hurt with the news that I had been excluded and feeling sorry for myself I went up to Granny Nolan and cried on her shoulder.
Granny dispensed some of her home-grown psychology when she took my face in her hands and said "Fay can't have you in the wedding because you are so pretty no one will look at the bride."

I began to save my shillings to buy a wedding present.

Dad arrived home with a two volumed edition of Funk and Wagnell's Dictionary for me to use for my homework.
I felt the timing may have been to comphensate for the exclusion from the wedding.

PERHAPS I will refer to these tomes throughout my adulthood as well.

Fay spent hours every night sewing on crystal bugle beads and pearls that traced the orchid pattern of the lace that formed the top of her wedding dress while the wispy marquisette skirt was hidden in a pillow case to keep it pristine.

I sometimes went with Shirl to Mrs Esme Young's as she was fitted with the red velvet bridesmaid's frock which was also embroidered with pearl trim.
A matching hat was created to match.
Mum allowed me to choose a new outfit to wear to the wedding and Mrs Connor made me an olive green pinafore that I wore over a lemon voile blouse.
I also had a new tan 'topper' coat to match my new flattie shoes and my first pair of stockings.
On the big day I was allowed to take the photos with Shirl's box Kodak camera and that was really the highlight of my day.

Fay asked Aunty Doll to loan her something old.
Uncle Paddy gave her a brooch of his Mother's to wear.
It was a heavy leaf of gold on which was written 'Regards'.
Fay's wedding ring was made from embossed platinum mounted on yellow gold that had been cut to form scallops along the edge.

Fay and Shirl   *Margaret Legge & Shirl*

Aunt and Uncle had discussed with Fay and Mervyn the possibility of share farming and the young couple readily agreed.
Mervyn's future prospects were very limited, due to his lack of education.

The reception for the wedding was held in Corney's Hall and was catered for by local neighbors and the cake made and decorated by a family favourite Uncle Bill Nolan.

Mum's loungroom was full of wedding gifts with several water-sets that were the popular wedding gift of the day, several pieces of silver including a sandwich tray I had saved up to buy, crystal and a statue of the Divine Infant of Prague from Aunty Doll and Uncle Paddy.

The sandwich tray I bought was partly paid for with ill gotten gains as I found myself short by five shillings. I took the five shillings from the mantle piece that Dad had left for Mum to buy a rare Lottery ticket so I could pay off the lay-by in time for the wedding.

I received a substantial belting but never divulged what I did with the money.

The young people went to Sydney for their honeymoon before taking up the offer made by Currans.

I snuck a peek at the postcard Fay had sent her parents at which they had laughed together.

Fay had written that the happy couple had spent their days thus.

Morning -read a book. Have breakfast and go for a walk. Read a book. Have lunch. Go to movies. Read a book. Have tea. Read a long book. Etc!!

I was blessed if I could see what was funny enough to make my parents smirk and wink and chuckle with each other.

Peachman's property over the road from Unc's was rented for the newly-weds to live in.

A new bedroom suite, lounge suite and a kitchen setting of cream wood and modern green laminex were purchased.

The setting comprised table and chairs and a large dresser that featured cupboards below, then three drawers, one of which was larger in size and lined with tin to house loaves of bread, and upper shelves where lived crockery above the bench top adorned with biscuit tins, canisters etc.

The upper and lower sections were joined by the addition of wrought iron panels.

Curtains and cushions and recently acquired wedding gifts were employed and in no time the little house became a home.

During one of my frequent holidays at Good Forest Uncle Paddy took me down to McDonald's old farm at Good Forest to deliver some stock magazines. He stopped at the gate and pointed to a post and related this story. Unc, and his brother, Tom Curran, were returning from a wedding at Hartley in their horse and sulky contraption and as they approached the entrance to McDonald's farm they were surprised to see a bright light on the gate post.
They slowed down the horse and called out, but no answer came back.
Unc alighted from the sulky and walked towards the light but as he approached the light rose and began floating down the driveway.
The brothers followed silently and the light led them to the old house where Mrs McDonald lived.
Sticking close together they entered the house and found Mrs McDonald dead in her chair.
Unc vowed the two men were not inebriated and this story was as it happened.

It was also in this area Unc had fallen from his motor bike while taking home a local girl of whom he was very fond.
He had even confessed to one of his brothers just how sure he was about this particular lady who he believed was 'mad about him'.

He was so proud of his bike and sidecar and, by his own admission, he went just fast enough to impress her hoping to scare her into 'closer proximity'.
His calculations weren't accurate and instead of her throwing herself into his arms she was thrown from the sidecar as it tipped over.
She touched her face and saw a trickle of blood and in no small voice accused him of scratching her face before she slapped him soundly, calling him a 'mongrel', and never spoke to him ever again.

I quizzed Aunty Doll about being related to the Lithgow Martins after a student at High School announced we were cousins.
Aunt explained the relationship through Uncle Will, brother of Granny Ryan, and I was satisfied.
I imparted the information to Unc.
"So they are your forty-second cousins by the buttonhole are they"?he assessed.

Gordon McDonald was a huge man who had gigantic hands, feet and mouth.

He would attend the bush dances and sweep the ladies off their feet as most only reached the height of his heart.
I can remember the design on the buckle of his belt!!
Aunt always said his mouth was so big that his face fell in half when he opened it.

Unc went to Lithgow every few weeks to conduct any business he may have and to top up supplies to augment their self-sufficient life-style.
He always dressed in the same way with a vyella shirt over a flannel undershirt. Gaberdine trousers, elastic sided boots, tie and jacket and a wide brimmed felt hat.
I chuckled at the pairs of 'long johns' that adorned the clothesline on washing days during winter.
If the school holidays had started he would wait for me after school finished and we would head out to Good Forest in 'Bevie the Chevie' a lovely old 1948 model he had purchased new.

On the front grill, hung a canvas water bag full of fresh water.
It was simply referred to as a 'water-bag'.
You wouldn't go anywhere without one and the contents I recall remained relatively cool and sweet I guess because of the addition of lumps of charcoal.

Sometimes he would arrange for the delivery of livestock that he had purchased in Sydney's Flemington days earlier.

One regular drover who would meet the stock at Bowenfels and bring them out to Lowther was Tom Kelly.
Tom was a drover and was renowned for his unattractive looks and incessant chatter.
Unc would tell you that Tom fell from the top of the Ugly Tree and hit every bloody branch on the way down!
On one occasion having delivered the stock to Unc's sale-yards, Tom spat out his false teeth while laughing and they landed in the sheep dip, a deep race containing such delightful additions as poison that the sheep were forced to traverse before being permitted access to the other sheep.
The dip rid the sheep of ticks and other unwanted vectors.

Despite the valiant efforts of Unc and others the teeth could not be found.
Tom would have to wait 'til a later time when the race was emptied.

Time passed and eventually Unc found Tom's teeth.
The deep red wax plate with teeth adhered appeared intact.
Unc washed the teeth under the running water of the outside tank and put them aside until Tom's next visit.

When Tom eventually came he took the teeth around to the kitchen and asked Aunt for a poly cup (A poly cup was one without a handle that was kept for cooking individual steamed puddings in) and some boiling water from the kettle.
Aunt handed over the cup but warned Tom that it was inadvisable for him to place the wax plate in boiling hot water.

Tom became quite abusive and insisted.
He filled the cup and swirled the liquid within.

The water began to change colour as the deep red wax plate began to change shape and ceramic teeth began to sink gracefully to the depth of the water.

Tom began a stream of bad language and Unc warned him to curtail his foul outburst in front of a lady.

Aunt could barely contain her bubbling laughter and it wasn't until Unc bid Tom and his 'lump of red wax' farewell that they sat and laughed heartily about the saga of Tom's teeth.

It is amazing how one's sense of taste changes over the years.
Yet we can recall with accuracy the taste of special foods we met when a child.
Unc would buy crumpets that tasted like no others I have ever tasted.
They were brimming with yeasty taste that would be complimented with slathering's of home-made butter that we would add after toasting them on a wire fork at the fire-box of the fuel stove.
He also bought rounds of cheese that were a foot across and so heavy I couldn't lift them.
He would cut a slice that resembled a giant piece of sponge cake and we would carve slices from the chunk to top the fresh crumpets before toasting them on the open oven until the melted cheese began to bubble and escape.
The toasted bottoms would be crisp and crunchy and oh, so tasty.

Sometimes we would have the addition of thick bacon carved from the sides of bacon Unc purchased at the town butchers.

I couldn't wait for supper time after we'd finished playing cards each evening. Unc would also continue the holiday ritual of catching a feed of eels from the creek on his property and we would roll the pieces in flour before frying them in butter until crunchy and golden.
Sometimes the pieces would first be boiled to rid them of oil that had a fairly strong taste.

Although I particularly loved the cooked flesh piled high on crispy buttered toast for breakfast, I was known to repeat the treat at these evening feasts when I substituted the toast for evening crumpets!

I have always loved seafood of all kinds but few compare with eel in my opinion.

Unc killed his own meat and he insisted lamb was tasteless, so we always had two-tooth or even hogget.
Every bit of the beast was used and in the case of a steer the cheeks were turned into a rich casserole and the tail transformed into a large pot of Ox tail soup, attesting to the belief that you wasted nothing.

Following a roast dinner there would be several days of cold meat and either salad or veggies.
There would be cold meat and salad, cold meat and hot vegies, meat patties and potato hash pie to punctuate the repetition.

The blood from the slaughtered animals was caught in a dish as the beast was hung to bleed before the skin and entrails were removed.
The blood is the first thing to start to spoil.
The blood was then mixed with herbs, rolled oats and onions and boiled in a cloth until well set.
The resultant 'black pudding' when cooled was sliced and fried in butter creating a tasty morsel popular with farmers.
The liver was thinly sliced then added to a flavor-some pan of fried onions and apple to which a generous portion of bacon had also been added before being drowned in gravy.

The liver cooked quickly and the jug of gravy was added to the pan immediately before serving.

This dish was served with a selection of veggies that included mountains of mashed potatoes.

Intestines were gathered and washed in readiness for the sausage making operation and the heart stuffed and baked after a time in the pressure cooker.

Kidneys were combined with lesser cuts of steak to make delicious Steak and Kidney pudding and minced with a hand mincer and the resultant minced steak utilized for a dozen different dishes.

There were chunks of topside sent to the butcher for corning or placed in a barrel of brine to achieve the results at home while others were seasoned and roasted as pot roasts.

Thin slices of beef were cured in salt and hung in the old dairy.

Bones were chopped and boiled to make soup and soup stock before being dispersed to the yard dogs who had already enjoyed the inedible entrails.

The entrails were delivered to the dogs in a wheelbarrow.

Then there were different types of steak to tempt the taste buds for the main meal.

Aunty would send me to choose veggies for lunch and I would bring back potatoes, pumpkin, beans, peas and maybe silver beet.

I would relate what I had picked and Aunt would argue that the silver beet was spinach. I would argue back.

She did this every time and I would never change my mind and nor would she. Invariably she would have the final word with "You bloody Ryans think you know everything."

I was surprised when Unc came home from digging a grave at Lowther cemetery with his neighbours told us he'd had a 'near miss' with a large black snake.

Apparently as the grass was quite long the men present had set fire to it and the offending snake had appeared from the corner of a subsiding grave and literally charged at the men who were all armed with shovels.

The snake was 'dissuaded' from further travel and when chopped in half thirteen small snakes emerged.

Unc maintained the snake had swallowed the babies when she had sensed danger.

I suggested the snake was a species that gave birth to its young alive and Unc was aghast at my 'ignorance'.

No amount of explaining could convince my hosts of the possibility.

Again Aunt had the last word "You bloody Ryans think you know everything."

PERHAPS many years later Aunty will relate to my children the information that 'not all snakes lay eggs you know' and I will resist the temptation to mouth 'We bloody Ryans did know everything after all!'

When Aunty Doll went to her Country Women's Meeting and I was left to my own devices. One particular afternoon, I decided to make a fruit cake.

I found the recipe book and made numerous trips around to the old dairy where the huge jars of ingredients were kept.

I filled the baker's basket with ingredients-fruit, sugar, butter, two types of flour, one dozen eggs, Aunt's home made candied peel and crystallized cherries etc.

I creamed the butter and sugar and golden syrup stopping frequently to lick the delicious mixture from my fingers, then added the free range eggs with their bright orange yolks one at a time.

Carefully sifted flours, brandy, then vanilla from the tall Watkins bottle and a large amount of dried fruit was combined.

After the addition of all of the ingredients the mixture was spooned into the carefully prepared tin lined with numerous layers of fitted brown paper.

Then into the oven it went.

I settled down to study the other recipes in the hand written books which included the 'Widden Cake' an old Irish butter cake recipe that had been made by generations as a Wedding Cake.

Aunty Doll made a passion fruit icing to enhance this special treat and with the taste of homemade butter making a unique contribution, the resultant finished product was a taste of unequalled comparison.

Yum.

Unc came up from his chores to have a cuppa and he sang my praises loud and long as he carefully banked up the old fuel stove.

I must confess I was pretty pleased with myself too as the unmistakable smell pervaded the whole homestead.

Aunt arrived home and joined the chorus of praise.
Finally I took the cooked delicacy from the oven and placed it on the rack to cool in the tin. We decided the cake would be cut for supper.
The normal routine was followed and an evening of cards followed.

Then came THE moment and Unc readied himself for the honor.

With a minimum of pressure he attempted to slice the cake.

Nothing happened.

He tried again with a little more pressure.
Nothing happened.
He bounced the knife on the cake's surface and it bounced off.
Unc started to laugh and I began to cry.

Aunt had a closer look and as she carried out her examination she shrugged her shoulder. She took the kerosene lamp and beckoned me to follow her around to the dairy.
"Show me what jars you used" she said.
I pointed them out.
When I pointed to the two jars of flour that were several jars apart, she shook her head.
"That isn't flour" she said "That's plaster of Paris.
Perhaps I should have put labels on the jars but I know where everything is love" she apologized.
The following day as we saddled the horses to drive some cattle out to Black Ridge, Unc appeared with the 'different' cake and said 'We'll take it out with us".
When we arrived at our destination Unc beckoned to me to stand at the peak overlooking a deep valley.
'Make a wish" he said.
"I hope I never make a cake like that ever again" I blubbered.

Unc held the cake aloft. "Well my wish is that in fifty or sixty years some clever fellow from Sydney University will come along and announce he's found an unknown fossilized rock cake in the middle of the Blue Mountains!"
And thrusting the cake forward we watched as it bounced, cavorted, rolled and careered down the mountain side on its way to the deepest of valleys.

Perhaps it will be a little while before I cook another cake at Aunty Doll's but, she and Unc will encourage me at every opportunity.

Aunt was the secretary of the Ganbenang/Lowther Agricultural Society and never missed a meeting.
I always teased her that she was sweet on the President, Mr Archie Thompson.
Mr Thompson was then the current owner of 'Lowther Park' where my great-grandmother, Annie England, had been born in 1849.

In our house paddock at home was an old white horse called Peter who had been 'turned out' to live out his days in relative peace.
That was not withstanding my presence.

David aboard Peter the Horse

One day when Mum was particularly busy polishing floors I managed to catch the elusive beast and maneuvered him to the post and rail fence.
I then carefully climbed the fence and mounted him much like a rodeo rider would do.
Peter reacted in much the same way by bucking me into the air as high as a space-craft headed to the moon.
The exhilaration of this moment faded rapidly as the realization dawned that gravity had taken over and I was headed downwards.
I don't know how long I lay there but I know I had the headache of all headaches for weeks after and the dizzy spells took some time to abate.

I would eat my dinner so as not to arouse suspicion and then go outside and vomit it all up.

No way would I tell anyone what had happened.

I was too ill with a substantial dose of concussion to risk having my person shaken up by a substantial paddling to my rear end.

If, in some dim corner of you cranium, it has occurred to you that I may have encountered a trauma of some magnitude that could account for my current ramblings, I offer the aforementioned story in my defence!

I would spend nearly every holiday out at Aunty Doll and Uncle Paddy's farm on the Jenolan Caves road at Good Forest for many years.

Being a jewellery buff I was particularly interested in Aunty's newly remodeled engagement ring.

Some years before Aunt had taken some small items from the leather pocket situated on the inside of the passenger's side of the Pontiac and later she discovered one of the two diamonds in her ring was missing.

She searched the pocket, even getting a shoe maker to undo the stitching, all to no avail.

Sometime later she won a substantial amount of money in the Lottery and the first thing she did was to have her ring fixed.

It was really very pretty and she was delighted with the result.

She would allow me to clean and polish her jewellery and I was permitted to wear the large rings around the house.

One I referred to as 'my ring' was a garnet with a gold rope around the stone that had been mounted on a plain gold band.

The ring was actually Granny Ryan's wedding ring and the garnet had been on Uncle Joe's watch chain and he had given it to Aunty Doll.

Aunt promised me I would inherit the ring but she didn't tell my cousin who took it and discarded the stone because it was scratched and had the gold melted and made into earrings for his daughter.

She also had a terrific collection of brooches, many of which she had inherited from her mother-in-law, Rose Curran.

She had given me a brooch in the shape of a gold map of Australia with three tiny garnets on the surrounding circle.

This ordinary little piece was special because it had been made from Granny Ryan's Engagement ring also known as a 'keeper'.

Uncle Paddy had known the Ryan family all of his life and he clearly remembered Aunty Doll as a preschooler when he had reason to see the family at church activities. With sixteen years age difference he did not anticipate marrying her, but in 1926 that is exactly what he did.

The old farm house was made of corrugated iron and was usually painted with whitewash and dark green paint.
The house had a front verandah, two doors and two windows at the front.

Currans House Good Forest

The verandah posts were medium sized tree trunks, hewn by Unc's Dad, Tom Curran Snr.
The left door led into the verandah room or shearer's bedroom and was used only when necessary. Iron beds were covered with cretonne covered 'Waggas' made from opened wheat bags that had been joined together.
It was thought the weighty blankets would provide extra warmth.

The view from the verandah was absolutely glorious, surrounded as we were by the magnificence of the Blue Mountains.
At night we sat on that front verandah and observed the twinkling of the city lights of Katoomba, Blackheath and Mount Victoria opposite us.
These iconic cities were separated from us by the vast and picturesque Kanimbla Valley.

The second door off the front verandah led into the lounge room which featured a huge open fire built of rough, local stone.

One of my regular duties was to collect pine cones and store them in a chaff bag so they could be used as kindling to light the fires.

They were most efficient as fire lighters and emitted a lovely fresh smell as the burned.

Another fire lighter was mandarin skins.

The skins were saved and dried out on the cooling stove.

When required they were placed amidst the kindling and lit with a match.

They would catch readily.

The added bonus was the very pleasant aroma that was emitted.

To the right of the lounge room was the main bedroom which housed the enormous, ornate iron bed, a dressing table with winged mirrors, a gigantic set of cedar drawers and cretonne curtains across two corners of the room behind which was a rail on which to hang one's clothes.

On the left of the main room was a second bedroom with its big bed and small cedar draws on which stood a matching, delightful, hinged mirror with tiny drawers below, and numerous religious pictures with scary illustrations of Hades, fire and brimstone.

All of this section of the house was lined with horizontal lining boards which ushered in the numerous insects and draughts through the obvious gaps.

Lighting consisted of kerosene lamps and flickering candles held in an arrangement of candle holders.

The rooms were small and cosy.

The nearness of the bedrooms allowed pillow talk to be clearly heard.

On one occasion I heard a conversation of my hosts discussing why they were so fond of me and Aunt said she thought I was the most honest child she had ever met.

I was touched and resolved never to give her reason to change her mind about me, and I never did.

Little did I know how many family and friends I would offend by perpetuating that decision and on many occasions since I have been accused about my honesty being 'brutal'.

They also discussed their own two children Luke and Hillary, who had been stillborn.

One was a year older than me and the other a year younger.

I had no idea that they had babies and I promised myself that if I ever had babies of my own I would share them with this bereft couple.

Bizarrely, they contributed to the Medieval belief that their babies, having been born dead and therefore not christened, would not be able to go to 'heaven' but would forever remain in an imaginary place called purgatory.

It would not be until the reign of King Henry V111, that this belief was questioned, yet Aunt and Uncle still believed the fallacy in the nineteen fifties.

Outside at the rear of the structure a large laundry was added.

The copper was accompanied by a set of two wash tubs and a huge bath that sat unevenly on the earthen floor that had been covered with discarded wheat bags and old mats.

There was storage space for towels and the few toiletries that were available at that time.

One I clearly recall was the 'Old Violets' talc which Aunt used liberally to dust her many creases following a bath.

Aunt was the first female form I had seen without clothes and as I was taken aback with the scars she bore I enquired further.

She explained she had undergone a hysterectomy that had left a wound from her breast to her pubic area.

She may not approve of my sharing this personal piece of information with you at this time but in truth this was a rare operation for that vintage and necessitated six weeks hospitalization followed by three months light duties.

Mum was much more 'coy' than Aunt and always maintained that Dad had never seen her in less than a slip (petticoat).

I remember when Mum had 'a bad back' she wore her corsets to bed!

There was also the fact that David slept with Mum and Dad until he was about seven and I don't think it is any co-incidence that he was the youngest in the family!

Uncle Paddy's parents, Rose and Thomas Curran, had lived in the old house and when they died they left the house to the boys.

Consisting of three bedrooms, lounge room and kitchen the house nestled close to the dividing fence to the Dowler property.

Ironically the stone, beehive shaped bread oven and woodheap were actually on the neighbour's property.

Unc 'bought out' his brother, Tom, and inherited the contents of the house and the eight hundred and four acres.

I particularly loved the country kitchen.

The sizeable room was lined with the same lining boards as the other rooms 'upstairs'.

It should be explained that the two sections of the house were built on two levels and one gained access to the upper section by ways of a huge block of local sandstone that acted as a step.

The years of wear had worn a groove in the stone, a record of the many footsteps that had gone before.

The floorboards almost rested on the soil beneath in the kitchen.

The walls were adorned with old calendars on which were found pictures of the Duke of York and his Duchess who would later become the King and Queen of England. (George V1 and Elizabeth the Queen Mother of Elizabeth 11.)

The numerous cake storage tins featured similar adornments.

It was unusual for Catholics to be royalists but Aunt felt a special fondness for King George and Queen Elizabeth because she had served them when they visited Jenolan Caves as Duke and Duchess of York.

The couple had stopped at Wilson's Half-way House for refreshments during a Royal visit in the 1920's.

There was an old black fuel stove of generous proportions next to an open fireplace that was whitewashed after every use.

Suspended from the chimney above was a substantial chain that could be attached to a giant kettle or griddle pan.

Such were the dimensions of this cavity it had space enough for several people to sit.

The griddle pan made the best ever pikelets.

The kitchen table was covered with lino on which a large slab of marble lived.

The marble was in frequent use for the making of scones and pastries.

The old pine dresser held many treasures as well as some practical items like china canisters, a glass cased clock that had been fashioned in Sydney many years before, a tea set in white that looked as though it had been dipped in oil to create a rainbow finish, and the daily china- plates, bowls and cups.

An old timber cool-safe would soon be replaced by a new, modern, electric refrigerator

Behind the old solid wooden door a set of shelves housed all manner of articles covered by a curtain.

The pots and pans lived in a similar structure in the 'lobby' outside of the kitchen.

A single paned window was hinged to open wide on sun shining days and closed by tying the discarded leather shoe lace that was nailed to its frame to a protruding screw.

The scene from this window took in the vista that included Mt Wilson in the distance.

I spent countless hours investigating the contents of the dresser and its drawers and learning of their origins.

There were gold seals featuring galleons intricately carved into a ring, another with tiny perfect roses carved from ivory, ancient porcelain and china and wonderful clocks that played delicate tunes, brooches and buttons and exquisite tins once used for snuff storage.

They really belonged 'upstairs' with the impressive collection of ruby glass and a special calico bag that housed Uncle's mother's wedding gown.

The gown was so tiny and delicate with its layers of the finest lawn, hand sewn with layers of fine lace.

It still sported the stainless steel pin that held the high neck erect. Margeurite Evans, who had been Aunty Doll's flower girl with my cousin Gwen Rolfe, once donned the dress and we took some photos.

I suggested to Aunt that the dress should go to Uncle Paddy's niece, Rosemary Curran, the daughter of Unc's brother, Tom, but she refused.

Wedding dress of Rose Curran worn in the 1860's

I was offered the dress but refused. I felt strongly that the rightful owner should be a descendant of Rose Curran.

Aunt donated the dress to a local museum so it would stay in the district and she was very upset when the owner sold the business to a Sydney firm.

During summer holidays we made numerous trips to the 'old garden' to collect fruit in the big fruit baskets.

The original Curran family home had been built on this sight and the ancient fruit trees were still bearing luscious reminders of days past.

Apples, plums, apricot, berries, figs, gooseberries, pomegranites, mulberries, pears, loquats and nectarines all made their way into the preserving pan, or jars, for future consumption.

I didn't enjoy picking the prickly gooseberries because the prickles hurt my hands.

The Old Garden

Not a small amount was consumed before it even got near the processing.

Shirl received a letter from Ken calling off their engagement.
She was heartbroken.
She had persuaded him to contact his estranged parents after several years rift and he had returned to Victoria eventually, thus creating a tyranny of distance that would impede their relationship.
As she wrote constantly and shared the local news she also mentioned the arrival of three male migrants that had been adopted by the neighbourhood and Kenneth Louis did not approve.
Shirl had been aware that the family did not overwhelmingly approve of her during her visit south and suspected her religion may have been a major cause.

PERHAPS I was a better judge of character than the family thought!

As Aunt and Uncle were devout Catholics I had to accompany them to Mass each Sunday when it was held in the tiny, iron-clad church at Lowther.
In the adjoining churchyard several generations of my family are buried.
According to the month of the year Aunt would sometimes be rostered to supply the flowers for decorating the church.
Late in winter we would pick huge bunches of Japonica from the large, overgrown Japonica found in the old garden and combine it in vases with greenery.
In the Autumn the masses of fruit tree twigs would accompany chrysanthemums of the same shades.
We would cut bunches of blossom in pinks and white and a variety of greenery to add bulk in Spring and choose shorter vases to house display the vibrant daffodils and other flowering bulbs.

After mass, which was only conducted monthly, we would take the flowers home and re-arrange them in giant preserving jars for own exclusive enjoyment.

Frequently my paternal Grandmother, Sarah Jane, was present at Mass, together with my Aunty Cis (Julia Agnes).
Now Aunty Doll and Aunty Cis did not speak to each other and though Aunty Doll told me not to acknowledge her sister, I would give her a little wave and she would return the greeting with a smile.
I loved this little game and played it often until Aunty Cis's early death at fifty seven.

Aunty Doll would look in Aunty Cis' direction as the plate was handed around and she would tell us that Aunty Cis had only put coins on the plate. "As tight as a fishes bum" she would state with disgust.

Aunty Doll couldn't understand why I went quiet (she called it sulking) when she commented on leaving the church "Did you see the silly bloody hat Cis had on?" and I wouldn't answer.

Each time I ask why the sisters did not acknowledge each other Aunt would tell me you don't need people in your life who do not treat you as you deserve to be treated especially those with whom you had shared your love.
I didn't understand her reasoning.

Perhaps, I, too, will eventually be just as guilty as Aunty Doll and make the decision not to communicate with people I genuinely care for but who did not treat me as I deserved to be treated.

Les had three other Taylors in his class named Anne, Allan and Ross.
Not one of the Taylors was related but were all friends, especially Anne and Allan.
Allan was exceptionally good looking and a very nice boy.
Eventually Anne 'moved on' and Allan and I became an 'item' and could even be seen occasionally holding hands over the next two years!
Such brazen behavior for two fourteen and fifteen year olds who even indulged in a kiss or two on occasions!!

Actually we practiced so frequently we were declared champions for the longest kiss at a birthday party we all attended!

Dad was not impressed with my school report which clearly showed how little interest I had in Maths 1.
It was the comment written by Mr Boffinger, that held his interest.
It read "If Beverley took as much interest in her schoolwork as she does the opposite sex she would be an outstanding student."

The School Ball was announced in June 1952 and Mum said I could go if I stayed at Taylors for the night.
I had intended saving for the big event when Alan presented me with my ticket that cost three shilling (thirty cents).

I was overjoyed at this grown-up gesture and have the ticket to this day!

I renovated a frock of Shirl's she had outgrown and, with my very handsome partner, set off for a memorable evening of dancing and fun and laughter It was a wonderful night.

We were even able to have a photo taken and Alan bought me a copy
Two fifteen year olds- Bev & Alan

LITHGOW HIGH SCHOOL

𝔄nnual 𝔖chool 𝔅all

will be held in the
Recreation Ballroom, Lithgow

FRIDAY, 13th JUNE, 1952

(Under auspices of the Lithgow High School P. & C. Assn.)
ADMISSION 3/-; SPECTATORS 1/-.

SUPPER.   P. E. GAUCHET, Pres.

The memento ticket.

Shearing time at the farm was a busy time.
The sheep to be shorn were brought in from outlying paddocks and housed near the house paddock.
The shearing shed formed part of the shed complex that adjoined large sales yard nestled under those three huge pine trees.

Local shearers were engaged and the wool press oiled and cleaned in readiness.
The hand held clippers or shears were checked and made ready for use though some of the shearers preferred to use their own tools.

The following Monday morning, bright and early, the operation began,
The sheep were herded into the holding pen amongst the sale yard and each shearer made his choice of animal.

The sheep was thrown on its back and the shearer proceeded to remove the wool in long smooth strokes down the length of the beast while he was resting on a 'cradle' of a wide band of leather roped to the ceiling.
The men laughed and joked as they worked and not a small amount of bad language was shared.

As each fleece was removed completely the 'rouse-about' picked up the fleece whole, threw it on the slatted table, and then removed the dags swiftly and deftly.

They then placed the soiled extras in a bin erected for just that purpose.
('Dags' were the soiled bits of fleece).
He, the 'rouse about', then rolled the fleece up and placed it in a huge iron press that was lined with a squared Hessian bag.
The strong smell of lanolin intermingled with the sweat of the men and the unmistakable odour of sheep poo.

At exactly 10am 'Smoko' was served by Aunty and me and as we rounded the corner of the shed we would invariably hear the shout "Ducks on the pond."

The significance escaped me for years until I read it was a common warning to the shearers to tone down the language as women were approaching.

The workers attacked giant mugs of steaming hot tea and trays of scones.
Today it may be plain, hot scones served with lashings of butter and jams, tomorrow tasty offerings loaded with cheese or mixed fruit or extra sweet sultanas, all slathered with butter.

Then back to the job until lunchtime.

In the old kitchen the unmistakable smell of roast lamb pervaded the air accompanied by huge pans of roast vegetables-potatoes, pumpkin, onions, sweet potato, carrots, parsnips.
Then there were the greens-peas, beans, silver beet.
And huge jugs of tasty gravy concocted from the tasty pan juices, flour and the water strained from the greens.

As Unc traditionally carved the roast with his favorite well sharpened carvers the men would wash under the running tap and then join their hosts around the old lino-topped table.

Unc loaded the plates with huge mounds of the succulent meat and the shearers piled the plates high with their choice of vegetables.
In no time at all the plates were completely cleaned with extra slices of home-made bread.
Then followed sweets of baked bread and butter pudding to which a generous amount of home- made jam had been added to compliment the stewed fruit and cream.

Again the huge mugs were filled to the brim and as the last remnants were drained it was time to return to the wool shed.

So that the men didn't get tired of roasts after a couple of days we would be treated to a meal of hot corned beef or a pumped leg of lamb accompanied by boiled veggies of all types and colors.

The cabbage was cut in half and boiled in the boiler with the meat, then drained of the water and mashed with a large dollop of butter.
The mashed potato had finely chopped onion added with a nob of butter or cream to ensure a creamy texture.
Parsnips, turnips, carrots, pumpkin, squash, broad beans, peas. Yum!
Then pies, oozing with fruit from the 'old garden' and custard and cream. Yum! Yum!

After helping Aunt do the dishes I was allowed to go to the shed and sweep the floor and pick up any dags that may have escaped the bin.
Despite my size I would try to throw the fleece onto the table.
Not a few times the shearers would tease me and pick me up and put me in the press. If it was empty I had no chance of escape because I was so short.

I loved these special times especially when Aunt allowed me to help with the cooking.
My favorite creations were old fashioned slide buns full of fruit and liberally sprinkled with sugar and spices together with patty cakes iced with passion fruit icing.

After much nagging on my part I even had special clothes consisting of bib and brace overalls and a tartan shirt (just like the cowboys wore in the movies) which were housed at the farm to wear on these special occasions.

I had suggested that wearing skirts while riding horses was not a ladylike thing to do and my hosts got the point.
Aunty made a joke of my reluctance to part with the clothes long enough to have them washed!
The irony was I hated cowboy movies and anything remotely related.

Depending on the sheep numbers the shearing was spread over one or two weeks and then things returned to normal.

We would saddle the horses and take the now naked sheep back to their particular paddock.
The shearing shed would be cleaned and the wool bales branded with Curran's brand and taken by truck to the wool buyers.

Cleaning the wool shed gave me the opportunity to examine all of the contents of this huge space.
Built of slit tree trunks (slabs) embedded into the earth and sheeted above with corrugated iron the shed housed many surprises one didn't see in ordinary storages.

I was particularly taken with the huge bellows attached to a forge.
Measuring a good eight feet I could only imagine what tasks this apparatus had performed in the past.
When a big black-smithing job was required Unc would light a fire in the coal pit and pump the bellows gently to allow air to filter through the coals and then let it burn until a glowing bed of red coals gave off a bright blue flame.

The metal was then placed in the coals until it became red hot, then removed, placed on the anvil and shaped by hitting it with huge, heavy hammers.

A noisy finale then ensued when the metal was plunged into a waiting bucket of cold water.

There were crank handles used for starting cars.
The iron crank was inserted into a hole found in the front below the engine and turned rapidly with emphasis on the downward thrust.
If the engine didn't turn over at once you repeated the process until it did!

Then there was the fine old sulky with its brown leather upholstery that remained in pristine condition.
There was the selection of bridles and saddles sitting astride a little fence that delineated the shearing and garage sections including a side saddle chosen by ladies in a former time.

Huge horse collars used for ploughing hung on huge hooks on the wall.
The collars, shaped like horse shoes, were placed around the neck of the horse and then attached to long reigns and the plough.
The farmer walked behind the plough 'steering' as it created furrows.
It was hard physical work.

I pestered Unc to let me use that saddle once-and only once- as my back ached for days!

I could not begin to describe the discomfort that ensued and each time I see pictures of the Queen astride a horse I moan for her.

If needed I was allowed cut chaff with the mechanical chaff cutter.

I would turn the handled and sneeze a hell of a lot as the hay became chaff suitable for the nose-bags.

The nose-bags were made from hessian and hung around the neck of the beast.

They would be placed so that the horse's nose and mouth was in contact with the chaff within so they could eat at their leisure.

They was often used during rest times or distances away from home.

There were rare and interesting tools for every purpose that took my fancy and a selection of beautifully crafted whips of varying sizes.

I pestered Unc to show me how to learn to 'crack' them and it took a while not to get the slim leather around my legs.

I hated it even more when the end wrapped around your face causing a stinging sensation that quickly turned to sharp pain.

Thereafter I would practice during every visit and I derived great satisfaction from hearing the unmistakable 'crack'.

My all-time favorite thing there was the old Edison Phonogram with its cylindrical records and on many a wet winter afternoon Unc would bring in the box to the lounge room and play us such tunes as 'If Those Lips Could Only Speak' and 'Barney McShane' both of which I still sometimes hear myself singing.

Shaped like an ordinary box the lid lifted to expose a mechanical arm that lowered a needle so that it came in contact with the cylindrical record that had been slipped onto a solid felt cylinder of similar size.

A handle was inserted and one of us would turn it with a consistent rhythm.

Two little doors were opened to carry the noise which was piped through a giant horn-like structure all shiny and bright that had been mounted on top of the 'box'.

Boxes of books that Fay explored during her visits lived high in the loft of the shed.

I loved the huge bins designed to hold the chook food while keeping the mice out of the containers.

Currans had the richest colored eggs I have ever seen with yolks that were bright orange.

Free range in the 'top orchard' the chicken's diet was augmented with pollard, bran and wheat and millet.

The 'shed dog' was named Jessie and she let you know if anyone came within a hundred yards of the farm.

The rest of the working dogs had housing in the 'top orchard' beyond the house. 'Lady' and 'Bandy', 'Bluey', 'Banjo', and 'Tiny', to name just a few.

Aunt had an expression that niggled me that related to any workers she had namely "Why keep a dog and bark yourself".

I heard her say it in relation to Mervyn and I spoke out telling her it was rude.

At that time Fay and Mervyn were not getting along with Aunt and Uncle and the plans to 'share-farm' were becoming less attractive.

Fay didn't like being left on her own during the day as Mervyn worked the farm and as she was expecting her first baby and was even more emotional than normal.

Uncle Paddy found it hard to actually relinquish the reigns and adopt any modern methods of farming with which Mervyn was familiar.

Unc was very careful with the money expecting the young couple to live the meagre lifestyle they themselves chose.

Fay was insistent that a regular wage should be paid and voiced her objection to following the self-sufficient lifestyle chosen by the Currans.

She failed to grasp the spasmodic nature of a farm's income.

It was Mervyn's intention to increase the number of stock by rearing poddy calves until maturity that would give the young couple an income of their own.

Fay was not prepared to help in this endeavour.

There were lots of tears and arguments and conflict.

When Regina was born in April, 1952, Aunty refused to let Mervyn take the car to visit his wife and baby at the hospital in Katoomba.

That was the last straw.

Whether it had something to do with her own unresolved grief at having lost her own babies I have never worked out but what could have been an ideal situation, where the young hard working Mervyn could have gradually taken over running the farm, with Unc given access to his pottering around the place he loved, well into old age, we will never know, but it is for sure that both couples missed out badly.

How enriched would Aunt and Uncle's lives have been with the inclusion of the Hasler kids and how much more love, compassionate direction and learning experiences would those kids have gotten from this couple with so much to give.

Fay was a difficult personality and so was Aunty Doll.

I have always felt great sorrow when I have considered how beneficial this relationship could have been to both parties.
There were certainly no winners in this sad saga.

Mum and Dad severed their relationship with the Currans too and when it was suggested I should follow suit I refused to do so pointing out that I felt they had backed the wrong party and I had no intention of severing my special relationship with people I loved.
So forceful was my rejection of their suggestion that Dad said to Mum "I think we've said enough" and the topic was never re-visited.

A new church had been built in the outskirts of Lithgow and Aunt and Uncle paid for the statue to fill the niche on the front of the church.
I think it was a statue of St Francis.

If anyone was very tall and thin Aunt would describe them as 'a long streak of misery'.
I challenged her to say if this description was of Mervyn and she answered, "If the cap fits wear it."

As many as ten dogs were kept as working dogs for cattle and sheep muster and to catch rabbits which, as I have said, in the fifties were a huge problem despite the recent introduction of myxomotosis.

Unc daily trudged through the 'top orchard' on his way to the cow bail to milk the cows.

He and Aunt would never use yesterday's milk in their tea and although they breakfasted early they refrained from having a cuppa until milking was finished.

A jug of milk was taken to the kitchen and the remainder taken to the dairy where it was put through the pristine, stainless steel separator.

With its different spouts facing different directions the milk flowed through into different containers for milk and cream as the handle sang a whirring song.

The cream was left to thicken and what wasn't eaten was churned into butter by mixing until the butter separated into curds and whey.

The resulting buttermilk was set aside for cooking and the remaining solid washed several times with fresh water until all remnants of milk had disappeared.

Salt was added to taste.

Rinsed in clean, strained water from the old, square tank until the water became clear, the dollop was tipped onto a plate.

Then, with the aid of butter pats, the butter was shaped and plated ready for use and placed in the cool safe in the very, high roofed dairy.

A special gift popular with youngsters in my day was a small Autograph album.

Most of us had the entry:-

Roses are red,

Violets are blue

Sugar is sweet,

and so are you.

It would be signed by a loving friend or family member.

I particularly liked my Uncle Doug's contribution in mine that read:-

Of all the albums I have seen

Some are red and some are green

But in Africa where I have been

All bums are black.

Not to be outdone Uncle Peter wrote:-
I wish I was a glo-worm
A glo-worm's never glum
How could you feel down-hearted
When the sun shines out your bum?

My book disappeared not long after I showed this entry to Mum.

Aunty Doll's best friend from girlhood was Pat Eames.
Pat had two children, Bill and Aileen.
Bill was notorious for wriggling his ears- especially at the dinner table.
More than a few bowls of soup were spluttered at their table when soup was on the menu.
Bill was nearer Shirl's age (and sweet on her for a long time) and Aileen was my age so it was natural we would become friends.
We would catch up whenever I was out at Lowther and write to each other in between visits.

I was fascinated to overhear Aunt mention Aileen was adopted which made her a 'special', special friend.
Aileen had 'everything' in my opinion except a ring like the one Shirl had given me.

It was dainty and made of gold with a small round sapphire in the middle of a gold wire circle and it had two dainty gold flowers and two gold leaves on the sides.
The relationship between Aileen and me was so special I allowed her to wear my ring when we were together!

Many changes were afoot when electricity came to Good Forest.

A refrigerator was purchased first, followed by a toaster, electric kettle, Mixmaster and iron and, in every room of the house, a brand new light.

No longer would we light the wax candles to guide our way to the bedrooms at night or sit closer to the kerosene lamps to view our handwork.
Suddenly the old shed came alive with electric shears and gone forever was the traditional, iconic and proverbial 'click' of the obsolete tools.

257

Uncle exchanged money for some large tapestries illustrating scenes of Eastern countries.

One was a scene in Egypt featuring the Pyramids and Sphinx.

A long discussion followed as I explained about the Seven Wonders of the Ancient World.

Unc was fascinated.

Aunt was less so and I waited for her to say "You bloody Ryans.........."

But, she surprised me.

The visual images were mounted on the horizontal floorboards that lined the walls of the old house creating a panorama as distant from the lush surrounds as it was possible to imagine.

Aunt complained about family members who had received pieces they never paid for.

As I lived in the nurse's home where no adornments were permitted on the walls I was given a small one to use as a mat.

Aunty Doll's cousin, John England Jnr, had married Tom Curran's (Unc's brother) sister-in-law, Philomenia Cullen and they built a tiny house opposite Currans which boasted the most glorious view overlooking the Kanimbla Valley.

I always felt that they would have the best view of any house in Australia and possibly the world as I knew it.

Most vividly I recall standing on the old verandah inhaling the majesty of the birth of a new day.

Unc was often called upon to find water on properties in the district.

He was what was called a water diviner.

He could take a forked stick or a piece of copper or fencing wire and walked around a paddock holding the device of choice out in front of him.

When he thought he had found underground water the device would begin to vibrate violently and Unc would indicate the spot.

I considered this to be some sort of hocus pocus until one day he offered the piece of copper wire to me and of course nothing happened.

Then Unc placed his huge hands on my shoulders and I began to rock so violently I could barely hold my feet.

My insides were trembling and there was this strong pull of gravity towards the spot Unc had indicated.

A well was ultimately sunk and at a depth of eight feet an unending supply of water was found.

During one daring episode at school, Les and his girlfriend, Jan, and Allan and I, decided a little 'pash' session was possible so we crept into the out of bounds, darkened 'theatre room' which doubled for the Music room.
The rows of adjoining seats had been pushed to the back of the room so we adjusted them to our needs and made ourselves comfortable.
No sooner had we done so when the door opened and in came Mr Nichols who proceeded to turn on the lights down the front of the room and start humming music he read from a book.
As we had instinctively crouched down to avoid detection we had little thought of long term comfort and though Jan and I were small and short and not too cramped for room, the same could not be said of the two six footers we were with!
The biggest difficulty was to remain quiet and suppress the giggles emanating from all four of us. If we had been caught we would surely have been expelled so the temptation not to make our presence known was paramount!

After what seemed an age the school bell rang and Mr Nicholls left us to scramble in all direction to avoid detection.
We laughed about that harmless little anecdote for years afterwards but I can assure you we were never tempted to try again.

On rare occasions I would be invited to go home to Amiens Street with my friend, Robyn, for lunch.
Although I really enjoyed the treat Mum was not happy about me accepting the invitation because she was conscious of the Mitchell's having so many children of their own to feed.

I suggested I invite Robyn to our house for a weekend and show her some Ryan hospitality.

On the afternoon of our arrival Mum greeted us with afternoon tea.
A beautiful cream sponge was served.
Robyn and I had a large slice each and then Mum offered Robyn another slice of sponge.

Before Robyn accepted Mum took a brush and shovel and swept up the imaginary crumbs we may have dropped!

Neither of us accepted her offer.

During a science lesson I was asked to read a definition of Aerobic respiration. I read it and for some unknown reason I have never forgotten what I read and I can quote the passage to this day.

It goes like this 'Aerobic respiration is the catabolic process of the oxidation of carbon containing foods in all living cells of animals and plants and results in the setting free of water vapour, carbon-dioxide and kinetic energy'.

One of my favorite times of day was after tea time when Shirl daily practiced her singing in the lounge room where her piano had been installed.

She would allow me to turn the pages of the music and sing along with her, often in harmony.

She taught me the appropriate areas to take a breath and I still have difficulty listening to modern singing where breaths are taken anywhere.

There were many memorable songs we shared.

'Because' and 'We'll Gather Lilacs' were particular favourites.

For my birthday Shirl gave me a brooch in the form of a spray of flowers made from diamante.

A gift from Shirl

This was my first 'grow-up' piece of jewellery.

In the mail came an envelope that housed a photo of a youth in cowboy gear complete with guitar.

On the back was a heart with the initials GR LOVES BR.

I was far from impressed by my unknown suitor and it was Mum who studied the postmark on the envelope and solved the mystery. "That's Gordon Rictor who lived down the lane" she guessed.

We were travelling into Lithgow on the bus when I saw a boy my age dressed as a girl, wearing high heels and lipstick.

I asked Mum none too quietly why he was dressed that way.

Mum shushed me.

It didn't matter how often I mentioned that boy after that time, Mum refused to engage in conversation on the subject.

I was interested to learn that new subjects were to be introduced in our second year for the external Intermediate Certificate we undertook at the end of our third year at High School.

Two that intrigued me were Biology and Art.

Dad was not impressed and argued they were both 'non' subjects and not near as important as Chemistry or Physics for example.

I insisted that they must be of value or they wouldn't have been considered.

I enrolled for them both.

By the time Dad made up his mind refusing me my choices it was too late for changes.

Of course I had to prove my interest and ensure I got good passes and I have never regretted my choices.

Mum was horrified that I enjoyed dissecting frogs that had been drowned in formaldehyde.

She didn't care for the many drawings I made of animals for this subject.

(I loved Biology so much when I undertook Higher School Certificate (Year Six) as an adult that was one of the subjects I chose).

3ʳᵈ Year (front third from right)

I was one of very few Aunties in my class and all of my friends heard of every milestone Regina reached.

I carried a photo of her in my top blazer pocket until it disintegrated.

Our first grandchild and niece Regina

Sport and school, boyfriend and movies at least twice a week, and frequent trips to Curran's, filled my life.

We had school trips to Bathurst and Mudgee where we were billeted by local families for a couple of days and bus trips to Sydney to compete in Choir competitions.

We were very successful in the Eisteddfod in which we appeared for the first time competing against the famed Fort Street Girl's High school.

We gained third place with eighty-five points, coming third behind the Champs.

All the hours we had rehearsed Bach's aria, 'Sheep May Safely Graze', was suddenly worth it.

Towards the end of third year, just as I was entering the room to undertake Intermediate certificate subjects I was told by a girl named Toni that she was meeting Allan after school.

I did not wait to ask Allan if that was true.

He had loaned me his watch for this occasion and after I had completed the challenge, while holding back the sniffles, I looked for him to return the timepiece and found him in conversation with the same Toni!

That was all too much.

He turned and smiled and gaped as he tried to catch his valuable wristwatch as it sped through the air in his direction.

I missed two further important exams as Mum would not let me go to school with the mysterious malady that ailed me.

I was an absolute mess with lots of tears, nose bleed, tummy pain etc.

Mum naturally thought it was my appendix.

Allan thereafter avoided me and refused to accept an apology sent through a mutual friend.

I never did find out if the rendezvous was for real or just imagined.

PERHAPS it was that jealous little episode on my part that put paid to my first sweet, innocent romance-and cost me two bloody Intermediate passes!

To add to the trauma our Intermediate results were published in the local paper for all to see.

How embarrassing!

At this time I had begun to think about what I would do when I left school. The opportunities for girls were so limited at that time with nursing, teaching, shop assisting or secretarial work the only choices.

I didn't think I was clever enough to be a teacher and I couldn't type to be a secretary so that left shop work or nursing.

I went to talk to the owner of jewellers called Moran's to see if he would take me on as an apprentice as I really loved the thought of designing and making jewellery.

He was quite shocked and assured me no female could possibly be a jeweller!

Frequently when Dad had pain in his upper left shoulder he would ask me to massage it hoping for some relief.

He would offer me his thanks and add "You have a beautiful touch Bill. You should go into the medical field where you can share your gift."

There was an added attraction to the idea of nursing in that you had to 'live in' at the hospital which meant I could leave home and live in the town with flush toilets and access to the movies, dances and Lithgow friends.
WOW!

It was approaching Christmas holidays and I applied to work over the holidays at Bracey's, the big mixed business in Lithgow.

I practiced what I would say when interviewed by Mr Eric Bracey.

Dad had fired 'rehearsal' questions at me for practice and I felt a little more confident.

I entered Mr Eric's office shaking in my boots.

"Beverley Ryan from Lidsdale eh?"

"Yes Sir" I mumbled.

"Grand-daughter of Rosie Nolan I presume."

"Yes Sir".

"Rose Nolan is one of my oldest and most valued customers and one of the most honest ladies I have known. You may commence on Monday."

And so ended my first ever interview.

Who said it wasn't what you know but who you know!

Somehow I was lucky enough to gain a place working in the toy section with my friend Robyn who was dressed as Snow White.

She got the job because she had such blonde hair.

When I suggested Snow White had black hair I was howled down.

We so enjoyed our new experience especially when Mrs Findlay came around every Friday with a basket full of flower sprays she had created from the flowers in her beautiful garden.

She charged us 2/6 or twenty five cents.
We pinned them on our shoulder and felt so grown up.

Everything was wrapped brown paper and tied up with string.
I mastered breaking string by twisting it around my palm and snapping it.

A very shy boy who worked in the shoe department was known to blush whenever I spoke to him and gave him a smile.
Other staff teased him unmercifully.
His name was Barry.
If the lingerie department got busy I would be sent over to sell the beautiful petticoats and matching panties that were always adorned with reams of delicate lace.
All were gift -boxed and had to be wrapped in tissue paper that matched the colour of the garments.

Shirl had been living in Lithgow boarding with a work mate at Fosseys, Mrs Thomas.
This enabled her to travel to Sydney every Saturday for her singing lessons at the Conservatory of Music after winning a scholarship.
Our sporadic bus service from Lidsdale did not allow for connections.
Just lately she had been driven all the way to Sydney by the new friend named Ray Jackson.
He had been on the scene for a few months now.
Ray was a promising bike rider who was employed by the State Railways as a shunter.
Sometimes I would be directed to accompany Shirl to Granny's of an evening where I would remain as she would catch the bus to Lithgow to meet Ray and go to the movies.
Sometimes Ray would be waiting at Granny's.
Not a few times he would give me an illegal cigarette.
Granny supported the 'young people' while being fully aware of Dad and Mum's objection to the relationship.
One of Ray's habits that was not well received was his predeliction to 'spout' his political views which was a rare thing to do at that time.

Ray was a card carrying member of the Labour Party and while that would have been endorsed by Mum, it would not have been acceptable to Dad.
Ray had a speech impediment that made listeners embarrassed as he spoke.

Perhaps Ray will abandoned his support of a working man's political party in due course.

Shirl was also regularly invited to sing at weddings.

School holidays and we were sitting on the back verandah on Saturday, January 6th 1953, when we heard a car pull up outside.
David looked and said it was Shirl and Ray.
Ray was not made welcome at our house so it was not unusual for Shirl to come in without him while Ray sat out the front in his Ford Pilot car.
As she appeared around the corner dressed in a beautiful pink and black dress and large black hat Mum remarked "Oh Shirl. You do look lovely. Have you been to a wedding today?"
Shirl answered in the affirmative.
"And who got married?" Mum asked
"I did" Shirl replied
Dad was seated at the dining-room table.
He took a look at the wedding ring, made a noise and continued reading the paper.

PERHAPS Mum and Dad would have to accept Ray now whether they liked him or not.

Shirl and Ray shifted into a Commission house in 'Wang and over the next couple of years were handy to do small jobs for Granny Nolan.
On one occasion they decided to repaint the kitchen that hadn't been painted for as long as I remembered.

They cleaned out the kitchen dresser so they could move it to get to the wall behind and they found some tins of condensed milk bearing the name of a brand that had been obsolete for many, many years.
Ray was curious to see what the contents were like after thirty odd years so he opened one.
The contents were completely caramelized and I have on the best authority that the taste was superb, especially when found in caramel tarts topped with dollops of freshly whipped cream.

In February I went to the hospital to make enquiries about nursing.
I was given some papers to fill in.

I met Anne Taylor who had begun her training that month.

I plied her with questions and she spoke with great enthusiasm about the course and lifestyle

I filled in the forms and gathered together references, results etc.

I did not mention my plans to anyone until Mum and I had words about me spending too much time out of school hours in Lithgow which meant I was catching later buses home.

I casually announced I would like to spend a lot more time in Lithgow when I left school soon.

Mum reminded me I couldn't leave home until I was sixteen.

A few days later, early on the Monday following my 16th Birthday, Mum called me for school and I rolled over in bed and told her I had left school and was commencing nursing that afternoon.

Mum was speechless and couldn't believe I was serious.

But I was.

I ask her if she would buy me a pair of shoes with 'crepe' sole shoes and a clock and she was so cross she refused.

So I rang Aunty Doll and she and Unc met me in Lithgow and furnished the requisites for my newcareer.

I reported to Matron Ashurst and she directed me to the Maternity ward where I would work until a new 'school' had commenced.

In charge of Maternity was Sister Everett.

"Have you seen in the Labour Ward yet Nurse"? she asked of me on the second day.

"No Sister".

"Then follow me Nurse" she called over her shoulder "But remember Lass, if you feel faint make for the door as we have a mother and a baby's life to consider and we cannot be concerned with fainting nurses".

"Silly old fool" I thought.

Well I followed her, and walked in on a lady called Fowler who was ready to birth her first child.

I did not make the door as I fainted and for two days afterwards I vomited whenever I thought of that poor woman splitting in half.

It was then I learned human babies do not arrive through the navel after all!!!

One of the girls offered me a cigarette and I went to the canteen and 'booked up' a packet of Gareth cigarettes and it would be a very long time before I would cease and desist this despicable habit.

Sister Pat, Fellow nurses, Sister Marj, (Bev hidden right)

That evening on the requests show on 2LT, a song was played for me called 'You Belong To Me' and a gift of a brooch with deep blue stones set in it was sent with a note wishing me a Happy 16th and saying how much pleasure my smile gave to others.

It was from my shy friend, Barry, who later became a Methodist minister.

Lithgow in the snow

Another card I received was from Barbara Wilson and the verse read:-
'The business of birthdays all started with Adam
And since he began it we've all of us had 'em.'
How true!

I purchased a cake of 'Palmolive soap' vowing to never use our family favourite called 'Protex' ever again.
For years I had tried to convince Mum that it burned my skin and she disregarded my complaint.
Another soap I didn't care for was called 'Lifebouy' and I learned Aunty Doll couldn't use that because it had a large amount of carbolic in it.
I suspected it could have been a relative of 'Protex'!

Uncle Paddy had a heart 'turn' and was admitted to hospital in Katoomba.

Aunty drove the Pontiac down to see him and coming home she was unable to get the car into gear as she drove through Mt Victoria pas- a well-known danger spot.
The car careered backwards and, with her in it, went over the embankment and flew through the air aimed towards the depths of Kanimbla Valley several thousand feet below.
Then, a miracle.
The car became wedged between two trees and as it rocked precariously a passer- by noticed the broken fencing and stopped to take a look.
He shouted to Aunt to keep still least the rocking car move and he promised her he would get help ASAP

Several hours later, as she was lifted up the mountain after being cut free from her prison, she realized her leg was badly broken as were several ribs.
She had lots of cuts and bruises but no serious internal injuries.
She would never walk without the aid of crutches again.

The Pontiac was so damaged it was converted into a utility to use around the farm.
It wasn't damaged again until I drove it into a tree stump when learning to drive!

Whenever I felt the need I took a short walk from the hospital two streets away to visit the Taylor family.
We would play records and Les would play the piano.

If it got dark he would walk me to the nurses' home where we would sit on the steps and talk for hours-and laugh a heck of a lot.

He described my sense of humor as 'self-deprecating', a term I'd previously not heard.

I missed him greatly when he went to Uni in Sydney.

I was transferred to the Main hospital and given a room at the corner of the nurses' home with a small window.

The sewing room superintendent came to examine the room and decided I should have a special curtain to compensate for the small window.

She invited me to choose something I liked and I pointed to pretty cretonne featuring varied colored carnations.

I then chose a pale green chenille bedspread and matching mat to compliment the solid maple furniture of bed, dressing table and wardrobe with its huge shoe draw at the base.

For the first time I had my own space.

Our uniforms consisted of a blue and white striped uniform over which was worn a crisp, starched, .white apron with matching cap.

Blue embroidered dots on the cap indicated the year of study.

Nurse Ryan

We wore warm royal blue woollen capes to and from the hospital, flat brown shoes with crepe soles and stockings in all weathers.
As stockings came in different shades when one was laddered we would place all of our odd stockings in a saucepan and boil them up so that the dye would colour all the same colour.
Who says recycling is a new trend?

I purchased my 'Principles and Practice Book For Nurses' with my week's pay.
In the Library I saw a verse that really spoke to me and I copied it into the front of the new 'Bible.
And here it is still remembered more than sixty years later.

'I expect to pass through this world but once; and any good thing, therefore, that I can do or any kindness I can show to any fellow creature, let me do it now; let me not defer it or neglect it for I shall not pass this way again'.
I found out in latter years that the verse was written by William Penn.

I introduced myself to my neighbor whose name was Pat Strickland.
Pat was a local Lithgow girl and she was a few years older than me.
We hit it off at once.
Some old school friends emerged like Lyn Lawrence from 'Wang public school and Fay Bingham from High school.
Norma Henry and Margaret Ironmonger were later additions.
And there was Anne.

Anne Taylor introduced me to her friend, Colin Glynn, whom she had gone out with a couple of times but claimed he was 'just a very nice friend'.
He was VERY cute I thought- and obviously the feeling was mutual!
So, for the next two years, we became an 'item'.
Even Leslie approved of the relationship.

I had known Col's twin cousins at school and our first conversation revolved around them.
Col sold his motor bike and purchased a two-toned Austin A40, registration number ADX571!
I was suitably impressed.

We played tennis, ordered numerous milkshakes at the Classic Cafe, went to church together and the movies a couple of nights each week.
Most evenings we spent parked in front of the nurses' home just talking.
It was a common practice for any of my fellow nurses to come and join us in the car out of the cold.

Col worked some nights as a projectionist at the best theatre in town.
He was an apprentice Fitter and Turner at the Small Arms Factory in Lithgow.
He had an older sister named Shirley and he lived with his Nanna in Wrights road.
His parents were divorced.
We loved each other's company and spent as much time together as we could around work and study commitments.

He would fashion me little eggcups and bowls in his classes involving the use of the new plastic material.
We shared a love of sport and had lots of mutual friends.
The only problem was my man could not dance all that well even though he would happily take me to dances and watch on as I danced with others.
It wasn't the same.

I feel my 'vintage' was indeed fortunate to have grown up in an era when dancing was such an important part of the mating process, i.e. the style of dancing where you moved around the dance-floor to the rhythm of the music in the arms of your chosen one.

I wanted to make my debut at the Catholic Ball and I much preferred Col as my partner but he couldn't learn the steps.
A mate of his was a terrific dancer and Col suggested he, Phil the friend, be my partner and he would take Phil's current girlfriend.
And that's what we did.

Aunty Doll and uncle Paddy offered to buy me a deb's frock because I only earned one pound, eighteen and six (two dollars eighty five) per week and it would take me ages to save up.
The condition was that the dress had to have sleeves and a 'respectful' neckline as both 'oldies' had been disgusted at the immodesty shown by some girls at recent balls.

I was happy to oblige though I did cheat a bit and have see-through sleeves of tulle.
The dressmaker suggested a peplin style which she maintained would accentuate my tiny waist.

PERHAPS...........................?

The neckline was a simple 'sweetheart' style.
For the top and peplin I chose a needle-point lace with fine gold thread on white tulle backing
Aunt approved.

Tickets were purchased for my parents and Aunty.

As Mum and Dad had missed Fay's Debutante Ball and Shirl had missed hers this was Mum and Dad's last chance to see a daughter 'emerge'.

We practiced our routine until the time arrived for the Marion Year Special event.

Mum rang to say Fay wasn't well and wasn't coping all that well with the new baby and that they were going down to Sydney as they were worried about her. They would not be attending the ball after all.
I cried.

The next day Dad made a rare visit into town and an even rarer trip up to the hospital to see me.

He apologized for the phone call and offered me a gift he had bought.

Inside the long grey box lay a dainty strand of pearls with a diamante catch.

"Wear these on Friday night and think of me" he said.

Dressed in my finery I asked my friend Pat to pin the red flowers in my hair and as she stood back to admire her handiwork she remarked "It's a pity you have such a small bosom as you just look a bit flat on top."

With that she rushed out of my room returning swiftly holding two sanitary pads and a pair of scissors in her hands.

She promptly fashioned the items into crescent shapes.

These she tucked inside my bra and jiggled the contents until she was happy with the result. "There, that's so much better" she giggled.

I had to agree, despite some misgivings and 'what ifs'.

Late that evening my boyfriend, shuffling around the dance floor with me, held me close and whispered in my ear "This really is your 'coming out' night isn't it?"

The Deb Of The Ball

Aunty Doll, Colin and Bev

I was on day duty with a senior nurse who was the daughter of a local minister. She was a quiet, charming girl whom we all respected, so much so we watched our language in front of her.

One particular day we had an unusual admission of a man with a hypoglycemic fit.

The patient was a miner and was the biggest man I had ever seen.

He was covered in thick black coal dust and had been placed on a bed covered with grey blankets.

Our first job was to wash the man and get him into some pyjamas, and, as he was completely unconscious we couldn't expect any co- operation from the patient.

We closed the screens to give our man privacy from the other seventeen patients in the men's medical ward.

We then gathered towels, basins of water, washers and soap and started the mammoth task.

We lowered the back rest and washed the face and hair.

First we stripped the upper part of his body by cutting off the clothes and, as I washed initially Nurse M washed the same area a second and third time.

We frequently changed the water running back and forth.

When the upper part of his body changed colour we moved to the legs where the procedure was repeated.

There was little conversation during this time.

When we prepared to wash the lower body of the gentleman, I donned gloves and cut the undergarments to allow removal.

Nurse M stood with mouth agape and without reserve said, some- what loudly "Oh Bev. Have you ever seen such a colossal tossle?"

The ward erupted with laughter and my fellow nurse covered her face with embarrassment at her outburst.

Her reluctance to leave the confines of the screened area when the job was finished was understandable.

I felt that way too and I hadn't made the comment

A night out for the girls (Bev 3ʳᵈ left)

With Pat and her boyfriend, George, we went on picnics down the mountains to Blackheath, Katoomba (where Col had attended St Bede's) or to Sunnycorner or Bathurst.

George bought an old car and the couple took themselves picnicking.

We made frequent trip to Curran's farm.

Aunty and Uncle really liked Col, but then he was a Catholic and they were very bigoted.

Pat was what was known as a 'bottle blond'.

She preferred her brown hair to be blonde and she achieved the change by rinsing it frequently with peroxide.

The most fashionable cut of the day was the 'Widgee' cut which was a short, well shaped cut with two curls combed down on either side of the forehead.

It was considered extra 'smooth' to have these two curls a different colour so I enlisted Pat's help by sharing her peroxide.

The result was disastrous as my very black hair turned out the brightest of orange.

We experimented with all manner of tricks to change the ghastly result and as I was expected home that night on 'days off' I really tried hard to source a solution.
In desperation, I found an old toothbrush and some black boot- polish and re-coloured the particular areas of concern.

We sighed with relief and I went to work.
After ten o'clock I went out home with Col as soon as I finished afternoon shift.

When we reached home we had a cuddle and a kiss in the car and I crept inside through the back door that Mum had left unlocked for me.
The following morning as I bid Mum good morning she popped her head around the bedroom door to say 'Hello' then cried "What have you got all over your face?"

I climbed out of bed and checked the mirror and the image reflected showed a face with several obvious, black, curl shapes that may have been made by what could politely be described as 'canoodling'.
Vera was disbelieving that I would be so stupid and her fear was not that my hair might be damaged and fall out but that I may have got black polish on her beautifully laundered pillow slips!

Dad questioned me about the people I had met since my last visit.
I mentioned a few patients and visitors.
Dad ask who the cook and cleaner were. I told him I had no idea.
Dad dispensed some advice.
"I suggest you make it your business to find out and you may well be surprised at what you learn. You see Bill, always remember if you show me a man I'll show you a story."

What wise words he imparted that day and I have found his message to be true throughout my life.

I was working in the Children's ward when a small boy was admitted with pneumonia.

He was tiny, pale, beautiful looking with blonde curls and big blue eyes.

He already looked like an angel.

It was obvious that he was dying yet we were not permitted to let his mother sit near him or hold him.

His mother, Ladorna, could only sit and sob in an adjoining room, waiting for me to tell her that her little boy had died.

That scene would stay with me forever.

I had to wonder about the people who made such rules and those who enforced them.

I would go to extreme lengths to avoid working in 'Kids' ward thereafter often swapping to work in the more difficult areas or long periods of night shift.

A new wonder drug had recently been introduced.

It was called Penicillin.

Penicillin came in two types, one of which was called Procain the other Chrystaline.

In order to administer the drug, (which came in powder form within a small glass bottle with a rubber top), one first had to choose an appropriate amount of sterile water from a range of glass phials, saw and break open the phial and draw up the required amount of water in a syringe.

The needle on the syringe was inserted through the rubber top and the water injected into the powder.

The bottle was then shaken vigourously until it was dissolved.

The 'mixture' was then drawn up in the correct dosage and administered intra- muscularly in the outer quadrant of the behind.

In the case of the Procain variety the process was the same but different in that the resuting mixture resembled liquid cement.

It was most painful to administer and receive having been housed in large syringes and the biggest sized needle!

I was able to earn a little extra money when a local Dr, Tony who was known to the family asked me to baby-sit occasionally.

Tony and his family would ultimately buy the Peachman's property where Fay and Mervyn had first set up house.

I also baby-sat for the manager of the shoe department at Braceys.

Mother's Day approached and I worked out my meagre budget.
I decided I needed to buy three gifts, one each for Mum, Aunty Doll and Granny Nolan.
I bought Mum a brooch with pale blue stones in a round design.
I bought Aunty a pair of earrings to match a garnet ring she had promised me.
I bought Granny a pair of Knights slippers that she always wore.
They were in her favorite colors of royal blue and maroon.

I couldn't wait to give them to her.

I went home on my day off and when I visited Granny I gave her the box and waited as she opened it.
She looked at me through her cataract covered eyes and raised her chin.
"What do we have here? Oh, how lovely. Just what I wanted, but you really shouldn't have spent all of your money."
"Well I wanted to buy you something special" I told her.
"Oh, is that so. I thought it may have been to repay all of those halfpennies you pinched when you were a kid" said Granny.
I was speechless.

Granny laughed. "Don't think you were the only one who took them because you all did it.
That's why I always kept a collection of those coins there on the dresser as I figured while you were pinching halfpennies you would not have the conscience to pinch anything else-and you never did."

As bath night was the night you also washed your hair it was natural to cover your hair towards the end of the week.
Scarves were very popular and a square was folded in half and tied around the head to cover the hair.
They were referred to as 'peasant' scarves.
Even the new Queen wore them.

Our Monarch, Queen Elizabeth 11, came to Australia for a Royal Visit.
It was planned that she would visit Lithgow and that the local park would be re-named Elizabeth Park during her brief visit.

She arrived as planned and was met at the Royal Train and driven in a motorcade to the park.
We were placed alongside the path in the park, escorting the patients who were well enough to attend the visit in a variety of chairs, both static and mobile.
As the party walked slowly toward the rotunda, the Duke followed the Queen, both nodding and waving to the assembled gathering.
One of the party looked in our direction and nodded in a general fashion, then came our way.
I stood next to Beryl Jackson and it was to her he directed his question.
"Your name wouldn't be Jackson by any chance would it?"
"Yes Sir" she swooned.
"Hmph" He muttered as he walked away, "Thought as much. I'd have recognized that conk anywhere."

Mrs G had a Manchester repair late in the afternoon.
I was delegated to sit with her until she recovered from the anesthetic.
There were no recovery rooms in those days or special care areas, so patients were returned to their wards.
Mrs. G was checked frequently throughout the evening.
Sister came around about nine PM and checked said patient then told me not to disturb her further but let her sleep.
I didn't feel right about the order, so before I went off duty I disobeyed my boss and examined Mrs. G.
I found her in a pool of blood and immediately rang the emergency bell.
Sister was so cross with me disobeying her order but fully aware our lady required a return to theatre to allay the haemorrhaging ASAP.

The next day as I read the days report I noticed the report compiled by said Sister.

She claimed she had carried out quarter hourly checks regularly throughout the previous evening.

I wrote my version of events that contradicted her account.

I was disciplined for correcting one of the sister's reports about a patient.
My punishment was that I had to wash every brass vase in the ward during my own time.

These medium sized brass vases had been donated by the Women's Auxiliary. Their normally shiny surface was dulled by the application of an oily film that did not detract from the appearance but meant the vase cold be easily washed in soapy water.

I thought I'd do a proper job and clean off all of the special film that covered them.

The result was that the vases forever after had to be polished as every finger mark clearly showed.

Although we were not permitted to accept gifts from former patients I did receive, and kept, a set of seven hand embroidered tea-towels sent to me by Mrs. G a month after her discharge.

The tiny card still bears testomy to her appreciation.

At least two of us knew exactly what had happened that fateful night.

Dear Nurse Ryan.
just a little thought for "The Box". Thank you so much for your kind attention
G. G

Something selected
Especially for you
And lots of good wishes
Go with it too!
from
Mrs. Glass

Col's 21st birthday approached and plans were made for a big party.

I made a new white dress on the new sewing machine that had been donated to the nurse's home.

I bought some fine black lace for a stole.

Other nursing staff to attend included Rae Williams who sang for us, Shirley Martin, Rita Fields, Marg Phelan and others.

They all voted it a terrific night.

George Pat Stan Raelene Marg Billy Rita Bill Cecily Phil Col Bev Brian

Shirley Glynn and Bev July 1954

Jean Taylor's sister, Betty, and her husband, Peter, arrived back from living overseas in Cocus Island with a fantastic imported car called a Mercury Montclair.

An American built machine it was big and black and sleek and really swish and absolutely unique in a relatively small town like Lithgow.

The townsfolk had never seen the likes.

It had been purchased by them from their former boss-a member of the famed Clunies Ross family.

It caused much comment.

Les had just gained his license and he was given permission to actually drive the vehicle.

He appeared at the hospital and invited me to go for a drive up and down Lithgow's main street with him and his friend, Gordon Sykes.

It was not Leslie's nature to skite, or show off, but he did that day.

That was a memorable day for three young country kids that one of them still remembers.

We were on night duty with a girl who was a known 'snitch'.

She had dobbed on us for smoking out on the fire escape while on night duty as well as several other violations of the nurse's code.

We were not impressed.

She had recently tried out a tongue clamp on herself and had run screaming into the adjacent pan room where I was scrubbing pans, begging for help.

The only way you could release the clamp was to apply more pressure to 'unlock' the device.

I left a triangular scar on her tongue and wished it had been someone else who had gone to her aid.

This girl was paranoid about accompanying any bodies to the morgue and would do anything to avoid this duty.

I called her up from children's ward downstairs and told her to meet me with a lantern in the lift-well to assist me with the trolley.

She didn't sound at all happy.

We maneuvered the trolley out of the lift then walked together down the long corridor and out the big doors and turned left in the direction of the morgue.

Half way there I instructed her to push the trolley and I would carry the lantern and open the door.

At that moment Pat, draped in a mortuary sheet, sat up.

'H' absolutely freaked out and pushed the trolley with all of her might sending trolley and Pat racing at high speed towards the corner of the substantially built bluestone morgue.

Pat was thrown in the air and sustained a broken collarbone.

'H' was last seen flying down Bridge Street at one hundred miles per hour.
We rushed inside to the small exchange and rang R, one of the local policemen who was on duty.
He was engaged to one of our nurses and knew us all well.
We left the rescue of 'H' to him and Pat managed to convince the powers that be that she was involved in a slight mishap during her meal-break.

'H' never snitched on me and as she didn't recognize Pat she couldn't report her either.

'H' eventually left nursing not because of our cruel joke but because she recognized what we all knew and that was she was one lousy nurse-and not a very nice person.

I have often pondered why 'H' was permitted to commence nursing when the entrance criterion was usually strictly adhered to.
'H' had an obvious social problem evident to anyone who engaged in conversation with her.
I think she was accepted more because of her Father's prominent position in the town rather than her suitability to undertake studies in that profession.

Coral Hill's general health was poor and her condition was deteriorating.
In her early twenties she was re-admitted to hospital with heart failure.
Shortly after Christmas she died.
I phoned Mum to tell her the news.
She was quiet for a time and I guessed she was crying.
She hung up the phone without saying good-bye.
I would discover later that she took off her apron, did her hair and phoned for 'Dutchy' Holland's taxi and went straight to Ilma's up Mudgee Road.
So, after ignoring each other's existence for twenty years, they came together to console each other and would not only re-kindle their friendship, but strengthen it, remaining close for the remainder of their days.

We were in a lecture theatre listening to a local Doctor whose topic was nursing in a mining area.

One of the nurses was an officious young woman who was very proper in speech and demeanor.

In other language she was a bit of 'snob'.

She posed the following question in her poshest voice.

"Oh Doctor. What precisely would you do if a pit pony kicked you"?

Dry L paused momentarily then said loudly "I'd kick the bastard back".

On another occasion the same Doctor asked if we had any questions we'd like to ask.

I asked him why a boy would appear in public dressed as a girl.

"He could have been a trans-gender boy" he answered.

I was none the wiser!

When I was finally admitted to the inner sanctum of the operating theatre I was in the adjoining autoclave room when I was directed to take a large stainless steel dish into the actual theatre.

Fully garbed in uniform covered with a theatre gown and my mouth and nose covered with a mask I hurried through the swinging doors and before I knew it I was standing holding the dish and the gift of an amputated leg!

It was so unbelievably heavy I nearly dropped my 'gift' and despite the covering of masks I could clearly read the humorous reactions of my fellow staff.

They, in turn, had little doubt that my hidden mouth remained agape.

I stood still, not quite knowing what to do next, until one of the nurses pointed towards the door and I made my hasty exit.

I would regret leaving the hospital before a full six months observing, and acting as theatre scout was served, but my fascination with the workings of the human body, both inside and out, would never wane.

We were invited to a dinner dance at the Marangaroo Air force base to act as partners for a contingent of English Officers who were visiting.

We would be chaperoned and transported to and from the venue.

I asked Col what he thought and he encouraged me to go.

We had a wonderful evening and despite the chaperoning, sparks began to fly between some couples.

Marangaroo Airforce Base

Bev and Derek

Christmas was approaching and I was asked what I wanted for a gift.

I had months before lay-byed car seat covers for my man.

I told him about a beautiful opal pendant and earrings I had seen.

I had no idea how much it cost.

Weeks later I noticed it had been removed from the shop window and I went in an enquired about it.

The shopkeeper said he thought it had been sold to a man as a gift to his wife.

I asked him the price and he said it was thirteen pounds!

I reeled on my heels and ask him why it was so expensive and he explained the setting of minute flowers and leaves was hand-made in individual tiny pieces by a specialist jeweller.

I closed my eyes and recalled the piece and stored the image in my mind to retain forever.

I was so relieved Col hadn't felt pressured enough to buy such a very expensive gift.

Weeks later I noticed opal earrings in the same window minus the pendant.

I commented to Pat that they looked the same as those I had seen previously.

We were on our way to midnight Mass that Christmas Eve and Col gave me a package.

I opened the cream plastic box to find resting on a bed of cream velvet the opal necklace.

I was overwhelmed and could not stop the tears from flowing.

"Oh Col it is really, really beautiful" I said. "Thank you, but I feel really bad. You should not have considered buying it when it cost so much. Do you like it too?"

"Not really Darling. I am really superstitious about opals as I fear they bring bad luck".

I laughed. "I'm not superstitious at all and I will treasure it for the rest of my life." I said as I placed the beautiful necklace about my neck and smoothed my new navy dress coat.

"I thought I saw the earrings in Miranes a few weeks ago" I told him.

"Yes. I couldn't afford the lot and Mr M was willing to split the set when I explained how you loved the pendant."

When we came out of Mass, Col's father met us. "Your Nana just died suddenly" he said.

One of our friends became pregnant and Col found out where she had been sent in Sydney to work in an institution until her baby was born.

There was so much shame and secrecy about pregnancies conceived out of wedlock in those days and the girls were ostracized and shunned.

Invariably they were sent away and the story spread that they had gone to stay with a relative or they had gone overseas.

Col broke the rules and went to Sydney to see her and was refused permission..

He ceased talking to the baby's father who didn't appear to give a hoot.

Others followed.

The father left town.

Another lass, who worked in our hospital dining room, also became pregnant. She and her boyfriend waited until her parents went on holidays then arranged a back-yard abortion to coincide with the girl's days off.

They figured she would be able to return to work after a few days and no-one would be any the wiser.

The 'expulsion' was incomplete and septicemia set in.

She was admitted to the hospital too late and we nursed her as she literally rotted away.

She had to be placed in an isolated part of the hospital to prevent the disgusting smell from pervading the entire building.

The only child in an adoring family, she died the most hideous of deaths and if that didn't frighten the daylights out of we youngsters nothing would!

I was returning to the hospital after days off at home when two local lads from Portland passed the bus on their motorbikes.

As the passed they tooted and waved.

They then slowed down as the bus passed and played the chicken game several times before old Claude gave them a loud pimping with the bus horn.

The boys got the message.

Several miles down the highway the bus was flagged down by one of the boys.

Claude pulled up and said I had best get off the bus as I was needed.

There leaning against the embankment of sandstone sat R where he had been thrown from his bike.

The top of his head had been completely sliced off.

Claude drove the bus to the nearest house that he knew had a phone and called for an ambulance.

A few months before the accident, R had been a patient and he was forever playing tricks on us.

One night he offered to wash my supper dishes so I promised to turn down his bed as I had to put out the lights by a certain time and he wouldn't be able to see.

I not only turned down his bed but poured freezing cold methylated spirit in the hollow of his mattress that was covered with a plastic cover and pulled the sheet so tight you wouldn't guess what I had done.

With lights out and me hiding behind a big fracture bed we waited.

In came R humming to himself.

He spoke in a very quiet voice to his immediate neighbours who didn't answer.

He removed his dressing gown and hopped into bed then let out a string of oaths that were intermingled with threats of what he would do to me when he caught up with me.

The entire ward was in uproar.

With his wet pajama pants around his knees I figured it was an opportune time for me to make my hasty exit.

The following afternoon I came on duty on full alert.

One of the men gave me a urine bottle and asked if I could empty it and return it before Matron did her afternoon rounds.

As this was not an unusual request I happily obliged.

As I opened the door that led to the pan-room I was ambushed, picked up bodily and plonked in a cold bath in full uniform, hat, shoes and all.

I then had to get out of the bath, escape the ward, cover one hundred yards to the nurses home, strip so as not to leave a wet trail to my room, find alternative clothes and get back on duty before Matron's entrance that was due in the next five to ten minutes.

I made it down the fire escape and ran through the big kitchen apologizing as I went, reached the nurses home where I stood and hollered "Help, Help". Heads appeared from all directions and my plight was quickly assessed.

Amidst lots of laughter I was dressed from the skin out borrowing collars and cap, even dry shoes that were too big for me.

I raced back to my ward and never mentioned the incident to any of the staff other than my friend Pat.

Matron commented that I should not come on duty with wet hair for fear I might catch cold.

If only she knew!

Pat, Dr Jerry and Bev

Col came up to visit in a very emotional state.

His father, Bede, while fishing down the South Coast of NSW, had gone missing, believed drown.

I had four days off from that night and he asked me to accompany him down to Bulli where the accident had happened

Mum and Dad surprisingly granted permission.

It was a sad and difficult time talking to Police, keeping journalists at bay, looking, but not being confident anything would be found, yet all the time living in hope as we trudged up and down the beach for days.

The empty boat had been found and the general feeling was that he had been taken by a shark.

It wasn't until a shoe with a man's foot inside was found that we left for home.

His body was never found and it would be seven years before he was confirmed dead.

Col thought our relationship was getting 'far too serious' and we decided to 'cool' it for a few months.

A few miserable weeks later a mutual friend became ill and Col visited her 'co-incidently' at the very time I gave out supper to the patients each evening, so I saw him every single day.

If I had a day off he would miraculously appear at my favorite haunts.

One evening when he came up to the ward he asked why I wasn't around and he was shocked to learn I had been rushed to theatre and had my appendix, which had burst, removed that day.

He begged the sister to let him see me and she refused because he was no longer my 'close' friend and I was too ill.

One of my nursing colleagues told him how I had been ill on duty with pain, vomiting and diarrhea and I had been sent to Matron's Office on 'Sick parade' the following morning.

She kept me waiting with door closed to her office while she spoke to the Manager.

When she opened the door she saw me doubled over and ordered me to stand up straight.

I fainted before I could follow her directions.

Shirl, who worked in Lithgow, was summoned to sign consent forms to allow the emergency surgery.

Beverley Ann Farmer

Sister Sheppeard thought my lovely swami pajamas were insufficiently warm and I awoke to find myself enveloped in her thick, voluminous, pink nightie that was many sizes too large.

I was so spaced out after the anesthetic I didn't care a dot.

I recalled how I felt I was spiraling out of control down a giant, grey, tunnel into oblivion while under the ether.

One constant visitor was by my side every single minute of every single visiting hour.

The romance was 'on' again, though was never quite the same from my point of view.

I saved up to go to Sydney to have my hair styled and cut at the master hairdresser of the day called Norman Floam.

Drawing of Bev by Lyn

On the train I met an artist named Lyn who was 'exceptionally' friendly. She wrote almost daily and phoned inviting me down to Sydney to Art Shows and to 'sit for her' and the like and she sent me a drawing she had done of me from memory.

Nurse J caused a ruckus when a pair of her white gloves disappeared from the clothesline at the nurses home.

We staggered off duty after a particularly heavy day and were not permitted into our rooms.

Matron went through everyone's drawers and laundry bags.

Dad was outraged at the violation of privacy and penned a letter of complaint to the administration.

I was never told if the gloves were recovered and didn't care.

It was exceptionally cold weather at the time and one night as Pat and I sat on my bed gossiping and laughing with our hot water bottles and feet tucked under the covers we decided to share our warmth and my bed.

I threw her a pillow down her end and we fell asleep.

Next morning when the night sister came to wake us for our six o'clock start she was shocked to see us in bed together and she immediately reported us to Matron, who in turn summoned us both to her office.

"You must know that you do not sleep with other girls" she began.

Pat and I exchanged glances.

We were both younger sisters who had shared a bed all of our lives until we went nursing!

"Do you understand Ryan?" she roared.

"No Matron. I've always slept with the girls" I confessed.

"What do you mean Nurse?" said Matron an octave higher.

I explained the family situation.

She asked Pat the same questions and Pat answered honestly.

Then the penny dropped and Matron's demeanor changed.

She could see we were absolutely innocent of her insinuations and so she gave us a brief account of Lesbianism.

We were nonplussed.

She warned us to be very careful in case we should 'become prey' "You will need to learn to recognize" was her advice.

As we made our escape I remarked to Pat "I'm pretty sure I've recognized already".

Until that time we had always walked arm in arm down the main street of Lithgow like other good friends or family members.

I suggested to Pat that we may have to change our ways especially if Matron was in sight.

Girls Night Out (Bev 8 th from right, back row)

Mona and Kaye graduated after their long four year training.

Another girl, Esme, had been through with them but she had recently been sacked because she had a fit of some kind.

She would move to Albury and start all over again.

A social evening was arranged in the Nurse's Lounge to celebrate the occasion and we were given special permission to have the boys attend.

Matron would be in charge of the distribution of bottles of drink and her glorious punch.

Naturally no alcohol was permitted.

Not a few of the boys owned hip flasks and as one attracted Matron's attention another one would empty his flask into the giant punch bowl.

As Matron's punch didn't appear to her to be popular she encouraged all present to partake.

She too, imbibed and by the end of the evening she shocked all present and smiled!!!

Rae Williams and I were invited to sing after Matron heard us sing a selection of songs in the shower when she did rounds one morning.

A group of us dressed up for a number called 'The Rich Maharajah of Magador'- He had ten thousand camels or maybe more', etc.

I was the head of a camel with nylon stocking over my head covering my new, very expensive haircut!

The Rich Maharajah, his slave and camel

I was on theatre duty and Dr L was conducting a tonsillectomy.

He was in a bad mood and was throwing instruments across the room and barely grunting at the staff.

The theatre sister was an extremely quiet 'gentlewoman' and in an effort to break the extreme and uncomfortable silence she said sweetly, "Oh. You have blood on your mask Dr."

The Dr answered "That's nothing to what I've got on my bloody liver today Sister."

Pat and George, and good friend Stan, wanted to have a weekend in Sydney, staying with Pat's sister, to celebrate Pat and George's engagement.

I was invited along because I was Pat's best friend.

Travelling by Sydney ferry most of the time we had a fabulous weekend visiting different venues,

Best Friends

Pat Stan Bev Sydney 19953

eating a Chinese banquet before going to Luna Park one night then attending a monster concert at Festival Hall featuring the one and only Louis (Satchmo) Armstrong who was accompanied by Ella Fitzgerald.

Working from the unstable boxing ring and playing to a very appreciative crowd they really had the enormous space rocking.

They played instruments and serenaded us with a wide selection of jazz and popular ballads.

We were all tingling when it had finished and we talked nonstop about the experience all the way back to Lithgow in Stan's car that was exactly the same as Col's.

I had been delighted to hear Fay and Mervyn had welcomed another healthy daughter whom they had named Maureen, though I was still hurt that Mum and Dad had gone to Sydney to assure them that Fay was managing rather than attend my ball.

I had reasoned that one of them could have gone to Sydney and one gone to the ball.

That seemed to me to be the fair thing but that was not what happened.

To express it mildly I was really 'pissed off' with my sister.

Following the 'falling out' of the Currans and Haslers and the end of the share farming agreement Mervyn suffered a 'nervous collapse'.

With a brand new baby and a wife, no income or place to live, he turned to his Aunt and Uncle in Sydney.

They already had Mervyn's sister and her new husband living there too and it was a small house.

I had visited the Haslers when they first shifted to Mascot where they lived with Mervyn's Aunty Mag and Uncle Bert.

On one such occasion Uncle Bert suggested I watch a young man play tennis next door on courts managed by Bert.

The young player was named Lew Hoad and together with his partner, Ken Rosewell, he would become famous as the world's best doubles player.

I also noticed how very attractive he was.

Although I loved my brother-in-law I was well aware of the distance in Fay and my relationship so I was positively overjoyed when I was invited to be god-mother to our newest family member, Maureen.

On the appointed weekend of the Christening we journeyed to Sydney and I had a legitimate reason to give the special new infant lots of extra cuddles and hope this would be the beginning of a very special relationship.

As I rocked her and cooed she regurgitated all over my brand new brick-red gabardine coat!

Fay was preparing a leg of lamb for roasting.

She cut off the shank.

When I ask why she did this she said Mum sometimes did so.

I ask Mum why she sometimes did that and she said her Mum sometimes did it.

I made it a point to ask Granny and she told me when she was first married she didn't have a pan big enough to hold the leg with its shank on, so she cut it off and sometimes made it into soup or gave it to the dog.

Neither mum nor Fay ever removed the shanks from their uncooked leg again.

The Haslers shifted to Harold Street in Matraville and rented a house from Joe Beecroft, a former Lidsdale resident who was a policeman in Sydney.

Outside the back door of Fay's house in Matraville lived a large frangipani tree.

The numerous cream flowers gave off a strong, sweet perfume.

I loved picking the flowers and threading them onto straws plucked from the straw broom.

The hollow straw enabled the water in the vase to refresh the flowers that would last for days.

I was feeling insecure with the change in my relationship with Col and I wondered about leaving my studies, home, my family, my friends- and him, and pursuing something a bit different.
I said nothing to anyone.
Standing on the terrace above the driveway into the hospital I measured my field of vision one day and realized it covered an area from where I had been born to the area where the cemetery was found!
I rationalized it would be possible to settle in that city and never move out of it, as many before me had done.
My entire life could be lived within that measured space.

I decided there was much more for me to see, do and experience.
I could only imagine what new adventures might await me.

By chance I met a girl from Portland named Joyce Deloraine and she told me she was planning to join the Airforce.
I quizzed her and decided I should look into joining too.
Here was an opportunity to travel without a chaperone, to see more of Australia, have a job of nursing about which I had learned much, a guaranteed place to live and a wage considerably more than I was currently earning.

It all seemed positive to me.
When I enquired further I was told the procedure and invited to Sydney to undertake tests.
I was warned that the intake took one out of every three who applied.
A medical followed on another day.
I went down to Sydney on an appointed day to learn my fate and was advised that I had been accepted and the next intake would begin in late July or August.

Mum and Dad were very disappointed with the choices I was making especially as the wartime WRAAFS had a 'bad name' according to Mum.

As she never knew one I was never sure how she gleaned this knowledge.

Dad gave me a lecture about completing what you begin and how I'd regret my decision and how I was fortunate to have had the educational opportunities that he had been denied.etc.
I pointed out his other daughters hadn't even started to train for anything and they'd had a very expensive education, unlike mine.

A very exciting occurance the week of my eighteenth birthday was the arrival of Shirl and Ray's first child, Deborah Ann.

Dad now had three grand-daughters and still no first grandson to inherit his gold fob watch as he planned and promised.

Deborah's Christening 1955

Not long after my eighteenth birthday I told Col of my plans and left the hospital. He begged me to reconsider.

On my last day our cranky old matron Ashurst called me to her office and delivered a sermon.

"Nurses are not made Ryan, they are born and you are a born nurse. You will rue this day" she said.

That was probably the nicest thing she had ever said to me.

I went out to Aunt's.

I saw a job advertised in the Sydney Morning Herald that required someone with nursing experience to care for two little girls, the children of a professional couple. Aunt offered to accompany me to Sydney for the interview.

In the morning I was woken early so we could be driven to Mt Victoria to catch the first train, The Fish. (Do I have to mention here the second train was The Chips?)

Breakfasted and suitable dressed in a lovely pale blue gabardine suit, high heels, gloves and matching bag and hat I was given the nod of approval by my Aunt.

She suggested I visit the loo as she did not want me using the train toilet.

Now, Curran's toilet was positioned a considerable distance from the house and I did not fancy walking the distance over uneven terrain whilst balancing on very high heeled shoes, so I decided on a detour. I made my way along the path and felt my way onto the grass, raised my rather tight fitting skirt, lowered my undies and step-ins that held in place one's stockings by means of suspenders, then squatted and urinated while hoping a cow, or sheep, that had escaped the nearby confines of the 'house paddock,' would not join me unexpectedly. I straightened my clothes and felt my way back to the path, waiting there a short time to syndicate the long walk that should have been taken.

I washed my hands under the running tap and went inside.

We gathered our bags and stood waiting for our driver.

Unc entered through the back door and Aunt took him to task "Where have you been? We are ready to go."

Unc walked over and raised his foot onto a chair showing a water marked shoe. "That was a very close shave Youngin" he began to laugh.

Unc had also taken a 'short cut' to relieve himself and when I appeared very close to him he thought it wise to remain absolutely still least I get a fright and 'fall off my high heels'.

In the pitch blackness I had peed on his foot!

As we both laughed, him with merriment and me with embarrassment, Aunt took us both to task for not going all the way down the back.

The trains of that era were driven by steam.

Adjoining the driver's compartment was a container of black coal that was shoveled into a glowing fire-box to supply the conversion to steam.

The train composed several individual box-like compartments each of which contained bench seats that comfortably accommodated eight passengers.

Access to the outside was through wood and glass doors.

Above the leather upholstered seats rested sturdy brass luggage racks. Adjacent to the racks were fine glass water carafes and glasses housed in highly polished holders.

Everything was spotlessly clean and I cannot recall ever seeing damage or graffiti of any kind.

Aunt considered Katoomba too near Mt Victoria to enjoy a lovely morning tea available at that station.

After the interview at a city dress shop we did a spot of shopping.

I bought a very expensive Mollinex overcoat in gun metal grey adorned with bobbles of tan and black wool.

It had a huge collar that you could fold up around your ears and I loved it.

Matraville 1955

A few days later I moved to Pymble and took charge of two little preschoolers, named Victoria and Alexandra.

Alexandra was nicknamed 'Bubba' and she suffered from asthma and required lung exercises.

One exercise I recall was she had to blow a Ping-Pong ball along the carpet.

I wondered about a Doctor who would suggest an asthmatic get so close to a dirty, dusty carpet.

Victoria was referred to as 'Tortie' and she helped raise the dust.

Mrs. Johnson, the housekeeper, agreed with my observation.

When Mrs. Johnno was off duty I was expected to do the washing and cooking. Every weekend the family travelled to the country, usually to Campbelltown district where they bought fresh fruit and veggies and dressed ducks from the many roadside stalls.

On one occasion when the kids were ill with bronchitis I left a pair of double bed sheets in the electric copper until they scorched.

I was docked a whole week's pay as the result.

I was intrigued that Mr and Mrs. went out most evenings.

That may not seem strange to you but it might if I add that they'd go in different cars and in different directions.

Then they came home and shared a bed!

A young train driver from Lithgow was a constant visitor on my days off.

On a rare weekend off we decided to see a new show in town called 'Carmen Jones'. It was a much hailed modern adaptation of the Opera, 'Carmen'.

Rather than catching a late train home with me and then catching a very late train back to Sydney if one was available, we decided to stay the night in town.

Don had booked rooms at the McLeay in Kings Cross because it was both cheap and central and as we had planned to spend the next day with Fay, Mervyn and girls we would only have one bus to catch from there.

I had never stayed anywhere by myself before but I had no problem sleeping until a young man entered my room at some ungodly hour of the early morning and placed a tea tray on my bedside table.

On the tray was a small dish containing two tablets. "Take these and you'll feel better" he said.

I was terrified.

I jumped out of bed and dressed hurriedly, grabbed my bag and headed for the outside, crouching on a park bench for the next three hours.

In the middle of King's Cross in the very early hours of the morning I was surely vulnerable.

When Don came out looking for me he was showered, breakfasted and well rested.

He wanted to return to the hotel and file a complaint but I just wanted to get a distance away.

I promised myself I would never stay by myself again and it would be more than thirty years beforeI would do so.

Aunty Doll and Uncle Paddy gave me a set of suitcases consisting of a large case and matching hatbox in a dark mottled grey.
I had gone up the mountains for a weekend specifically to visit Granny Ryan who was a patient in Katoomba Hospital.
In her somnambulant state she opened her eyes briefly when Aunty Doll told her I was there and she murmered "Vera."
I didn't correct her.

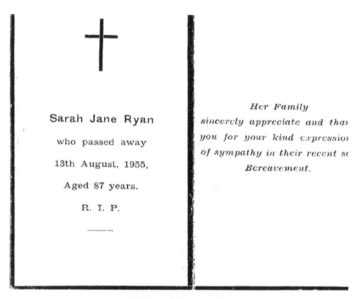

Sarah Jane Ryan

who passed away

13th August, 1955,

Aged 87 years.

R. I. P.

Her Family sincerely appreciate and than you for your kind expression of sympathy in their recent se Bereavement.

She died on August 13th, 1955 aged eighty seven.
She was buried in the Lowther Cemetery with so many of her family.

Late August came around and I was summoned by the Air force to attend a swearing-in ceremony in Sydney Central with a batch of new recruits.
I would be mustered as a Nursing Orderly.
We boarded the overnight train on August 30 that would take us to Point Cook in Victoria and an unexpected new life.
Cramped and noisy in the antiquated train carriage it appeared sleep would not be possible.

Then, a brainwave.

Being so short I would climb up onto the luggage rack and the other girls would place their luggage from there between the seats, creating a bench on which they could sleep top to toe!

Wrapped in my new expensive coat I snatched some shut-eye and tried to visualize what fate had in store for me.

I indulged in my favourite day-dreaming activity and saw myself marching through lots of different Airforce bases in all states of Australia.

We alighted from the train at Flinders Street Station in Melbourne and climbed aboard an Air force bus heading out of town.

Once inside the compound that was Point Cook Air force base we were caught up in the initiating procedures.

Uniforms were distributed, barracks allotted, rules displayed and a set of new suitcases doled out!

On top of the list of rules written in large type were these words:-

"STRICTLY NO FRATENIZING WITH MALE PERSONEL ON THE BASE".

We had been warned.

I had been allocated a room on the end of the building on the ground floor.

A space of eight feet saw a fence and beyond the fence was situated another barrack the same as ours.
Both buildings were two storied.

Just outside my room was a door that led to a small landing.
It was on this landing the very next weekend that a group of us engaged in some high-jinx.

Fun and games at Pt Cook on that fateful day

Our laughter caught the attention of a man seated on the first floor verandah of the opposite building reading a book.
He leaned over the rail and asked if we were the new recruits.
We were.
Then he asked where we were all from.
When he got to me and I said "Lithgow" he became animated.
"I trained at the Small Arms Factory there" he said. "What's your name?"
"Beverley Ryan" I answered.
"I'm Jack Potts. Are you any relation to Jim Ryan the golfer?"
"Yes. He's my father."
"Well that is amazing. Next to my fiancé I love golf best and it was your Dad who taught me how to play."
At that point in time he was joined by another fellow who carried some books.

Jack filled him in on the remarkable co-incidence.

His visitor appeared to be totally disinterested giving us the briefest of glances.

He thrust a pile of books at Jack and then hastily left.

Jack looked after his visitor, shrugged his shoulders, then kept talking, finally asking us if we would like to go for a drive in his car.

He explained he could only fit three of us in his little car but he would ask a mate if he would take the rest of our small group.

Shortly after we joined Jack and he introduced us to his friend whose name was Phil.

He was the intruder on Jack's verandah earlier.

We were 'steered' to one or other car.

I was directed to the bigger car owned by the 'friend'.

Joan sat next to 'Phil the friend' and I sat near the window.

Sally, Joyce and Gwen sat in the back of a cream Holden sedan with the registration number GGD809.

Sally, Bev, Rod and Gwen and GGD809!

We went to a place called Bacchus Marsh through a lovely Avenue of giant trees affectionately known as the Avenue of Honor.

We stopped to stretch our legs at a cafe where we all had a milkshake.
As we prepared to return to Point Cook, Joan climbed into the front seat as before and Phil closed the door.

He took me by the elbow and directed me to the driver's side, opened the driver's door and gestured for me to sit in the middle.
He took off his sports coat and handed it to me to hold.
I thought little of it until we arrived home and as we prepared to alight Phil took me by the arm until all of the girls left, then asked me if I would like to go to the movies the following Friday night at the drive-in.

A drive-in no less!

I had heard of such places but had never seen or attended one.
Well I was here for some new experiences so I said "Yes".
I thought it appropriate to ask him what his surname was.
"Farmer" he replied.

Each morning thereafter, as I joined the breakfast queue to toast my bread on the giant cylindrical toaster, a certain Corporal Farmer would mysteriously appear at my shoulder anxious to exchange niceties, despite the no fraternization rule.
If I decided on salad for lunch and lined up in that area, so did he.
How 'co-incidental' that we should find ourselves standing together in the tea line each evening!

On the Friday night I attended my first ever drive-in with him.

We talked a lot without the problem of disturbing other patrons.
Turning down the speaker Phil asked me to share with him my plans for the future.
I shared my immediate plans of remaining in the Air force for four years while accepting any posting I was offered so I could see as much of Australia as possible.
"Well Beverley Ann Ryan I think you had best think about changing your plans because I am going to marry you and I am not waiting four years to do so."
I laughed heartily.
"No way. I'm not interested in marrying anyone, least of all you" I told him.

I had known him for five days.

Then followed an interesting period of 'courting' by my new friend who had an answer for every objection to a continuing relationship I could muster-and there were many.

There was a big age difference of eleven years I explained that would mean we were from different generations almost- not a problem as he thought I was 'very mature' for my age.

There were religious differences, me a Catholic and him C of E which meant we would have different aleigences -not a problem as his Father had been a lapsed Catholic for years and religion was no impediment to his parent's union.

Education differences, I had left school with form three and knew I had much to learn whilst he had finished school and undertaken a journalistic career.

Surely he would have to feel superior while I would feel intimidated- not a problem as he looked forward to watching me 'grow'.

Big experience difference, he had travelled and lived and worked overseas and interstate while I had been nowhere and had seen nothing- no problem as most of his friends hadn't travelled as much as he had and he didn't consider them to be different.

We knew nothing about each other-we would have the rest of our lives to learn.

And then there were the all-important ambitions.

Mine, as I had told him, was to travel and learn while his, as he told me, was to marry me ASAP.

My evening study time was encroached upon as we continued to meet each evening-despite the rules.

Phil would park his car at the common fence line to make it easier for me to slip out of the end door to join him.

I was aided and abetted by my fellow recruits who covered for me on many occasions.

One such 'rookie' was Bernie from Geelong.

It was Bernie who taught me how parochial were Victorians when it came to Football!

In the shared shower room I was accosted by a WRAAF corporal who I had seen at the Dental Section when we had gone for Dental check-ups.

She sidled over to me as I cleaned my teeth all big and bossy and turned off the running tap.

"A warning" she snarled. "Keep your hands off Phil Farmer."

"I haven't had my hands 'on' him YET" I retorted and I turned the tap on again.

We went for another drive to Bacchus Marsh one weekend where Phil introduced me to his best friends, Jack and Annie Williams, and their small son, Tony.

Jack took Phil to the small kitchen and was heard to say "Where did you find her Mate? She's bloody gorgeous. Grab her while you have the chance Mate."

"I have every intention of doing so" was the reply.

Baby Tony crawled over and pulled himself up against my knee. I picked him up and after a short time he fell asleep.

Jack was impressed. "Look at that Mate. She's even got the touch."

He went inside and came out holding a black lacquered music box. "This goes with him" Jack promised as though this small box would swing it in Phil's favor.

We left after tea and I thought if you could have such nice friends you have to be pretty nice yourself.

On the trip home we discussed music and I mentioned how I had enjoyed 'Carmen Jones'.

Phil scoffed and mounted a tirade towards those who took it upon themselves to coin classical music for popular purposes.

He struck me as a proper musical snob and I hoped I might be wrong in my summation.

Phil announced that his sister, Elaine, and her friend, Rosemary, would be coming to Point Cook to witness the Trooping of the Color.

Even though he was well aware of the risk I would be taking, he asked me to join the party as he really wanted me to meet a member of his family.

My friends rallied around and found sun glasses, wig, hat etc. and I slipped out of the barracks hoping no one would recognize me and praying one of the girls would answer roll call in my absence.

Elaine was obviously VERY surprised to meet me and her friend did not appear impressed at all with my attendance.

After the formalities we headed to my barracks so the girls could attend the Powder Room.

Half way there we were met by my Staff Sergeant Fraser, who saluted Phil, nodded in the direction of the ladies then said in acknowledgement of me "Ryan".

PERHAPS Amy Fraser had seen a wig and sunglasses before.

We went to the Melbourne show and I couldn't help but be impressed with the extent of my companion's knowledge.

The range of subjects this knowledge covered was astonishing.

He bought me a tiny carved rickshaw and insisted I sit for a scissors artist who cut profiles of your face.

PERHAPS I was becoming a little bit interested.

In the centre of Melbourne I stopped to gaze in jewellers, a habit I'd followed since childhood.

"Which engagement ring do you like best"? I was asked.

"That one with the emerald surrounded by diamonds" I answered without hesitation.

"That's not a proper engagement ring" I was told in a most emphatic manner.

PERHAPS my interest had just waned.

Every time we were together he asked how soon I would marry him.

If I greeted him with the question "Did you have a good day?" he would answer

"Yes. It was a day closer to marrying you".

He told me of his experiences overseas and showed me loads of photos and slides he had taken in Japan and Korea and more recent ones of his sister's wedding.

I learned of his journalist days on the Sunraysia Daily and his adventures and experiences in Western Australia working in a hospital, on a farm at Beverley with the Whittington's, or on the railway.

I learned how he loved motor bikes and how he had been involved in a bike accident in Western Australia when he ran into a milk truck.

He still bore the scar on his little finger.

We visited St Patrick's Melbourne to see the architecture and compared the structure with Cook's Cottage.

We combed the Botanical Garden and drove to Healsville and Maroondah Dam coming home via the Acheron way, marvelling at the spring flora and giant trees.

Melbourne in the Spring of 1955

When the results of our final exams were posted I was very pleased with the marks I attained considering the time spent in Phil's company that should have been devoted to study.

Our graduation took place at the Southern Cross Hotel, considered 'THE' hotel in Melbourne at that time.

Even interstate I had heard of the hotel specialty of Bomb Alaska for sweets. It proved to be as good as its reputation!

I received notification of a posting to 3 RAAF Richmond in NSW.
I would be mustered as a Medical Orderly in the hospital there.

After a visit to the Art Gallery in Melbourne it became obvious that our taste in Art and sculpture varied very much.

I mentioned the differences as he again discussed the subject of marriage on our trip home.

I questioned his expectations of marriage.

He shook his shoulders.

He just knew he wanted something 'different' to the marriage of his parents.

He thought he wanted a 'companion' and he wanted a 'family'.

I commented on the different marriages in my own family and confessed I had only very recently considered the subject.

Buoyed by the treasures we had witnessed at the gallery I likened my idea of marriage as being like a block of granite that could be chiseled into something beautiful and lasting by the careful application of a craftsman's tool.

If, in the event of a thoughtless action, the chisel wasn't applied thoughtfully, then a chip would result that could disfigure the masterpiece.

Graduation Pt Cook 1955 Back row 4ᵗʰ from left

The comment that was made was to the effect that it was 'a novel analogy'.

I was somewhat shocked when my friend offered to take me to a hotel for a drink.

I reminded him of my age and the law that stated the drinking age was twenty-one and I wasn't about to abuse that law.

The night before I left for NSW, overwhelmed with a mixture of new emotions, I agreed that I would 'think about' marrying him 'sometime in the future'.

No sooner had I marched in to the new base when the letters began to arrive.

Each mail delivery, both at morning and in the afternoon, brought another eloquent love letter to my mailbox.
Flattered beyond belief I read and re-read the mushy lines like:-

'Darling posted one letter to you this morning and is writing another this evening. See what you have done to me? Never mind, I like it,'
Or:-
'Despite the very brief time we have known each other I find I love you very dearly. These words come so easily to the lips when you are in my arms and in saying them now I am not just thinking of the present but am looking forward to the next fifty years, when the fullness of time makes inroads on the freshness of youth and a family takes its toll of figure and temper,'
And:-
'I am sorry that I will never be able to give you all that you've been used to having but I can offer you all of my love and hope that part way makes up for it.'
Plus:-
'The lack of money means we will have to struggle together for some time but if you are the wife I think you're going to be you won't mind the odd year sneaking past in its stockinged feet.'
Also:-
'When considering in the same vein the other girls I have told you about there were always doubts existing somewhere. With you, my Darling, there are none'.

Suitably punctuated with terms of endearment, the contents of the box with the blue ribbon began to bulge!
There was the occasional phone call and even a telegram or two, all professing undying love.
I was delighted to find a 'boyfriend' who communicated so readily.
I shared one of my letters with Mum thinking she would be most impressed.

She read the letter, raised her eyebrows and said'
"They don't always mean what they say you know."

A long weekend was gazetted at the end of October which would include
Melbourne cup day. Phil planned a trip up to Richmond.
He claimed he couldn't wait to see me.
Upon his arrival he came to the hospital to pick me up as I came off duty
from night duty. He drove down the road a ways and pulled to the curb and
kissed me.
"Do you like it?" he said.
"Funny question. Your technique hasn't improved as I recall" I thought.
"The ring" he said. "Do you like it?"
I looked and my heart sank.
The ring he had placed on my finger was everything I disliked in rings.
"Not really. I don't think I could wear a ring like that" I truthfully answered.
"I sold my motor bike and cashed my insurance policy to buy that" he
confessed.
I felt awful but it didn't improve my opinion of the ring.
"Couldn't you exchange it for one we both like?" I queried.
"Absolutely not." was the curt and final reply.

Somehow I knew this was not what I envisaged an engagement should be.
I had no idea he would want to get engaged before we had discussed the
timing.
He had not actually asked me to marry him, but had told me.
This step was a complete surprise to me at that time.

Perhaps it was my tiredness that was making me feel both sad and disappointed.
I climbed into the back seat of the car for some sleep as Phil negotiated his
way to Harold Street in Matraville where Fay and Mervyn lived.
We stopped to buy some meat and fruit and the lady at the fruitshop commented
on my nice nails and made no comment about the brand new ring.

I introduced what was to become the newest member of the family.
Mervyn took Phil to the 'local' to share a couple of beers to celebrate the
engagement.
In the afternoon I took the two girls to the shop and bought Phil the top-
selling book for the month of October.

As the last letter I had received from him referred to my sprinkle of freckles across the bridge of my nose and stated he would like to kiss each one, I signed the book 'from Freckles'.

The following day we drove to Lidsdale and Phil asked Dad if we could get engaged.
Dad said it all depended on me.
Phil, full of fear and trepidation, formally requested my hand in marriage.
Dad told him a one handed daughter was not of much use to him so he had best take all of me!
Mum looked at my ring and commented "That isn't the sort of ring I expected you'd pick."
I assured her I hadn't.
"Your father did a similar thing to me" she shared.

PERHAPS I would learn to like mine as much as I liked Mum's.

I took Phil up to meet Granny Nolan.
She looked at Phil from feet to face then asked me "How old is this young man Bevie"?
'Twenty nine Gran", I answered.
"And how old are you now"?
"Eighteen Gran" I replied.
"Well. You be careful my girl. It's often these old ones that are the worst!"

I didn't expand on the conversation or the message implied.

We both returned to work and I was surprised to be summoned to the office of Matron Schultz.
Pam Schultz was in her thirties and had been in Japan in the early fifties.
She was charming and I had not been surprised to learn she was 'keeping company' with a fellow officer.
She acknowledged my knock and asked me to close the door.
I felt decidedly uncomfortable.
Then she said "I heard you became engaged at the weekend nurse."
"Yes Mam."
"Aren't you going to show me your ring?"
I felt in my pocket and withdrew the ring, placed it on my finger and offered my hand. "Congratulations Lass" she said. "Can I share a secret with you?"

315

I nodded in the affirmative.

She withdrew from her pocket an engagement ring of a large sapphire surrounded with diamonds that she placed on her finger.

Then she came around from behind her desk and gave me a big hug.

On my way out she told me another girl from my intake had also got engaged that weekend.

I detoured to the library where this Maureen O'Sullivan worked as an Educational Officer and offered my congratulations to a very surprised girl.

I did not disclose the source of the news though I did tell her the emerald surrounded with diamonds that she wore was nicer than Matron Shultz' and much, much, nicer than mine.

The correspondence continued.

Phil complained about the small amount he received from me and it was difficult to explain there was very little to write about when you worked all night and tried to sleep during the very hot days.

After a demand for a 'long' letter I wrote one on ten feet of toilet paper and my attempt at humour was not well received.

The gang at work threw in and bought me a Morphy Richards iron.

I thought it very swish.

I had no idea Phil had an identical one.

I told everyone we were 'thinking' about getting married the following Easter.

I had been working night duty for extra leave and saving to buy an air ticket to fly down to Melbourne, but the price was prohibitive. It would take six weeks' pay.

A fellow nurse suggested I apply for an Air force flight on one of the planes that flew from Richmond to Laverton.

It was my intention to stay at Jack and Annie's to look after Annie and the babies when she came home from hospital with the new baby as neither she, nor Jack, had any family to call on.

Jack met me and we drove to Bacchus Marsh where I would live for a week.

On the Saturday Phil took me to Melbourne to Elaine's flat in Sth Yarra for an engagement dinner she had prepared.

I wore my new watermelon pink dress with an accordion pleated skirt and black lace stole- and THE ring.

During the evening Elaine asked me what my taste in music was and Phil piped up and told her I liked 'Carmen Jones'.
She looked askance as her brother had done.

PERHAPS there are at least two musical snobs in this family I figured!

Phil announced he wanted to get married at Christmas when he had some leave.

He had sussed out Jack and Annie and they had agreed we could stay with them until we got somewhere of our own in the Marsh.

A couple of weeks later I made a trip up the mountains and spoke to Les.
He thought I was moving too fast and he suggested I should wait awhile.

He reinforced his philosophy- if there are any doubts- don't!
I had to confess there were some, not least of which was my reluctance to move so far from my friends and family knowing it would probably be years before I would see them again.
I could only anticipate a terrible wrench.

It was difficult to imagine an existence foreign to my experience of life as I knew it.
I talked honestly about Phil and confessed that I felt my feelings weren't being considered and it would be an easier transition if I was given more time.

Les suggested a list of plusses and minuses.

He asked me to start with a few small minuses.
"He's a lousy dresser. He has awful thin lips. He keeps saying 'aint' when he actually has a great vocabulary, he's not wise with money, he's a bit bossy, he never says thankyou, sometimes I don't know if he's a really happy person, he doesn't have many friends and he can be boring sometimes. I also wonder how come he's so old, yet has never married." I replied.
"Now plusses" said Les.
I answered very quickly "He is very clean and smells wonderful, is quite shy, he is very bright, very persistent, he writes great letters, he laughs with me, he has gorgeous eyelashes and I have an uncontrollable urge to run my hands

through his lovely wavy hair and touch his delicate skin AND he has a really, REALLY nice bum."

Les threw back his head and laughed. "How could I possibly compete? With an attribute like that you will surely marry him". Now tell me. Could you live with him on a desert island? Does he have enough knowledge to keep you safe and well? Does he appear to be the type who can provide for you? Can you envisage him as the father of your children?"

I needed no time to ponder the answer.

PERHAPS Leslie would be right.

I told him I had given Phil a book to mark the occasion of our engagement and I felt a bit mean when his gift was worth so much more than mine.
Les looked at me and took my hand. "Believe me it is Phil who got the bargain" he said.

"PERHAPS I might be able to write a book of my own to give him one day" I said.

Les laughed heartily.
"I can't see you ever writing a book. You are too impolite. You have to write words that people like to read and you are too blunt. A bullshit artist you are not Miss Ryan and I fear that's a pre-requisite for a writer."

"What about if I wrote about myself and my life?" I suggested
"You would have to live long enough to have a story" he advised.

PERHAPS I will.

I filled in working an extra shift for Isla who was on day duty.
At this time in history all young men were required to undertake National Service by training in the military for six months.
The society was divided in their approval of such an undertaking but I never met a recruit who objected to the practice.
And I met more than most as it was me and my fellow orderlies who administered the many inoculations it was deemed necessary for these young men to receive.

We devised a little game as we prepared our numerous needles and phials and observed the anxious Rookies who lined up ready for our attack.
We would try to guess which boys would faint.
My method was to pick the big, good looking, macho guys and my score was usually very good!

One of the girls complained about the attentions of a patient who felt he had the right to 'grab' her as she passed his bed.

She was afraid to complain because he was a sergeant.
As he had broken his leg his stay was expected to be lengthy.
One of our special staff members, Ron, a lovely fellow who really looked after us and who was a higher rank, offered to speak to him after I reported the problem.
After second thoughts I decided to speak to him myself and to hell with his rank.

As I stepped around the door to his room I recognized him as one of the Air force personnel from our dinner at Marangaroo the previous year and he had definitely been one who had been 'extra' friendly with one of the nurses for many weeks after.
He had been overheard telling his roommate how jealous his wife was and asking the other patient not to mention how attractive the nurses were when his wife visited that day.
Tommy, the patient, had lost an arm in an accident in Japan.
He referred to the stump as 'Baby San' and he suffered severe psychological problems which caused him to scream with pain in the missing arm.
He did not care for his room-mate at all.
He very rarely smiled or showed any interest in anything or anyone.
He listened disinterestingly and rolled over without a word.

I made my entrance.
Having recognised the man in front of me I immediately changed my line of attack.
"Sergeant I........ I believe you have been harassing one of my nurses despite her request that you desist.
Apparently you think all young ladies with whom you come in contact find you irresistible like M. in Lithgow.

319

I'm sure your wife will be shocked with accounts of your dalliances when she visits this afternoon".

My patient, recognised me from the Marangaroo visit years before.

"My God. I know you" he exclaimed.

It was then our big, strong, brave, (good looking) creep wiped the leer from his face and began to blubber, begging me to say nothing to his wife and agreeing to any condition I suggested.

That included a written apology and a promise to treat our girls with respect in the future.

Tommy became animated for the first time since admission and his rare laughter could be heard bellowing throughout the entire ward.

Every time I saw him after that he would bow and address me through "Baby San" and the Christmas card he left the ward for the first time to buy for me, was signed by his alter ego with a message 'You go get them'.

The summer weather was very warm and living in antiquated barracks with no fans or air conditions made comfort impossible.

Isla and her fiancé, Ken, Ron and I would sometimes walk down to the river after tea to cool off before our shift.

As I could not swim I had to suffice with paddling and splashing in the cool water while the others really took advantage of the river.

On this occasion as I sat on the bank I had been joined by Isla who was a strong swimmer who usually spent every second breast stroking back and forth.

She had complained of feeling 'off color' and we put it down to the oppressive weather and her recent illness where she had been administered a transfusion, but when she had to rest several times on the way home complaining of severe stomach pain we were convinced she was really ill.

We barely made it back in time to go on duty and I told Flight Wilson about her symptoms. "That girl sounds as though she has Hepatitis" he said.

"She can't. She's my bridesmaid in two weeks." I told him.

PERHAPS he will be right in his diagnosis and I will be wrong in mine.

ACW Beverley Ryan

Isla offered me her wedding dress to wear after her own wedding was postponed for a second time. It was not my choice of dress but as Fr Murphy had said I was not permitted to wear a slack suit, and I hadn't the funds to buy a dress, I had little choice.

I purchased a pair of pale blue shoes and, although my least favoured color, I made two pale blue slips and a two layered veil of blue and white to attach to a very fine straw hat I had.

I ordered flowers with ribbon trails in the same blue as my slips.

Another friend, Jan, stepped in as a replacement for Isla and she would wear a blue nylon frock of mine in that I had planned to wear as a 'going away' outfit. She would carry a small bouquet like mine.

Not being a morning person I was horrified when Fr Murphy said the only time available on Christmas Eve was at ten o'clock in the morning!

I rang Phil to suggest another day but he reminded me Jack had booked a return flight to Melbourne and he couldn't afford to lose the cost of the fare that could not be exchanged.

And so the wedding planning was completed.
When I shared with Dad that Phil didn't want any of his family at the wedding
he shook his head and remarked "Decidedly odd. Is he ashamed of you or something?"

Shirl had invited Fay and family to Goulburn for Christmas some weeks earlier and they had both declined their invitations to the wedding.

Flight Sergeant Wilson was the first male 'nursing sister' I had ever met.
Not only was he a trained General Nurse but he was also one of the first men to be permitted to undertake midwifery training in Australia.
So 'female dominated' was nursing in those days very few hospitals would allow males to train as nurses.

Flight was very experienced, yet he was only a Flight Sergeant and was out-ranked by his much younger female contemporaries who became Officers immediately they joined the force, despite their being less qualified.
It was a ludicrous situation.

I went up the Mountains to see Aunt and Uncle and have my last weekend with them.
It was a nostalgic occasion.
I sat laughing as all of the old sayings became etched in my lexicon.
When I mentioned a family member who was a snob Aunt summed her up thus
"She thinks her shit doesn't stink."

When I suggested the snob would not be impressed with Aunt's description she added "She can kiss my foot."
When talking about a dog that had died suddenly Unc, who had found the animal, described it as being 'as dead as a doornail'.

As Unc left the table to return to work he would say "This sitting here won't buy the baby a dress or pay for the one it's wearing."

When the offspring of dull parents followed in their parents footsteps the saying to describe them was 'You can't make a silk purse out of a sow's ear'.

If you criticized someone for displaying the same behavior as you Unc would say "That sounds like the kettle calling the pot black."

If a second 'go' at something was called for he would say, "One rip never tore a sack"

If you passed wind Unc would comment "An empty house is better than a bad tenant."

If Aunt didn't agree with someone she would label them as "Silly old goat."

If I asked what we were going to eat for dinner Aunt would say "Bread and pullet."

If I said we had that yesterday she would answer "Well we'll have duck under the table as a change and if you are lucky we can have windmill pudding if it will go round."

When someone annoyed them they would comment "She made my blood boil."

If anyone was inebriated they were described as being 'as full as a boot' or "as full as a country dunny at a Sunday School Picnic."

'As dear as sin', 'What Tommy rot', 'A mouth like a Cocky's cage', 'Tight as a fleas bum', there were so many classics they shared with me and I was forever surprised and delighted with their extensive repertoire.

My all-time favorites I still use include 'He's as happy as a worm going fishing' and the classic to make a point that goes like this: - "If you burn your bum you sit on the blister!"

Sitting playing cards I turned to Unc and asked him if he had any advice for me on the eve of my wedding week.

He looked at me seriously and said "Just you remember Youngin, 'it' has to be fed and 'it' won't eat bread!"

He asked me if I would like to wear a brooch of his Mother's as something old.

Beverley Ann Farmer

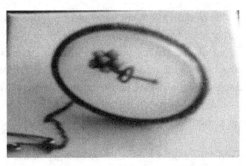

I chose a white shell one with delicate adornment of forget-me-nots in turquoise.
A gift from Uncle Paddy-Something Old

Aunty Doll and Uncle Paddy

On Wednesday afternoon I was woken with a request to report to the hospital. I staggered out of bed, showered, dressed in uniform that included day requirement of a white butterfly veil and reported as required.

When I walked through the staff room to get a cuppa I was confronted with a lovely afternoon tea celebration just for me.

I was presented with a pair of large vases, a table cloth and serviettes, and a pair of salt and pepper shakers to add to my growing collection.

My bridesmaid, Jan, and good friends Jean and Ron, had arranged the surprise for me.

As I left, the staff who wouldn't be attending the wedding lined up and gave me a hug and wished me well, all except Ron.

I commented sarcastically in his direction as he was leaving that I appreciated the hug and kiss I didn't get from him!

He turned around and came back into the room and taking me by the upper arms he kissed me so passionately I went weak at the knees.

He turned and left the room.

I shook my head as I gathered myself and asked of Jean "What was THAT all about?"

"He's in love with you" she answered "Has been since he first saw you."

I spent my waking hours of Thursday sorting out what clothes I could fit in my limited luggage.

Much of what I had would have to be given away.

I packed the emerald green everglaze dress I loved and the vivid yellow cotton.

The new taupe dress and the navy coat frock had to come too.

Would I have need of sundresses living in a much colder climate?

I couldn't possibly leave the black velvet frock and coat I had for that 'posh' wedding at St Mark's, Darling Point.

Lined with watermelon pink satin that matched the pillar box hat it had been the nicest outfit I had ever owned.

It was also the most expensive!

The uniforms supplied by the Airforce had to be returned though we were able to keep the large and small suitcases.

That meant I had two large, one medium hatbox and one small case to transport all of my belongings, including winter gear.

I also required a container for my range of make-up that had cost a fortune.

I had to be ruthless and allotted a container for winter, summer, shoes (of which there were many in a variety of hues) and the smallest one for jewellery, squashed hats, gloves and handbags.

My room-mate, Dorothy, promised to forward some coats I could not find room for at a later date-but never did.

After finishing work on the Friday morning I caught the train to Lithgow then the bus to Lidsdale.

Shortly after lunch Phil and Jack arrived from Victoria.

The boys were summoned and Mum and I were driven to Betty White's to have our hair 'done'.

The men went to the pub and overstayed their time and, in consequence, we were not picked up at the appointed time.

Mum was very cross and she called the one and only taxi to take us home. In due course the men realized the time and raced to Betty's, then came home. Mum was so mad by then she locked the door and told me to be quiet. Dad knocked and called to no avail and Mum steadfastly refused to answer the door. Then Jack Williams spoke up "Bugger them. Let's go back to the pub then." "No you won't." Mum yelled as she threw the door open.

We picked up Jan and Jean from the station in time for tea. After tea as we sat out the front in the car I gave Phil a gold ring with an onyx stone and he seemed as pleased with it as I had been with mine.

He gave me a blue satin dressing gown.

I asked to take a peek at my plain, wide, gold, wedding ring I had asked for. In the box was a narrow, heavily embossed, platinum number on a gold band. "What the...Why would you buy a ring like that?" "I thought it would look better with your other ring." "But it doesn't match anything all covered with hearts and it's mainly silver in color and it looks lousy on my dark skin. After all I am the one who is going to wear it." I tried it on and as I guessed it looked ordinary.

I noticed it was too big for my finger and I queried why he had chosen one so large. My clever husband-to-be rationalized that because I would be wearing the ring all of the time he figured it should be bigger to allow for swelling as my hand became accustomed to the constant chaffing. I told him I thought if anything the ring would settle on my finger and therefore should have been smaller than the engagement ring. Not for the last time neither of us could see the other's point of view.

Jack appeared and I expressed my disappointment.

'You've got a lot to learn Mate." he suggested "You'll be hearing about this blunder for the rest of your bloody life. I'm telling you Mate they never forget."

PERHAPS Phil will learn what insight his friend has!

We were still giggling about Jack long after he and Phil had left for Curran's farm to stay the night.

We three girls climbed into our old bed in the back bedroom where I had slept as a kid and after several warnings from Mum to get to sleep we finally stopped talking and laughing.

This time tomorrow I will be an 'old married woman.'

Mum woke us with trays for breakfast in bed.
Scrambled eggs, juice, toast, butter, jam, teapot, sugar and milk were crowded on the trays.

We fought for the bathroom with me taking advantage of my importance for the day.
I starched the petticoats and ironed them before scalloping the edge of the veils.

Now bathed and dressed and wearing more make-up than was the norm I waited for Unc to arrive in "Bevie the Chevie" and we headed for Lithgow.
As I settled on the pale blue leather seats I painted my fingernails on the way in and wasn't a bit nervous as I prepared to walk down the same isle that had previously been traversed by my parents and two sisters.

I reflected on the years that had gone before and the people who had contributed to who I was.

My name is Beverley Ann Ryan.
I am the daughter of James Francis and Vera Ryan,
the granddaughter of Sarah Jane Dowdell and Bernard Arthur Ryan,
the great granddaughter of Annie England and William Dowdell,
the great,great grandaughter of Catherine O'Neill and John Dowdell,
the great, great, great granddaughter of William O'Neill and Sarah Morning
and the great, great, great, great granddaughter of Garret Morning and Mary Owens.

I, (and my genes), am about to advance toward an unknown destiny.

Will it be a destiny that matches my hopes and dreams for my future?

PERHAPS, PERHAPS, PERHAPS.

Recipes to share.

Granny Nolan's Ginger Sponge

Two papered tins	4 eggs (separated)
5oz(155gms)castor sugar	Half oz(915gms)plain flour
3oz(90gms) cornflour	Half teasp bicarb soda
1teasp cream of tartar	pinch salt
1teasp ginger	1teasp warmed golden syrup
1tablesp boiling water	

Beat egg whites until stiff. Gradually add sugar, beat well. Add yolks. Sieve all dry ingredients together twice and fold into egg mixture. Add syrup. Stir in boiling water. Bake 20 minutes in moderate oven 375(190c) until centre springs back when pressed with thumb.
Fill with mock cream made by combining butter and castor sugar until smooth.
Gradually add chilled water and stir. Drain water and repeat process once more until un-dissolved sugar is washed away.
Liberally sprinkle top with sieved icing sugar.

xxxxxxxxxxxxxxxxxxxxxxxx

Aunty Glad's Pot Roast.

Choose a corner cut piece of topside.
Fresh breadcrumbs
teasp mixes herbs
2 teasp curry powder
1 diced onion
Salt & pepper
1 tablesp butter

With a sharp knife slit a pocket in the meat. (Butcher will do this for you)
In a dish combine fresh breadcrumbs, mixed herbs, finely chopped onion, salt, pepper, curry powder, large knob of butter and bind together.(Amounts vary depending on required amount.)

Stuff into pocket. Sew sides together (or thread with skewers and bind with string)and place in large pan with dripping and hot water. (1 cup each)
Cook slowly on stove top checking liquid level frequently. Top up as required.
Allow half hour for each pound weight (Double time for K's.)
One hour prior to serving add potatoes and pumpkin.
Remove meat and vegetables and use juices for a tasty gravy by adding a small amount of flour and water from other boiled vegetables.

xxxxxxxxxxxxxxxxxxxxxxxx

Jam Roly Poly (1)

Half cup butter	2cups SRF
Cold water	Jam
half cup sugar	1tablesp butter
1cup boiling water	

Rub butter into flour until it resembles breadcrumbs. Add enough cold water to form stiff dough. Roll out and spread with liberal amount of jam. Roll up like Swiss roll and place in pie dish. Make a syrup of sugar, butter and boiling water. Pour over roll and bake in hot oven for 30 minutes.
Serve with custard or cream.

xxxxxxxxxxxxxxxxxxxxxxxx

Suet Roly Poly (2)

Half quantity suet to flour (eg 4ozs suet, 8ozs flour)
Pinch salt   teasp sugar
water

Mix to stiff dough.Spread with jam or syrup. Roll into log. Wrap in greaseproof paper then floured cloth.
Tie the ends and cook in boiling water for 2-2 and a half hours.

xxxxxxxxxxxxxxxxxxxxxxxx

Beverley Ann Farmer

Vera's Ice Cream

Half pint of cream
1 tin condensed milk
Egg whites (Beaten)
Beat the ingredients together then add eight passionfruit.
Freeze. Take out of freezer and re-beat to increase volume.
A teasp of glycerine can be added to decrease iceing.

xxxxxxxxxxxxxxxxxxxxxxxxx

Old Fashioned Rock Cakes

Half pound flour
3oz butter
Pinch salt
1teasp baking powder
ozs currants or sultanas
2 sm eggs
3 ozs sugar
grated lemon peel

Rub butter into flour, add salt, baking powder, sugar and mix well. Add fruit
and well beaten eggs. Put in rough piles on greased tray. Sprinkle with sugar/
spice mixture. Bake till firm and golden in fairly hot oven for 15 minutes.

xxxxxxxxxxxxxxxxxxxxxxxxx

Family Sago Plum Pudding

1 tablesp sago
1 cup milk
Half cup sugar
3ozs butter
1 egg
Half teasp cinnamon
1 tablesp golden syrup
half teasp bicarb

pinch salt
1 cup raisins
1cup soft breadcrumbs

Wash sago, soak overnight in milk. Cream butter and sugar, add egg and syrup.
Dissolve soda in milk and sago, stir I salt, raisins, cinnamon, crumbs. Pour
into greased mould and steam for three hours.

xxxxxxxxxxxxxxxxxxxxxxxxxx

Granny Nolan's Egg Salad.

6 Boiled eggs
I lettuce finely shredded
2 teasp powdered mustard
Salt and pepper
Vinegar
Small teasp sugar

Slice eggs. Remove yolks and place in dish. Mash with fork.
Add mustard, S and P and sufficient vinegar to form consistency of sauce.
Place shredded lettuce in dish.
Sprinkle with sugar.
Arrange rings of egg white over lettuce.
Pour over yolk mixture and serve with cold meat.

xxxxxxxxxxxxxxxxxxxxxxxxxxx

Ration Cake (No eggs or butter)

2 cups sugar
2 cups hot water
2 tablesp dripping(or margarine)
1 teasp salt
1 cup seeded raisins
1 teasp cinnamon
1 teasp mixed spice

Boil liquids for 5 minutes. Allow to cool.
Add 3 cups plain flour, 1 teasp baking powder dissolved in 1 teasp hot water.
Bake in square tin 45-50 minutes.
Commence with hot oven and adjust after 15 minutes to slow oven.

xxxxxxxxxxxxxxxxxxxxxxxxxxxxx

Fresh Mint Sauce

Fresh mint leaves
2 teasp sugar
Half teasp salt
Half cup boiling water
Half cup vinegar

Dice and crush mint in pessel Add sugar and salt. Add boiling water and allow to steep.
Add vinegar to taste. Place in screw top jar and store up-side-down in fridge.

xxxxxxxxxxxxxxxxxxxxxxxxxxxxx

Gnat Bites

Take 1 dessertsp of Epsom Salts and dissolve in 1 cup of boiling water.
When cool put in small bottle and dab on skin to prevent bites.
If this mixture does not work effectively drink the liquid and expect to run too fast for gnats to catch you!

xxxxxxxxxxxxxxxxxxxxxxxxxxxxx